P9-ELU-354

The Rise and Fall of
the Bulgarian Connection

The Rise and Fall of the Bulgarian Connection

EDWARD S. HERMAN and FRANK BRODHEAD

 SHERIDAN SQUARE PUBLICATIONS, INC.
NEW YORK

Publisher's Note: This book is one of a series of in-depth studies of current intelligence- and media-related issues. For a catalog, please write to Sheridan Square Publications, Inc., P. O. Box 677, New York, NY 10013.

First printing, May 1986.

Library of Congress Cataloging-in-Publication Data

Herman, Edward S.
  The rise and fall of the Bulgarian connection.

  Includes index.
  1. John Paul II, Pope, 1920-   —Assassination
attempt, 1981. 2. Espionage—Bulgaria. 3. Disin-
formation—United States. I. Brodhead, Frank.
II. Title.
BX1378.5.H48   1986   364.1'524'0945634   86-6582
ISBN 0-940380-07-2
ISBN 0-940380-06-4 (pbk.)

This book is a compelling exposé of the plot behind the plot—the concoction by the Italian secret services of a Bulgarian Connection in the attempted assassination of the Pope.

The reader of this book is faced with staggering proof that the media utterly failed to meet acceptable standards of care and professionalism. *The Rise and Fall of the Bulgarian Connection* is a serious and realistic assessment of the handling by the western press of a propaganda trick; it shows how the press was led by a handful of journalists linked to the CIA into accepting as proof a fabricated story.

In following this case, lawyers were disheartened by the erosion of the principle of the presumption of innocence. And just as the legal system failed to probe the case against the accused Bulgarians in accordance with that presumption, so the media ignored information suggesting hidden political motives behind the accusations.

The book is a chilling indictment of our so-called "free" press, a press which abuses its freedom by omissions, by half-truths, and by stirring the continuation of a Cold War climate. It deserves to be read and remembered.

—**Seán MacBride, S.C.**

Seán MacBride is a recipient of the Nobel Peace Prize (1974), the Lenin Peace Prize (1977), and the American Medal of Justice (1978); former Chief of Staff of the Irish Republican Army, Foreign Minister of Ireland, and United Nations Ambassador; U.N. Commissioner for Namibia, and author of the UNESCO Report on The New World Information and Communication Order; current Chairman of the Board of Advisers of the Institute for Media Analysis, Inc.

The Institute for Media Analysis, Inc. is a non-profit educational institution devoted, in part, to the study of western media disinformation and deception operations. This book was prepared with the assistance of the Institute and members of its Board. For further information about the Institute for Media Analysis, Inc., please write to: IMA, 145 West 4th Street, New York, NY 10012.

Contents

"Destroy his fib or sophistry: in vain—
The creature's at his dirty work again."
—ALEXANDER POPE, 1735

"After a disinformation effort has been launched,
if it gets into replay it can be manipulated
for long periods of time using assets in
other areas and be revived at will."
—CENTRAL INTELLIGENCE AGENCY, 1982

Preface

On March 29, 1986, a jury in Rome, composed of two judges and six lay members, concluded that three Bulgarians and six Turks charged with conspiracy to assassinate Pope John Paul II should be acquitted for lack of evidence. The decision was an abrupt and, for many, surprising end to four years of claims and speculations about the "Bulgarian Connection." During those years the charges, linked in the media to more general accusations that the Soviet Union stood behind "international terrorism," regularly found their way into the headlines: "Dramatic new revelations. . . . " "The investigation is continuing. . . . " "Bulgaria today angrily denied. . . . " "U.S. officials refused to speculate. . . . " Long before the trial began, the flow of leaks from a supposedly secret investigation, and repeated assertions by supporters of the Connection that the evidence was abundant and compelling,[1] conditioned most people in the West to believe that the Bulgarians were guilty.

From its inception, however, the case had rested on the testimony of the would-be assassin, a young Turkish terrorist named Mehmet Ali Agca. It was therefore somewhat disconcerting to those who had taken the charges seriously that on the opening day of the trial, in May 1985, Agca's first sentences to the court announced that he was Jesus Christ, and that he had returned to warn of the imminent end of the world. He revealed further that he held the occult secrets of Fatima, that the Pope supported him in his claims to be Jesus, and that mysterious forces in Rome wanted to kidnap him and set him up as Pope. To prove his claims about being Jesus, and incidentally to support his charges against

---

1. Paul Henze, in a 1985 update of his book, *The Plot to Kill the Pope* (New York: Charles Scribner's Sons, 1985), wrote that the case for Bulgarian involvement has gotten "continually stronger" and the "evidence" for the Plot has "steadily accumulated to the point where little rational doubt is now possible" (p. 196).

the Bulgarians, he offered to raise the dead in the presence of President Reagan and other world leaders.

The prosecutor, Antonio Marini, claimed that Agca was deliberately sabotaging the case. Others maintained that Agca was just having some good fun, or that he was mysteriously signaling his Bulgarian collaborators to rescue him from jail.[2] Still others asserted that Agca was mad. The case became a shambles, but dragged on for almost a year. Agca agreed to dozens of conflicting versions of the truth, shifting major claims two or three times within half an hour. He launched into tirades about the Soviet Union, or western imperialism, and then became confused when the judge sternly reminded him about the here and now of the case. He withdrew in protest from the trial several times, each time returning with an even more improbable explanation of his shifts in testimony. But he stuck to his guns that he was Jesus Christ, come to announce the end of the world.

While the prosecution successfully developed a coherent case for a papal assassination conspiracy by Agca and perhaps a dozen of his associates in the Turkish rightwing movement called the Gray Wolves, the case against the Bulgarians made sense only if one believed it already.[3] Not a single witness was produced during the trial to support Agca's claims that the assassination plan was hatched in Bulgaria, that he had plotted with Bulgarians in Rome, or that he had collaborated with Bulgarians on the day of the assassination attempt itself. Despite a lengthy summation before the court in which Marini frequently implied that the Bulgarians stood behind the assassination attempt, this was so much rhetoric: While asking for prison sentences for Agca and three of his Turkish collaborators, the prosecutor was compelled to recommend dismissal of the charges against the three Bulgarians for lack of evidence. The jury, in its turn, however, acquitted all of the defendants of the conspiracy charges.[4]

2. The prosecutor also suggested this in his final summing up, although he never indicated how the Bulgarians could have rescued Agca, or why, after Agca had given up "signaling" he still failed to produce any confirmable evidence about Bulgarian involvement.

3. The present writers have always maintained that the claims and demonstrations of a Bulgarian Connection were deficient in both logic and evidence. While this position has been sustained in the trial and court judgment, we show in this book that the fatal weaknesses of the case were quite apparent when the Connection was at its peak of popularity (see especially Chapter 2).

4. In Italian criminal law, in addition to a finding of guilty or not guilty, there is a third possibility, a finding of not guilty because of insufficient evidence. Thus, failure to prove a charge beyond a reasonable doubt does not mandate, as it does in the United States, a

The trial in Rome raises many questions. If the only evidence against the Bulgarians consisted of assertions by an imprisoned and half-crazed criminal, why did anyone in the Italian state apparatus take them seriously? Did Agca think up these charges himself, or was he coached and supplied with information by people who somehow gained access to him in his solitary confinement? And how was the claim of a Bulgarian Connection sustained for four years in a Free World media that prides itself on investigative reporting and skepticism about sources? Was this a case of massive disinformation, beginning with planted stories and then growing to a universally agreed upon version of the truth? Or was the media's cooperation with the myth of the Bulgarian Connection simply a series of journalistic mistakes, taking the error-ridden Italian judicial process at its word and elaborating on the story from there?

In this study of the rise and fall of the Bulgarian Connection we attempt to answer these questions. Its main thesis is that the only Bulgarian Connection in the plot to assassinate Pope John Paul II existed in the minds of its originators and spokespersons in the West and in the selective coverage of the topic in the western mass media. The story of the "rise" of the Connection is therefore the tale of how and why this politically useful story was put over by a small coterie of U.S. journalists who we believe to be propagandists and disinformationists, most notably Claire Sterling, Paul Henze, and Michael Ledeen.[5] More broadly, *The Rise and Fall of the Bulgarian Connection* is a case study of how the mass media of the Free World function as a propaganda system.

The "fall" of the Bulgarian Connection may be something of a misnomer. While the case against the Bulgarians has been dismissed, it does not follow that the public will now be provided with sufficient information about the failed case to alter their well-ingrained perceptions

finding of not guilty.

5. Claire Sterling's September 1982 *Reader's Digest* article, "The Plot to Kill the Pope," launched the Bulgarian Connection in the western media. Paul Henze, former CIA station chief in Ethiopia and Turkey, wrote influential background reports proposing a Bulgarian Connection shortly after the assassination attempt. These reports were used by many major media outlets (see Chapters 6 and 7). Sterling elaborated her views in *The Time of the Assassins* (New York: Holt, Rinehart and Winston, 1983), while Henze later produced *The Plot to Kill the Pope* (New York: Charles Scribner's Sons, 1983). Michael Ledeen, though playing a lesser role, served to link the ideas of Sterling and Henze to the Reagan administration and to the influential Georgetown Center for Strategic and International Studies. We analyze the product and influence of these, the Big Three, in Chapters 5, 6, and 7.

of Bulgarian and Soviet guilt. In our analysis of the rise of the Connection, we stress that the initiation and handling of the case in Italy, and the willingness of the western media to accept uncritically a stream of implausible allegations, were based not only on western preconceptions and prejudices, but also on the serviceability of the Plot to important political interests. Both external pressures and internalized preferences caused the Italian courts and the media to follow blindly a politically convenient western party line. And just as the party line was followed uncritically, so alternative lines of fact and argument were not pursued, and dissent from the preferred view was rarely admitted to public inspection.

With the case against the Bulgarians now rejected by an Italian court after a lengthy trial, the mass-media sponsors and supporters of Sterling and other proponents of the Connection will have no interest in explaining to the public why they were wrong and how the public was manipulated into accepting a myth. Earlier critics of the Plot will not be honored for their foresight, but will continue to be marginalized. The creators and disseminators of the party line will not be subjected to close inspection and serious criticism, but will be given further access to the media, now to explain the legal setback. And out of their explanations the Bulgarian Connection will arise like a phoenix, available once again for regular service by conservative politicians and pundits.

The bases on which the Bulgarian Connection will be revived became clear in the mass media's coverage (or noncoverage) of the waning days of the trial. It is apparent that media creators of the Connection like Claire Sterling and Paul Henze have not been discredited, and that the media will recycle themes already advanced by Sterling, Henze, and others in explaining why the case was lost. For example:

● It will be argued that the case failed because western legal standards require excessive evidence in order to protect the innocent. Of course, Sterling and the mass media operated on principles precisely the reverse of this great western tradition, asserting for years that the Bulgarians and Soviets were guilty prior to any judicial rulings. They work both sides of the street, arguing guilt beforehand and explaining away a decision of non-guilt on the basis of western presumptions of innocence! So while the KGB really did it, this couldn't be proved with the overly cautious and soft legal system of the West.

● In explaining the loss of the case, Sterling and company will also return once again to the cleverness of the KGB in hiding its guilt beneath a web of proxies. Initially they charged that the very absence of evidence was proof of Soviet guilt, because the professionals of the KGB were always careful to establish "plausible deniability," and left no clues behind. As there were no clues, *ergo*, the Soviets did it. Sterling and Henze abandoned this line when the case rested on Agca's claim that three or more Bulgarians openly paraded around Rome with him, hosted him socially, and participated in the May 13, 1981 shooting. With the loss of the case, we believe Sterling and Henze will return to the plausible deniability argument, assuming, probably correctly, that the western media will once again fail to challenge them with facts or the record of their somersaults.

• Sterling and Henze will also contend that the case was lost because the western powers failed to cooperate fully with Italian authorities in bringing the KGB to heel. Sterling has made this point frequently, arguing that the Reagan administration has been fearful that revelations of Soviet misbehavior would undermine détente![6] It is testimony to the power of ideology and interest that this Orwellian nonsense has not interfered in the least with Sterling's credibility as an expert.[7]

• It will be contended further that Soviet threats coerced the Italian government into voluntarily losing the case, again to preserve détente.[8] Before the 1985-86 trial, while the case was under investigation by Judge Ilario Martella, Sterling, Henze, and the mass media periodically claimed that the Bulgarian Connection was being built in the face of strong political opposition. They have never acknowledged the existence of potent vested interests and biases *favoring* the pursuit of the case.[9] And as Martella shared the Sterling-Henze preconceptions, he was consistently lauded as hardworking and conscientious and his investigation was found to be meticulous and thoroughgoing.[10] With the

6. "I think there's been a deliberate effort by certain sections of the government not to take a public position that would concede any possible Bulgarian-Soviet connection because they consider it a destabilizing factor in the East-West power balance for the public to know such things." ("Why Is the West Covering Up for Agca? An exclusive interview with Claire Sterling," *Human Events*, June 26, 1984, p. 54.)

7. See Chapters 6 and 7 for an analysis of Sterling's conspiracy theories, overall record, and hegemonic position in mass media expositions of the plot from August 1982 to mid-1985.

8. A *Wall Street Journal* editorial of January 21, 1985, states that: "Claire Sterling, the Rome-based journalist and terror expert, says the Italian judiciary [sic] is scared to death the politicians will insist on such a coverup [a deal where Antonov makes a limited confession and is released]."

9. These are developed at length in Chapters 4, 6, and 7.

10. We show in Chapter 5 that while Martella was hardworking, his biases and conduct of the investigation left everything to be desired.

thoroughgoing and open trial[11] yielding a rejection of the Bulgarian Connection, the powerful supporters of the Connection will resort once more to a *political* explanation of this (to them) untoward result.[12] When the disinformationists succeed, it is because the truth is on their side; they lose only because of the intrusion of "politics"!

● Finally, it will be alleged that an enormous and uncontested Soviet disinformation campaign affected the climate of opinion in the West, contributing substantially to the loss of the case. This has already been a primary thrust of Sterling, Henze, and their close allies at the Georgetown Center for Strategic and International Studies, the primary sources for media commentary on both the case in Rome and "international terrorism" in general.[13]

We predict that these rationalizations will be given far more exposure than any analyses showing the case to have been an obvious fraud from the beginning, and one which survived only by virtue of media connivance.[14] While most journalists and editorial writers in the respectable media will no longer make outright assertions that the KGB organized the plot to kill the Pope,[15] the contrary case—showing that the Plot was

11. The Martella investigation was not open. This allowed its biases and evidential weaknesses to be kept under cover until the trial forced them into public view.

12. This was greatly facilitated by prosecutor Marini's closing statement in the trial in which he suggested that the case was lost because the judge refused to allow sufficient time to call all the necessary witnesses. The mass media quickly latched on to this opportunity to rationalize the loss of the case. (See, *e.g.*, Elisa Pinna and Luca Balestrieri, "Conviction of Bulgarians in papal plot trial seen as unlikely," *Christian Science Monitor*, March 14, 1986; John Tagliabue, "Acquit Bulgarians, Prosecutor Asks," *New York Times*, February 28, 1986.) These articles fail to note the following: (1) that the trial was exceptionally lengthy and called a very large number of witnesses; (2) that it had been preceded by a two-year investigation which presumably yielded relevant and usable data; and (3) that Marini's effusions may have been a political gesture to protect the Italian establishment from attacks for having brought a case and having expended substantial resources where not even a diligent prosecutor could ask for a verdict of guilty.

13. "The International Implications of the Papal Assassination Attempt: A Case of State-Sponsored Terrorism," A Report of the CSIS Steering Committee on Terrorism, Zbigniew Brzezinski and Robert Kupperman, Cochairmen, CSIS, 1985. For a further discussion of this document, see Appendix E. On the hegemony of *western* disinformation in the national perception of the Bulgarian Connection, see Chapters 6 and 7.

14. See Chapter 7.

15. The editorial page of the *Wall Street Journal*—sometimes known as the "ideological page"—is a notable exception. Any claim that puts the enemy in a bad light finds a welcome home there, whatever the credibility of the source, implausibility of the allegation, or existence of incompatible facts (which are duly suppressed). One week before the prosecutor himself asked for dismissal of the charges against the Bulgarians for lack of

a hoax and analyzing the earlier propaganda outpourings asserting KGB guilt—will still not get much airing. Furthermore, the right wing, now well represented in all parts of the mass media, will be quite free to continue to assert Bulgarian-Soviet guilt. Old, fabricated, and disproved anticommunist tales never die, they merely fade into the dimmer background of popular mythology.

We make no pretense that this book provides an exhaustive treatment of the Bulgarian Connection case. Our objective, instead, has been to provoke serious debate on both the substantive issues involved in the case and its treatment by the media. Toward this end, we have tried to give a coherent and factually accurate alternative analysis to the standard version. We have provided information about the Turkisĥ background to the assassination conspiracy, and have explored the Italian context in which the Bulgarian Connection was fabricated. We have also attempted to set the scene in the United States itself, where the case found a warmly receptive audience, and where disinformationists and the media played an important role in originating and developing the case.

We have gone into considerable detail to show the remarkable lack of both coherence and empirical support for the standard version of the Connection as expounded by Claire Sterling and Paul Henze. The weaknesses and chameleon-like shifts in the ingredients of the party line[16] raise serious questions about how and why the line came into being and dominated the field so thoroughly for an extended time span. In short, the independence and integrity of the mass media are at issue. We therefore devote considerable space to evaluating the quality of the media sources in the case and the processes whereby a party line was institutionalized.[17]

evidence, the *Journal* editorialized that "the question now is not whether there was a Bulgarian Connection but when it began" (February 19, 1986). This was based on the prosecutor's strongest flights of rhetoric and resort to weak hearsay evidence immediately before his abandonment of the case! It would be entirely out of character for the *Journal* to wait for the presentation of the *defense* case, or the decision of the court; it is the prosecutor who is saying what the editorialists want to believe. For the *Journal*, when Agca says something compatible with their preconceptions, he "admits" it; when he says something incompatible with these beliefs, he "attacks his own credibility." This is the language used by Gordon Crovitz in a *Journal* Op-Ed piece on February 12, 1986, entitled "The Bulgarian Connection Still Holds." We may be sure that the Bulgarian Connection will "hold" indefinitely for the *Journal* as its truths are independent of the world of fact.

16. See Chapters 2, 5, and 6.
17. See Chapters 6 and 7.

The inadequacies of the mass media's performance on the Bulgarian Connection were hardly a consequence of a poverty of materials; they were the result of a failure to ask questions, to follow leads, and to use readily available documents. As we describe in Chapters 2 and 7, the media did do some investigative work on the Turkish right wing and the Gray Wolves—the true locus of the plot to shoot the Pope—immediately following the assassination attempt. Once the party line—the Bulgarian Connection—was firmed up, however, all such leads were abandoned and any context for the case incompatible with the line was ignored.

The failure of the western media to meet its own alleged professional standards is illustrated and dramatized by comparing its handling of the case to that of a single reporter, Diana Johnstone. It is our belief that between May 13, 1981, and August 1985, Johnstone, writing on the Bulgarian Connection and related issues for a small weekly newspaper, *In These Times* (circulation about 30,000), conveyed more relevant facts, used more pertinent documentary materials,[18] and provided more intelligent analysis and insight on the Bulgarian Connection than the entire U.S. mass media taken together—radio, TV, newspapers, and weekly news magazines.[19] While this is a testimonial to Johnstone's abilities, it is also indicative of structurally based blinders that hamper and constrain mass media investigative efforts and reporting. These obstructions are apparently not applicable to a reporter working for a small, nonestablishment publication.[20] This contrast, and the overall mass media per-

18. We will show in Chapter 7 that the U.S. press completely ignored a major 1984 report of the Italian Parliament on a rightwing conspiracy, P-2, that had penetrated a secret service organization, SISMI, which played an important role in getting Agca to talk. Also entirely unmentioned was a major court report of July 1985 that described repeated corrupt behavior by SISMI, including the forging and planting of documents. These reports, along with other materials available to but ignored by the U.S. media, were regularly employed by Johnstone.

19. Citations to Johnstone's writings will be found throughout the text below and in the index.

20. On September 12, 1985, Ralph Blumenthal wrote in the *New York Times* that "more than a thousand news articles" had appeared in Italy in the previous 18 months on the story of Francesco Pazienza, a key player in any analysis of the origins of the Bulgarian Connection. Many of these articles claimed that Pazienza was involved in the manipulation of Agca in prison, while most of the rest related to abuses with which Pazienza was a party as a member of the intelligence agency SISMI and often in collaboration with U.S. disinfor-

formance on the Bulgarian Connection, suggest that on major foreign policy issues the mass media is systematically unable to seek the truth and serves instead to dispense system-supportive propaganda.[21]

The authors are indebted to numerous individuals for help in translating documents, discussing the issues of this complex case, and reading and evaluating parts of the manuscript. We would like to make special mention of the following: Wolfgang Achtner, Feroz Ahmad, Sister Elvira Arcenas, John Cammett, Noam Chomsky, Alexander Cockburn, Kevin Coogan, Ellen Davidson, Doug Dowd, David Eisenhower, Franco Ferraresi, Gianni Flamini, Anna Garbesi, Anna Hilbe, Diana Johnstone, Martin Lee, Bill Montross, Ed Morman, Ugur Mumcu, Njat Ozeygin, Donatella Pascolini, Nicholas Pastore, Jim O'Brien, Mark O'Brien, Muieann O Briain, Ellen Ray, Bruno Ruggiero, Bill Schaap, Hayden Shaughnessy, Helen Simone, and Lou Wolf. We owe very special debts to Howard Friel and Andy Levine. Frank Brodhead would also like to thank Christine Wing and Benjamin Boyd for their support and great patience during this project. Finally, the authors want to express their gratitude to Carol and Ping Ferry for their generous financial assistance. The authors remain responsible for the content of this book.

mationist Michael Ledeen. During this 18 month period, however, the *New York Times* never discussed Pazienza, with the exception of a single, brief news article in the Business Section of the paper on March 25, 1985. Our hypothesis is that this systematic avoidance was a result of the paper's commitment to the party line, which would be disturbed by reference to Pazienza and his shenanigans. Again, Diana Johnstone was not subject to this kind of self-imposed prior constraint and could use these voluminous and highly relevant press materials freely. (See further, Chapter 7, under "The *New York Times*-Sterling-Ledeen Axis.")

21. An interesting case study could be done on the timing of media investigations and disclosure of the stolen wealth of the Marcos family. Although the Marcoses' looting occurred over an extended period, the U.S. mass media were exceedingly quiet and their investigatory zeal reined in on that subject until the U.S. government withdrew its support from Marcos in late 1985. At that point, as if by a tacit signal, there appeared a flood of disclosures. While Marcos was a valued ally, his looting was off the agenda; with Marcos in process of ouster, his looting was freely discussed.

1. Introduction

O n May 13, 1981 a young Turkish gunman fired shots at Pope John Paul II as the Pope's vehicle circled slowly through the crowd in St. Peter's Square. Gravely wounded, the Pope was rushed to the hospital. His assailant, Mehmet Ali Agca, was tackled by a nun and captured by the crowd. The Italian police soon reconstructed his movements prior to the shooting, seeking to determine his motives and accomplices. Yet when Agca was brought to trial in July 1981, little of this information was produced in court; his aims were still unclear and no co-conspirators were named.

Agca's crime was committed in the fourth month of the Reagan presidency. From the outset administration officials and supporters sought to link the assassination attempt to the Soviet Union and its allies, in accordance with its new stress on "terrorism," and in aid of the new plans for a military buildup at home and the placement of advanced missiles in Western Europe. This effort did not bear fruit, however, until the publication of an article by Claire Sterling in the September 1982 issue of *Reader's Digest*. Sterling maintained that the attempted assassination, previously thought to have been the work of a rightwing gunman, acting either alone or as a member of a Turkish rightwing network, was in fact instigated by the Bulgarian secret services, and behind them the KGB. This latter claim took on particular significance because at that moment the heir apparent to the terminally ill Leonid Brezhnev was Yuri Andropov, who had been the head of the KGB at the time of the assassination attempt. Thus a successful linking of the KGB to the shooting would seriously cripple the prospective leader's ability to project any moral claims for Soviet policies were he actually to succeed Brezhnev.[1]

1. Andropov received little notice in the West as a possible successor to Brezhnev until the death of Mikhail Suslov in January 1982. An article by Don Oberdorfer in the *Washington Post* on April 3, 1982, mentioned Konstantin Chernenko as a likely succes-

The claim of a Bulgarian Connection received apparent confirmation in November 1982, when Agca declared that several Bulgarian officials residing in Rome had assisted him in his crime, and that the plan had originally been laid while he was passing through Bulgaria in the summer of 1980. Two of the named officials had returned to Bulgaria, but one of them, Sergei Antonov, deputy director of Balkan Air, was immediately arrested. With the heightening of Cold War tensions, and European debate and demonstrations over the scheduled deployment of new U.S. missiles reaching their peak, Agca's accusations found a ready and uncritical reception in the western media. While no independent evidence linking Agca to the Bulgarians, or the Bulgarians to the crime, was forthcoming, Agca's mere declaration and its apparent confirmation by the arrest of Antonov all but convicted Bulgaria in the western press. Leaks of Agca's evolving claims, which soon included a Bulgarian-instigated plot to murder Lech Walesa, served to keep the pot boiling. Despite severe problems of fact and logic, the Italian judicial machinery ground slowly but steadily through its investigations, culminating in an official indictment of three Bulgarians and six Turks on October 25, 1984. A trial of these indicted individuals began on May 27, 1985, and ended with the acquittal of the Bulgarians on March 29, 1986.

It is our judgment that the media's uncritical, even enthusiastic, embrace of the case developed by Claire Sterling and the Italian prosecution was not merely wrong, but also points up the more general propaganda role played by the press. As we will show below, the credibility of Agca, the primary (in fact, *sole*) witness—based on his character, history, political affiliations, circumstances of imprisonment, and shifts and contradictions in testimony—is close to zero.[2] Furthermore, the logic of the case, as advanced by its leading proponents, was seriously flawed and rested ultimately on Cold War premises.[3] We believe that similar evidence and arguments put forward in a case not helpful to western political interests would have been objects of derision and quickly rejected and buried.[4]

sor. It was not until Andropov was appointed to an important new post in the Party Secretariat on May 24, and resigned from his position as head of the KGB two days later, that he was regarded publicly in the West as a leading candidate to succeed Brezhnev. This period of the emergence of Andropov coincides with the sudden decision by Agca to cooperate and name his alleged Bulgarian collaborators.

2. See Chapters 2-5.
3. See Chapters 2, 5, and 6.
4. For example, imagine the response of the West if a lifelong leftist terrorist, after

A Dual Conspiracy

Where the creators of the Bulgarian Connection see one conspiracy, we see two. The first was a conspiracy to assassinate the Pope. The second was a conspiracy to take advantage of control over the imprisoned Agca to pin the assassination attempt on the Bulgarians and KGB. We, like Claire Sterling and her associates, believe there was a conspiracy to assassinate the Pope. But who were the participants? In the Sterling model it was the Bulgarians and KGB. But throughout the investigation and trial in Rome, the only evidence of Agca's linkages that was not based on his word alone (and that of Claire Sterling and company), suggested a conspiracy rooted in a Turkish neofascist organization called the Gray Wolves. Its members assisted Agca in escaping from a Turkish prison in November 1979; aided, financed, and sheltered him during the 18 months prior to the assassination attempt; and cooperated with him in carrying it out. There is extensive evidence in the final report of Investigating Magistrate Ilario Martella, and in the record of the Rome trial, of these continuing and intimate contacts between Agca and the Gray Wolves network in the months prior to the assassination attempt. Investigations into Agca's background in Turkey have also placed him squarely in the midst of an intricate web of political rightists, drug dealers, and gun runners—a large proportion also Gray Wolves—who were the only known participants in the conspiracy to shoot the Pope.[5] We develop these links, and the possible motivations that might have led Agca and his associates to attempt to kill the Pope, in Chapter 3.

The main focus of our work, however, is on the second conspiracy, which used the imprisoned Agca to advance various Italian and New Cold War political interests. The Rome trial, while discrediting the Bulgarian Connection, greatly strengthened the hypothesis that Agca was coached to implicate the Bulgarians. This conspiracy was implemented

being held captive in a Bulgarian prison for 18 months, suddenly confessed that he had acted for the CIA, several of whose officials he identified from a picture album showed to him by the Bulgarian secret services!

5. Up to the time of the trial it was thought that Agca had one or more Turkish accomplices in Rome at the time of the assassination attempt. The trial raised doubts about any on-the-scene accomplices of Agca, although it has not diminished the force of the evidence that Agca was moving through the Gray Wolves network in his passage through Europe to the rendezvous in Rome. See further, Chapter 3, pp. 53-55.

by the Italian secret services and their allies in the Vatican and the
Mafia, with assistance from other members of the Italian government,
their friends in the Reagan administration, and the press.[6] We believe
that a powerful analogy can be drawn between the "confessions" extracted during the Soviet political trials of the 1930s and Agca's "confessions" of 1982 and 1983. In Chapter 4 we describe the domestic and
international forces at work in recent years which encouraged the Italian
initiators to press Agca into implicating the eastern Bloc in the Plot. We
also discuss the background of the Italian security services, which were
mobilized early in the Cold War era as an activist, anticommunist instrument of U.S. and conservative Italian political aims.[7] These services
played an important role in rightwing destabilization strategies of the
1960s and 1970s, including efforts to plant fabricated evidence on the
Left. We discuss the massive rightwing conspiracy *Propaganda Due*, or
P-2, which was exposed in a major scandal shortly after the assassination attempt against the Pope in 1981. An Italian Parliamentary Report
on P-2, issued in July 1984, showed that those agencies of the Italian
state which held Agca in captivity, which had daily access to him, and
which participated in the investigation of his evolving claims, had been
thoroughly penetrated by P-2.

The gradually accumulating evidence that Agca was induced to implicate the Bulgarians by means of both positive incentives and threats is
spelled out in Chapters 4 and 5. We also describe the weaknesses of the
Italian judicial process in its investigative phase, which combined major
violations of judicial and scientific procedure in handling evidence with
a flow of timely leaks that allowed numerous Cold War points to be
scored by proponents of the Plot. We show in Chapter 5 that Judge
Ilario Martella was an ideal choice to pursue the investigation, quietly
dignified but dedicated to proving an *a priori* truth.

The Italians did not decide to pursue the Bulgarian Connection entirely on their own. Italy is a part of the Free World, and it was caught
up in a web of larger interests. The Reagan administration's rearmament
plans and antiterrorism campaign provided encouragement, ideological

6. We believe that this conspiracy was loosely organized and tacit, not centrally directed, and with a number of participants pursuing the same end quite independently,
some playing their role knowingly, others contributing innocently in the belief that they
were merely expressing or eliciting a self-evident truth. (See the beginning of Chapter 8
on the multiple invention of the second conspiracy.)

7. See Chapter 4.

support, and political backing for such an initiative.[8] Encouragement and support came in part from the pressures built up in the U.S. mass media, but they also flowed through more direct channels. The penetration and manipulation of the Italian state by the CIA and other agencies of the U.S. government is a matter of public record, confirmed by the Pike Committee of the House of Representatives[9] and by many independent Italian investigations. In Chapters 4 and 5 we describe this background of manipulation and quasi-dependency. We also discuss some of the recent evidence in Italian court documents and in the press revealing linkages and cooperative ventures between officials of the Reagan administration and agents of the Italian secret services. We show that the team of Michael Ledeen and Francesco Pazienza, which had already achieved a notable success in manufacturing the "Billygate" scandal in 1980, was virtually directing U.S.-Italian relations during the Reagan transition era. This team was well positioned to encourage the second conspiracy and disseminate information linking the papal assassination attempt to the Bulgarians and Soviets.

We also show that the Bulgarian Connection had already been concocted in documents fabricated by the Italian secret services only days after the assassination attempt, and that the idea of getting Agca to tell this story had arisen early from several different sources. There were numerous avenues through which interested parties in the secret services, Mafia, Vatican, and other political interests could persuade, threaten, and instruct Agca on a proper confession. The evidence suggests that Agca was induced to confess properly by a variety of individuals and interests, sometimes acting alone, sometimes working in collaboration.[10] We believe that the Italian background and the interna-

8. Part of the conservative line on the Bulgarian Connection is that its prosecution suffered grievously from Reagan administration and CIA negativism and foot-dragging, rooted in a devotion to détente, with perhaps some assistance from KGB moles who have penetrated the government. This line, which stands the truth on its head, reached its finest flowering in the writings of Claire Sterling and in the Georgetown Center for Strategic and International Studies pamphlet on the papal assassination attempt. See Chapter 6 and Appendix E.

9. The "Pike Committee" was the Select Committee on Intelligence of the U.S. House of Representatives. Its report on the CIA's record, completed in February 1976, was never published by the government, but was leaked and made available by the *Village Voice* on February 16 and 23, 1976. It was issued in book form by Spokesman Books in England in 1977, with an introduction by Philip Agee, under the title *CIA: The Pike Report*. For some of its findings pertaining to the CIA in Italy, see Chapter 4, p. 73.

10. In the account of Giovanni Pandico, a former Mafia leader, now the chief state wit-

tional New Cold War political context are essential to understanding the Bulgarian Connection. It is this context which explains why many individuals with access to Agca were anxious that he confess, and why the western political and media environment was receptive to an implausible confession. This essential background, however, has rarely been mentioned by the *New York Times* or the major media sources in the West. Thus, while featuring prominently the report of Prosecutor Albano and the final report of Magistrate Martella in 1984, the *Times* and its mass media associates completely ignored the sensational findings of the July 1984 Italian Parliamentary Report on P-2 and the major July 1985 Italian court report on the multiple abuses of Francesco Pazienza and SISMI, the Italian intelligence agency with which he was associated. The only "politics" which the media allow to enter the discussion of the Connection is the Soviet concern over Solidarity and the Polish upheaval, which happens to coincide with the interpretation of the motivations for the assassination attempt developed by Claire Sterling and her associates.

The reasons for this dichotomous treatment seem quite clear. If the media is playing a supportive political role, it will not only concentrate its attention on reports and political themes damaging to the enemy, but it will also ignore any information that would suggest hidden political motives behind the case or cast doubt on the quality of our allies (the supporting cast). This allows commentators such as the *Wall Street Journal*'s Suzanne Garment to endorse the Bulgarian Connection on the basis of the integrity and even superior wisdom of the Italians: "Mind you, this is the Italians—no American hawk paranoids but instead people who live with a new government every thirty days. You simply cannot doubt their word."[11] While it would be interesting to examine Garment's view that political instability is a source of sound political judgment, the more important point is that not only *can* we doubt the "word" (and the political processes) of an Italian state machinery saturated with P-2 cadres, but we *must* do so if we are to arrive at the truth behind the Bulgarian Connection.

While the U.S. media have suppressed the Italian context of the Bulgarian Connection, their treatment of the involvement of U.S. citizens in the creation of the Connection attained an even higher level of prop-

ness in a trial of the Naples Mafia, it is suggested that a number of convergent interests—Mafia, Vatican, and secret services—worked together in getting Agca to talk. See below, Chapters 4 and 5.

11. *Wall Street Journal*, June 15, 1984.

aganda service. Here the very individuals actively participating in the manufacture of the Plot were mobilized to serve as the main media sources of information on the subject. The most important investigative work—or, we should say, creative writing—in establishing the hypothesis of the Bulgarian Connection was done by Claire Sterling, Paul Henze, and Michael Ledeen. Their writings in the *New York Times, Christian Science Monitor, Reader's Digest,* and other publications, and their frequent appearances on the MacNeil/Lehrer News Hour, the Sunday television news programs, and before Senator Jeremiah Denton's Subcommittee on Security and Terrorism show them to be the media's commentators of choice on the Bulgarian Connection. That these individuals have long records of CIA and other intelligence agency connections and disinformation service has not been disclosed to the American public. We discuss their role and performance at length in Chapter 6. In Chapter 7 we describe the remarkable dominance which they have been able to exercise over the U.S. mass media in the dissemination of the Plot.

This pattern of media bias is a uniform characteristic of Red Scare eras. In every such period, as during the Palmer raids (1919-20) or the McCarthy years (1950-54), hysteria and bias overwhelm any sense of fair play, justice, and concern for truthfulness. A wave of passion and propaganda establishes guilt beforehand and makes doubts seem subversive. While Red Scares require a favorable climate of opinion in which to develop, they do not simply emerge spontaneously; rather, they are cultivated and stoked by prospective beneficiaries and their agents.[12] The Bulgarian Connection met a need in the emerging New Cold War comparable to that met by earlier Red Scares. We believe that it was similarly created and stoked by Claire Sterling, Paul Henze, Michael Ledeen, and their governmental and media allies.[13] These influential disinformation specialists, linked to both the Reagan administration and to the Italian secret services, first created and packaged the Bulgarian Connection, and then helped sell it to the Italians. Finally, in a scenario worthy of Pirandello, they became the terrorism "experts" and commentators to whom the *New York Times,* the *Christian Science Monitor,*

12. See Robert Murray, *Red Scare: A Study of National Hysteria, 1919-1920* (Minneapolis: University of Minnesota Press, 1955); David Caute, *The Great Fear: The Anti-Communist Purge Under Truman and Eisenhower* (New York: Simon and Schuster, 1978).

13. It was also simultaneously created and stoked by Italian intelligence and other local sources. This was a case of multiple invention and causation. See Chapter 8, pp. 206-09.

the MacNeil/Lehrer News Hour, and the NBC Nightly News turned to elucidate and evaluate the real story of what the nefarious KGB was up to.

2. The Evolution of the Bulgarian Connection

his book is a case study in the response of the West—of its intelligence agencies and mass media, intellectuals and disinformationists—to an act of terror. The response was complex, but the "Bulgarian Connection" was its most important outcome. The Connection did not emerge full-blown from a single source; it grew piece by piece over a period of four years, and many hands contributed to its manufacture. In this chapter we will examine the craft of these many laborers, and look at the evidence, claims, and hypotheses with which they constructed the Connection.

The Preliminary Version: A Turkish Conspiracy

Looking back, it seems amazing that the story could have been turned around so swiftly and smoothly, before the eyes of several hundred journalists gathered in Rome from the four corners of the globe to cover the papal shooting. The truth was close enough to touch for a fleeting instant, and then it was gone. At the first sign of a probable conspiracy, government and Church leaders perceived the dangers of exposing it. A wall of refracting mirrors went up overnight, deflecting our vision at every turn.[1]

So begins Claire Sterling's argument that a great international cover-up was organized to conceal the conspiracy that supported Agca's attempt to kill the Pope. At the very outset of her study of the Bulgarian Connection, Sterling characteristically distorts elementary aspects of the historical record to make it appear that—against the callous indifference

1. Claire Sterling, *The Time of the Assassins* (New York: Holt, Rinehart and Winston, 1983), p. 5.

of the West and the active disinformation efforts of the East—she has rescued the truth about the Soviet-Bloc conspiracy to kill the Pope. What was "the truth that was close enough to touch"? According to Sterling, Italian authorities determined immediately after Agca shot the Pope that he had been aided by "other persons who remain unknown," as Attorney General Achille Gallucci put it in his arrest order. Judge Luciano Infelisi, who signed the order, noted that "for us, there is documentary proof that Mehmet Ali Agca did not act alone." These quotations, from the May 15, 1981 issue of the Turin newspaper *La Stampa*, are cited by Sterling at the beginning of her book. They are immediately contrasted with a statement from the *New York Times* of the same day that "Police are convinced, according to government sources, that Mr. Agca acted alone." For Sterling, this was the beginning of the cover-up.

As she develops this line of thought in the introductory pages of *The Time of the Assassins*, Sterling makes four points:

1. Italian officials were initially convinced that there was a conspiracy to kill the Pope, and then suddenly retreated on this issue, saying that there was insufficient evidence;

2. The western media generally followed this lead, dropping any investigation into the possibility that there was a conspiracy to kill the Pope, and taking as true Agca's claim to be "an international terrorist" acting alone;

3. The conspiracy that the Italian authorities initially detected was one involving international terrorists and Soviet-backed organizations; and

4. The Italian authorities and the western media backed off from investigating this conspiracy because of their overriding interest in maintaining or supporting détente.

Was there a cover-up? It is evident from a simple reading of the western press in the days and weeks following the assassination attempt that the question of a conspiracy was very much alive. A day-by-day account of the reporting in the *New York Times* and the *Washington Post* for the first ten days following the assassination attempt, which we present in Appendix A, clearly shows that Sterling's "wall of refracting mirrors" was completely ineffective in stemming the media's pursuit of a possible conspiracy. We also know from leaked documents and published accounts of the investigation that up to the time of Agca's trial,

Italian officials continued to pursue the possibility that he had help.[2] The conspiracy under investigation, however, which Sterling fails to see,[3] was a *Turkish* conspiracy, based in the shadowy rightwing network called the Gray Wolves and in its parent organization, the Nationalist Action Party of Turkey. To the extent that there was any official hesitancy in investigating this wider conspiracy, therefore, it can only be inferred that someone or some institution was reluctant to explore any possible links to international fascist networks that might compromise Italy's NATO allies.

This finding, moreover, was reflected across the board in the U.S. media. Summaries of the evening news broadcasts of the three major U.S. television networks reveal a sustained interest in Agca's Turkish roots.[4] *Time* magazine, in its first issue after the assassination attempt, described Agca as a "right-wing fanatic" and connected him to the Nationalist Action Party.[5] Similarly, *Newsweek*'s (far more extensive) coverage placed Agca in the world of the Gray Wolves, even speculating on more far-reaching connections to European fascists as well.[6]

Finally, we must point out that this preliminary model seemed so compelling that it convinced even Claire Sterling, who made what were perhaps her most cogent remarks on the Plot in an interview with *People* magazine immediately after the papal shooting.[7]

Some people are saying that the Russians plotted this because of the Pope's role

2. For example, on May 25, 1981, SISMI turned over to investigating magistrate Domenico Sica the names of 11 Turks with whom Agca was known to have associated in West Germany and/or Switzerland, and who were wanted by Turkish police for "subversive activities" in association with the Gray Wolves (SISMI document number 1356904). Among the 11 Turks named were Mehmet Sener, Abdullah Catli, and Oral Celik. On May 27, 1981, DIGOS, the Italian anti-terrorist police, forwarded to Judge Sica information about 17 "suspected Turkish citizens" who were known to have links with Agca (DIGOS document number 051195/81). This latter document was published in *Espresso* on December 6, 1982. (See Sari Gilbert, "3 Bulgarians Linked To Shooting of Pope," *Washington Post*, December 8, 1982.) The DIGOS report of September 15, 1981, (see below, note 20) indicates that the investigation continued.

3. Just as Sterling can never see rightwing terror (see Chapter 6), so it is possible that she is unable to recognize a rightist conspiracy as a genuine conspiracy.

4. Vanderbilt University Television News Archive, *Television News Index and Abstracts* (May 14-25, 1981), pp. 831-902.

5. "Not Yet Hale, But Hearty," *Time*, June 1, 1981, pp. 34-35.

6. "The Man With the Gun," *Newsweek*, May 25, 1981, pp. 36-38.

7. "An Authority on Terrorism Offers A Chilling New Theory on the Shooting of the Pope," *People*, June 1, 1981, pp. 32-35.

in Poland, but I think that's crazy. If it was an organized plot by a serious group, I suspect there would have been a better getaway plan. Maybe this was a sort of kamikaze mission, but usually these people are skillful at escapes. There would have been some distraction in the crowd, some escape route. I could envision a small splinter group of Moslem fanatics with Agca among them vowing to get the Pope. But more likely he made the final decision alone.

Sterling saw a possible motivation for an attack on the Pope, noting that he "isn't perceived as just the head of the Roman Catholic Church, but as the supreme symbol of the intrusion of western civilization" into the Moslem world. She also noted that the attack occurred shortly after the release of the hostages at the U.S. Embassy in Iran, and in the wake of the attack on the Grand Mosque at Mecca, which in the Middle East was widely (but falsely) attributed to the CIA and Israel.[8] Sterling also argued that the Pope's trip to Turkey in 1979 had been highly inflammatory and "a terrible mistake." Finally, she placed Agca within the networks of the Gray Wolves, "the paramilitary wing of the neo-Nazi National [sic] Action Party."

This, then, may be taken as the preliminary paradigm of any possible "Connection" to Agca and the assassination attempt: a conspiracy which was rooted in Turkish neofascism, sustained by the European branches of the Turkish Right, and motivated by the problematic ideology of the Gray Wolves and the unstable personality of Agca himself. We call this the "first conspiracy." We will examine the Turkish roots of this conspiracy in Chapter 3, and show that no agents of the East were required to originate and execute Agca's assassination attempt.

The Challenges Confronting Sterling and Company

The facts unearthed by police and journalists that connected Agca to a Turkish rightwing conspiracy provided a formidable challenge to Sterling and her associates in their efforts to transform the case into a Soviet-based plot. As the case for a Bulgarian-KGB Connection was developed, logical contradictions also emerged that demanded (but never received) resolution. Some of the core problems were as follows:

Agca's relation to the "Gray Wolves." Those arguing for a Bulgarian

8. Agca had mentioned the attack on the Mosque and attributed it to the United States and Israel in his 1979 note in which he first announced his intention to shoot the Pope.

Connection were divided on whether Agca was always a KGB recruit who was simply using his Gray Wolves associations for cover, or whether he was in fact a genuine participant in rightwing activities and terrorism who was later recruited by the KGB. Claire Sterling, for example, told a congressional investigating committee in 1982 that Agca was "a sleeper," a lifelong Soviet agent who was activated only when a strike against the Pope became necessary.[9] Others have argued that Agca was recruited at the university, or while in a Turkish prison, or only later, in Bulgaria. But the only known *facts* are that Agca was continuously involved with Turkish fascists from his high school days.

Agca's stay in Bulgaria. A key element in Bulgarian Connection scenarios has always been the fact that Agca stayed in Sofia, Bulgaria for some days or weeks in the summer of 1980.[10] Sterling and NBC-TV claimed that the very fact of Agca's presence in Sofia proved Bulgarian guilt, because the Bulgarian police know everything and must have been "protecting" Agca. Thus, according to Marvin Kalb, it "seems safe to conclude that he had been drawn into the clandestine network of the Bulgarian secret police and, by extension, the Soviet KGB—perhaps without his even being aware of their possible plans for him."[11] This is a *non sequitur* that rests on a number of assumptions, some of them quite foolish. Agca came into Bulgaria on a false passport, and the flow of Turks through Bulgaria numbers in excess of a million a year. The assumption that the Bulgarians knew of Agca's presence is therefore unproven.[12] The further assumption that, if his presence was known, he must have been protected and recruited by the Bulgarians for some se-

9. "The Assassination Attempt on Pope John Paul II," Hearing before the Commission on Security and Cooperation in Europe, 97th Congress, 2nd Session (September 23, 1982), p. 7. She has never given evidence that this was so, but this has never been demanded of her by friendly congressional and media interlocutors.

10. Perhaps the most important aspect of his stay is that even Agca has rarely claimed contact there with any Bulgarian official. For a long time he claimed to have worked strictly through intermediaries, although eventually a Bulgarian official came into the picture. During the trial Agca disconcertingly took the new tack that on July 4, 1980, he had been introduced to the First Secretary of the Soviet Embassy in Sofia, who visited him in his hotel room!

11. "The Man Who Shot the Pope—A Study in Terrorism," transcript of NBC-TV program of September 21, 1982, pp. 44-45.

12. During his testimony at the Rome trial on September 22, 1985, Gray Wolves leader Abdullah Catli gave as one reason for Agca's visiting Bulgaria, instead of proceeding directly into Western Europe, the fact that the volume of Turkish traffic is so large that a Turk may enter Bulgaria without having to undergo very careful checks!

cret purpose is simple-minded Cold War ideology. *If* the Bulgarians knew who Agca was they may have been uninterested in him, or they may have failed to arrest him because of incompetence or indifference to the appeals of Turkish authorities, or they may have left him alone as a favor to Turkish smuggling interests with whom the Gray Wolves were linked.

The Bulgarian-Soviet motive. The issue of motive also bedevils various accounts of the alleged Bulgarian link. Why would the Bulgarians or the Soviets want to kill the Pope? Advocates of the Bulgarian Connection hypothesis have built a motive out of the situation in Poland between the election of Cardinal Wojtyla as Pope in 1979 and the proclamation of Solidarity in late August 1980. It was the Pope's support for Solidarity which is held to be the key to the Soviet desire to want him out of the way, and at one point it was even claimed that he had declared his intention to lay down the papal crown and return to Poland in the event of a Soviet invasion.

There are several very serious difficulties with this imputed rationale. First, Agca had already threatened to kill the Pope in 1979 during the Pope's visit to Turkey, long before Solidarity existed or Poland was in turmoil. This suggests the likelihood that the real explanation for the assassination attempt is to be found in Turkey. Second, the timing of Agca's alleged conspiracy with the Bulgarians also presents problems, as Solidarity was formed in late August 1980, while, according to Sterling, Agca's dealings in Sofia were largely completed by early July of that year. Third, there is no reason to believe that killing the Pope would have been useful to the Soviet Union, and the costs and risks of either a successful or a bungled assassination plot were great. The magnitude of the potential damage from such an effort has been demonstrated by the events which have unfolded since May 1981, as the attempted assassination was ultimately pinned on the Soviets on the basis of mere suspicion. Nowhere is the belief in Soviet complicity stronger than in Poland, and it is hard to imagine how any Soviet official could have expected that a successful assassination attempt would have quelled unrest in Poland. Furthermore, if an assassination had been convincingly linked to the Soviet Union, this would have had a devastating effect on Soviet efforts to oppose the new missiles planned for Europe and to advance the gas pipeline project, goals then considered by the Soviets to be of great importance. In short, this would have been an extremely foolhardy enterprise for the Soviet Union to embark on, and western analysts of

Soviet politics regard the Soviet leadership as cautious and not inclined to adventurism.[13]

Finally, there is some evidence that the Soviets regarded the Church as a *conservative* force in Poland. According to the Turin newspaper *La Stampa*, in December 1980 Vadim Zagladin, Vice-Secretary of Foreign Affairs in the Soviet Communist Party's Central Committee, told the Vatican that "Moscow does not intend to invade Poland, but that the Church should continue to use its influence so that certain situations do not escalate." (At this time western media and government officials considered a Soviet invasion of Poland imminent.) A second Soviet official, according to *La Stampa*, told Vatican Secretary of State Cardinal Agostino Casaroli that "If the Church committed itself to stem the ardor of the Polish strikers within limits acceptable to Moscow, then Moscow in her turn would renounce the idea of an invasion."[14] According to this line of thought, which has considerable support in the historical record, the Polish Pope, the Vatican, and the Polish Church acted as a stabilizing force in Poland; and the assassination of Pope John Paul II would only threaten the very stability the Soviets sought there.

Operational ineptitude: (1) hiring Agca. Each successive version of the Bulgarian Connection has also had to wrestle with the overall ineptness of the alleged plot. Why would the Bulgarians want to hire Agca in the first place? Of the hundreds of rightwing terrorists wanted by the Turkish government, Agca was probably the most notorious; and, as the events of his 1985 trial have demonstrated, he was personally unstable. As an anticommunist he would have little compunction in confessing to Bulgarian involvement. The hypothesis that Agca was hired by the Bulgarians in the summer of 1980, after his escape from Turkey's maximum security prison and then from Turkey itself, must contend with the fact that at just that moment Turkey and Interpol were issuing bulletins asking for his immediate arrest. In their respective reports, Deputy Prosecutor Albano and Judge Martella stressed Agca's notoriety, maintaining that both the Bulgarians and the Turks who allegedly assisted Agca should have known precisely with whom they were deal-

---

13. See, *e.g.*, George Kennan, *The Nuclear Delusion: Soviet-American Relations in the Atomic Age* (New York: Pantheon, 1982); John Lowenhardt, *Decision-Making in Soviet Politics* (New York: St. Martin's Press, 1981); and Jerry Hough and Merle Fainsod, *How the Soviet Union is Governed* (Cambridge, Mass.: Harvard University Press, 1979).

14. Cited in "The Papal Attack Background," *Intelligence Digest* (Great Britain), October 1, 1981.

ing and could not plead ignorance that "Farouk Ozgun" was in fact Agca, the wanted criminal.[15] Yet precisely this notoriety would have caused any intelligence service to steer clear of Agca.

Operational ineptitude: (2) the Sofia gambit. In explaining the lack of any direct evidence for Bulgarian or Soviet involvement, Claire Sterling and her associates have always retreated to the notion that the KGB is a very professional body that does things well, covers its tracks, and operates from a base of "plausible deniability." Thus the very lack of evidence, according to the Sterling school, pointed to a Soviet hand in the plot. In the version of the Connection developed in the second half of 1982 by Sterling in the *Reader's Digest* and by Marvin Kalb on NBC-TV, the implausibility of bringing Agca to a prominent hotel in Sofia to be recruited and/or to get his instructions was not mentioned. In the interest of maintaining plausible deniability, however, Sofia is the last place to which any Bulgarian co-conspirators would want Agca to be traced. If contact between Agca and Bulgarian officials were observed by western agents in Sofia—certainly a reasonable possibility—the logic of hiring a fascist to provide a cover for a Bulgarian- and KGB-sponsored plot would be badly compromised from the start.

Thus the presence of Agca in Sofia, rather than supporting a Bulgarian Connection, tends to undermine it. In fact, it more readily supports two alternative views. The first is that someone wanted Agca to be linked to Bulgaria before he got on with his assassination attempt, after which he could be worked over at leisure until he "confessed." The second, which we believe to be entirely valid, is that because Agca had stayed in Sofia, Italian and other western intelligence services and propagandists seized the opportunity to build a case which, with an induced confession, would be salable in the well-conditioned West.

Operational ineptitude: (3) the assassination attempt. Another major operational difficulty with the hypothesis of the Bulgarian Connection is the gross ineptitude of the assassination attempt. It is hard to imagine a more poorly managed plan of attack than the one employed in Rome. Agca not only failed to kill the Pope, but he himself was neither rescued

15. On a number of occasions Turkish authorities were notified that Agca had been sighted in Italy, Switzerland, or West Germany, and unsuccessfully requested that he be arrested. For some reason, no negative implications have been attached to the West German, Swiss, and Italian authorities for their failure to apprehend Agca, despite lengthy stays in their countries and repeated Turkish protestations.

nor killed. Writings and other items found in Agca's room and on his person after his arrest would have helped incriminate and identify him, even if he had escaped or been killed. On the whole there was nothing in this operation that even hinted at the alleged professionalism of the Soviet-Bloc intelligence services. Rather, the obvious amateurishness of the assassination tactics fits far better an operation managed by Agca and perhaps a few of his friends.

Operational ineptitude: (4) the Bulgarian involvement in Rome. The operational weaknesses of the alleged Plot reached epic proportions after Agca had declared that Bulgarian state officials met with him and guided his movements in Rome. Proponents of the case would have us believe that the Bulgarian secret service involved its agents in direct contact, planning, and tactical maneuvers with Agca up to the moment of the assassination attempt itself. Agca and two or three Bulgarians allegedly visited St. Peter's Square on each of the two days preceding the assassination attempt in order to make the final plans. Not one but two of the Bulgarians would allegedly drive Agca to the Square, and one Bulgarian official would use smoke bombs to divert the crowd's attention so that Agca could get a good shot and/or make a getaway. This would, of course, entail serious risk of a Bulgarian being arrested right at the scene of the crime, the very thing that hiring a Turk with right-wing credentials was supposed to avoid, according to the Sterling-Henze model!

In his early declarations implicating the Bulgarians, Agca even claimed that he visited Antonov and Aivazov in their homes in the Embassy compound; and in one instance, just days before the assassination attempt, he supposedly met Antonov's wife and young daughter. This latter statement was subsequently "withdrawn," but this was not done on the basis of scrutiny or ridicule on the part of the western press, nor doubts and investigative efforts by Martella. The accumulated contradictions and exposed lies, as we shall see, had simply become too top-heavy to sustain.

The lag in Agca's confession. It took Agca more than 17 months after his arrest to name his Bulgarian co-conspirators—six months after he had agreed to "tell all." Investigating Magistrate Martella never bothered to explain this long time lag. Sterling explained the delay as a result of Agca's expectation that the Bulgarians and KGB would get him out of prison. But she never indicated how the Bulgarians could do this without admitting guilt and once again contradicting the logic of employing a rightwing assassin.[16]

These weaknesses in the case were never overcome. The most interesting questions, therefore, are why, by whom, and how so implausible, undocumented, and internally contradictory a Plot was created and sustained in the Italian courts and in the western press for a three-year period.

The First Trial: Agca's Fast One of 1981

While there were immediate efforts to link the Soviets to the assassination attempt, when the Italian government brought Agca to trial in July 1981 any co-conspirators were assumed to have been fellow Turks and members of the Gray Wolves. Yet little was revealed by the trial, and no solid information about any possible conspiracy was forthcoming.

It is puzzling that the Italian authorities moved to try Agca so quickly, before the investigation of a conspiracy could be completed. One possible explanation is that Italian authorities wished to have him convicted and under their control, and feared that any delay would increase the possibility that Agca would be found mentally incompetent to stand trial. Media reports about Agca's childhood and Turkish background, combined with his wild lies under interrogation, raised the possibility that he was seriously deranged. Indeed, Agca's court-appointed lawyer—Pietro d'Ovidio, a frequent defender of rightwing criminals—asked the court to delay the trial until Turkish authorities could furnish the court with copies of psychiatric examinations conducted at the time of Agca's murder trial in 1979. The court ruled, however, that the contents of these examinations (which had allegedly said that Agca was medically competent to stand trial) were known through press reports, and d'Ovidio's request was refused.

At the opening of his trial, Agca maintained that he acted alone. "I did not want to talk to anyone about my plan to kill the Pope," he said. "I acted independently, in the name of truth above ideologies. I do not belong to any organization. International terrorism as I conceive it is not concerned with ideology. It needs no idea. It needs a gun."[17] Shortly

16. This issue is discussed below in this chapter and in Chapter 6.
17. Cited in Paul Henze, *The Plot To Kill the Pope* (New York: Charles Scribner's

after making this statement Agca announced that he would take no more part in the trial, and attempted to dismiss his lawyer. The prosecutor, saying that "no one can understand or even guess the reason behind this act," called Agca "the son of modern-day terrorism, that sinister affliction of our time," and described the assassination attempt as "symbolic patricide."[18] At the end of his three day trial, therefore, the jury deliberated for six hours and sentenced Agca to life imprisonment. He would be eligible for parole in 30 years.

The Court's decision, however, also observed that "the plea of guilty by the accused must not close the case, since it is necessary still to explore certain aspects of the affair and to throw light on the background from which a crime of this kind emerged."[19] Thus, when the Court issued its full 51-page "Statement of Motivation" on September 24, 1981, Agca was described as "only the visible point of a conspiracy which, though impossible to define, was widespread and menacing and devised by shadowy forces." The report described Agca's act as the "fruit of a complex machination orchestrated by hidden minds interested in creating new conditions of destabilization." Despite the Court's uncertainty over the precise relations between Agca and the Gray Wolves—"which not even the Turkish authorities were able to render intelligible"—the Statement of Motivation maintained that Agca was "not a religious fanatic" but a disciplined and well-trained terrorist well suited to carry out a "confidential task." "One must ask oneself," maintained the report, whether an organization which had broken Agca out of prison and supported him financially and in other ways between that time and the assassination attempt "would have permitted him to take a personal initiative that was not in keeping with a common plan worked out in advance in all its details."[20]

Sons, 1985), p. 7. We are citing the revised paper edition. The original edition was published in 1983.

18. Henry Tanner, "Italian Prosecutor Requests a Life Sentence for the Pope's Assailant," *New York Times*, July 22, 1981; "Manic Motives," *Newsweek*, August 31, 1981, p. 38.

19. *Martella Report*, p. 9(11). In citing Judge Martella's unpublished Report, we use two sets of page numbers. The first refers to the English-language translation made available to the authors by the International Association of Democratic Lawyers, a nongovernmental organization in consultative status with UNESCO; the second, in parentheses, refers to the original Italian version.

20. Henry Tanner, "Attack on Pope A Conspiracy, Court Says," *New York Times*, September 25, 1981; and John Earle, "Pope 'Victim of Hidden Conspiracy,' " *London Times*, September 25, 1981. The Court's Statement of Motivation was supported by, and

The Bulgarian Connection Emerges

The publication of the Statement of Motivation followed by three weeks the airing of a British television program on the assassination attempt which anticipated many of the ideas which were later developed as the "Bulgarian Connection." The program was produced by Julian Manyon, a rightwing reporter for Thames Television's "TV Eye"; Paul Henze served as a consultant. The broadcast claimed that the Pope was shot because of his inspirational relationship to Poland's Solidarity, an idea developed in the program primarily by Francesco Mazzola, the Italian junior minister in charge of the Italian security forces at the time of the shooting. Mazzola noted that, at the time of the assassination attempt, the Pope had recently met with Lech Walesa, and was about to announce his return to Poland to administer the last rites to Cardinal Wyszynski. According to Mazzola, the Soviets believed that such a visit would produce a potentially dangerous series of anticommunist demonstrations; and Mazzola maintained that the Vatican was convinced that this was why the Pope had been shot.

The "TV Eye" program also extracted several items from Agca's early declarations which were to re-emerge in Claire Sterling's *Reader's Digest* article, "The Plot to Kill the Pope." It claimed that Agca stayed in Bulgaria for 60 days, that his contact there with one Omer Mersan helped him to obtain his forged Turkish passport, and that Mersan introduced him to a mysterious "Mustafa Eof." According to Mazzola, Mustafa Eof was Agca's contact with the Bulgarian secret service and supplied Agca with money, documentation, and instructions. Eof supposedly met Agca again in Tunis, where he had fled following the murder of a Turkish Gray Wolves leader in West Germany. Mazzola maintained that Eof directed Agca's apparently random wanderings throughout Western Europe, which were all somehow directed toward the attack on the Pope.[21] The only evidence presented by Mazzola, Manyon,

probably drew on, a report by the anti-terrorist police force DIGOS, dated September 15, 1981. This report summarized information gathered up to that point on Agca's travels and associations, and traced the history of the assassination weapon from its Belgium manufacturer to an Austria gun dealer. *(Martella Report,* pp. 9-16(12-18).) Claire Sterling, in her account of the Statement of Motivation in *The Time of the Assassins*, neglects to mention that it connects Agca with the Gray Wolves.

21. Michael Knipe, "West Germans Now Believe KGB Inspired Attack on Pope,"

or anyone else that a conspiracy existed, however, was a photograph showing a figure fleeing from the Square, supposedly in the moments just following the assassination attempt.[22] Agca subsequently identified this individual as a Bulgarian, and still later as his Turkish friend Oral Celik, but never as Mustafa Eof. The latter has disappeared from sight, and may reasonably be presumed to have been a figment of Agca's imagination.

The Martella Investigation. The Court's conclusion that Agca had been part of a conspiracy returned the case to the Public Prosecutor; and on November 7, 1981, the Prosecutor appointed Magistrate Ilario Martella to conduct the investigation.[23] In accordance with Italian law, Martella was given broad powers of investigation during this, the "Instruction Phase" of the legal proceedings against Agca "and persons unknown." His function might be compared to that of a Grand Jury in the United States, in that he was not constricted by formal rules of evidence and there was no burden of proof on the prosecution. Like a Grand Jury, the Instruction Phase is supposed to be secret. The examining magistrate is also supposed to pursue lines of investigation that would demonstrate the innocence, as well as the guilt, of the accused. Finally, the Instruction Phase culminates in a decision whether there is sufficient evidence to bring the accused to trial.[24]

Martella began his investigation by re-interviewing the witnesses to the assassination attempt and by asking a team of forensic experts to investigate how many bullets had been fired. These efforts revealed little new information. The forensic experts concluded that one pistol had fired two bullets.[25] The eyewitnesses apparently had little to add to their

London Times, September 5, 1981.

22. This photograph, taken by Lowell Newton, is discussed below.

23. For a fuller treatment of Martella's handling of the Bulgarian Connection case, see Chapter 5, pp. 114-21.

24. G. Leroy Certoma, *The Italian Legal System* (London: Butterworth, 1985), p. 219; cited in International Association of Democratic Lawyers, *Report of the International Commission of Study and Information on "The Antonov Affair"* (Brussels: May 13, 1985), pp. 7-8.

25. *Martella Report*, pp. 22-27(25-30). Martella eventually concluded that a second gunman must have fired a third bullet. While there was disagreement among the witnesses as to how many bullets were fired, Martella never explained why he overruled his forensic experts in deciding that there must have been three bullets fired. It was this conclusion, and the equally shaky conclusion that Agca had fired only two bullets, which led Martella to state in his final Report that Agca had been accompanied by a second gunman on the

trial testimony, although Lowell Newton, the U.S. photographer who had taken the picture of a man running away from St. Peter's Square immediately after the shooting, who he said was carrying a gun, provided a detailed description of Agca's apparent accomplice.[26]

We now come to a critical period in the fabrication of the Bulgarian Connection. According to Martella's Report, sometime in late April 1982 Agca told the prison authorities that he wished to make a statement. The "new Agca" was suddenly voluble and cooperative, giving Martella for the first time plausible testimony on some of his Gray Wolves associates and connections.[27] Most significantly, Agca began to bring the Bulgarians into his story, at first incidentally and tentatively, but later moving them to the front of the stage.

Why did Agca suddenly decide to talk? On this question Martella's Report is silent, implying that Agca had simply decided to cooperate and tell "the truth." Claire Sterling and others committed to the validity of the Bulgarian Connection maintain that Agca decided to talk because he realized that his hopes of being rescued from prison by the Bulgar-

day of the assassination attempt. This unexamined aspect of Martella's Report, of course, provided the media with its headlines and lead paragraphs when the Report was released in late October 1984. The effect of this was to reinforce, if only subliminally, support for a Bulgarian Connection, even though the second gunman was presumed to be the Gray Wolves leader, Oral Celik, not one of the Bulgarians.

26. *Martella Report*, pp. 19-21(22-24). According to Newton, the man ran towards and past him, carrying a gun in front of him. Newton, who said he waited for the man to run past him before using his camera, later "pointed out a definite resemblance" between the running man and a photograph of Celik, according to a letter he later sent to Martella in April 1984. Soon after his original deposition for Martella, however, Newton had identified the man in the Square as identical to one "Ali Chafic," whose picture was circulated as a composite drawing by the Reagan administration after the "Libyan hit squad" furor in November 1981. ("Conspiracy to Kill the Pope," *Time*, January 11, 1982, p. 31; and James Coates, "FBI Probes Libyan Link to Pope Attack," *Chicago Tribune*, January 10, 1982.) It was later discovered that this secret official U.S. list of "Libyan hit squad" members included Nabih Berri and the names of other prominent members of the Lebanese Shiite party Amal and aging Lebanese parliamentarians; but this information was suppressed in the United States. See Duncan Campbell and Patrick Forbes, *New Statesman*, August 16, 1985.

27. Exactly how valuable this information was is hard to determine. Martella's Report only occasionally contains actual quotations from his interviews with Agca. More typically it offers summaries and reconstructions of Agca's responses to his questions. In light of the complete breakdown of Agca as a useful witness during the trial that began in May 1985, the accuracy of Martella's Report in even correctly reconstructing Agca's statements is seriously open to question. It seems very likely that Martella sifted from Agca's changing and conflicting statements a more-or-less logical version of what might have happened. Thus Martella's Report must be used with caution in reconstructing even the flow of the investigation.

ians—either in a jail break, through a prisoner exchange, or by being ransomed—would not be fulfilled.[28]

On the other hand, in December 1982, immediately after the arrest of the Bulgarian Antonov, a mass of details and allegations were published in the Italian press strongly suggesting that Agca was pressured or bribed to "confess." Martella's Report is notable for its failure to explore the possibility that Agca was coached; and, as we will see in Chapter 5, Martella was an important part of the machinery of an induced confession.

What and when did Agca tell Martella about his alleged Bulgarian co-conspirators? Throughout his "confessions" during the first week in May there was apparently only a single reference to Bulgarian cooperation. According to Martella's Report, sometime in early 1981 Agca contacted a Syrian in Sofia who had earlier attempted to help out with his passport difficulties. A few days later, Agca told Martella, they met in Vienna and, "during a meeting held in the presence of a Bulgarian diplomat named Petronov, [the Syrian] not only gave Agca the sum of 100,000 Austrian schillings but promised him that, if he managed to organize some terrorist attack against the European Parliament, NATO, or the Common Market, he would receive in return unconditional hospitality in Syria, Bulgaria, or East Germany."[29]

Agca's wild tale of a meeting in the presence of a mythical Bulgarian diplomat named "Petronov" was the only time that any charge of Bulgarian cooperation was recorded by Martella until late October 1982.[30] Then, under questioning about his companion or companions in St.

28. On December 20, 1981, Agca began a hunger strike that lasted for 10 days. Claire Sterling is fond of pointing out that Agca was repeating the Turkish scenario of 1979, during his trial for the murder of the Turkish newspaper editor Abdi Ipekci. That is, Agca's hunger strike was a "signal" to the Bulgarians to release him "or else," and when a suitable period of time had gone by Agca began to talk, as he had earlier threatened to do in Turkey before he was broken out of prison. (For a critique of Sterling's "signaling" theory, see Chapter 6, pp. 138-40.) Sterling and company also advanced the hypothesis that Agca began to talk when he was confronted with the "information" that his alleged Bulgarian co-conspirators intended to have him killed in St. Peter's Square, but bungled the job. This was also the conclusion of *La Stampa*, which reported that "What convinced [Agca] to talk were the conclusions of the investigators . . . who found out that Agca's accomplices, if the killer made it out safe and sound from St. Peter's Square, were going to eliminate him instead of bringing him to safety across the border." "Pressure on Agca Reported," *Philadelphia Inquirer* [UPI], December 8, 1982.

29. *Martella Report*, p. 45(50).

30. On January 27, 1984, Agca admitted to Martella that his story about Petronov was a figment of his imagination. This means that before October 1982 Agca had not named a single nonfictional Bulgarian in all of his extensive interrogations. *Martella Report*, pp. 407(534-35).

Peter's Square on May 13, Agca suddenly began to tell Martella about his Bulgarian co-conspirators. And a week later Agca picked three Bulgarians out of a photo album, telling Martella that these were the men who organized the assassination attempt on the Pope and assisted him on the day of the assassination attempt itself. Was this, again, simply a matter of Agca finally deciding to tell the "truth"? Or had something happened in the interim to persuade Agca not only to continue talking but to talk about the Bulgarians?

Art Anticipates Reality. Indeed, much had happened between the "new" Agca's confessions of May and those of late October. Most important, in the interim Claire Sterling had published her article in the *Reader's Digest* arguing that Agca was acting on behalf of the Bulgarians, and NBC-TV had broadcast its special "white paper," "The Man Who Shot the Pope: A Study in Terrorism." While neither of these efforts contributed any new information, they sketched a model of a "Bulgarian Connection" which was adopted and embroidered on by Agca.

Sterling's article, "The Plot To Murder The Pope," was published in the September issue of the *Reader's Digest*, which reached subscribers in mid-August. Despite the many lies and contradictions in Agca's evolving confessions, Sterling's *Reader's Digest* article relied heavily on Agca's May 1981 declarations that he had been trained at a Syrian/PLO camp in Lebanon, and that his primary political connections in Turkey were with the Left and not the Right. Both in the *Reader's Digest* and later, Sterling maintained that whatever links Agca had with the Gray Wolves were a cover for his real, leftist sympathies. Sterling found the chief link between Agca and the Bulgarians in the Turkish smuggler Abuzer Ugurlu, who she claimed worked hand-in-glove with Bulgarian authorities. Sterling also introduced Ugurlu's associate Omer Mersan, who was later to tell an Italian court that he had given $770 to Agca (who he knew under another name) at Ugurlu's behest. Out of these "links" Sterling created a chain of command by which the Bulgarians induced their agent Ugurlu to hire Agca to shoot the Pope.

Five weeks after Sterling's story reached the public, NBC-TV broadcast "The Man Who Shot the Pope: A Study in Terrorism." The program, which was narrated by Marvin Kalb, employed Sterling and Paul Henze as consultants. While many of its points had already been made by Sterling, perhaps the chief characteristic of the report was its stress on the Soviet's motive in shooting the Pope. According to NBC, the

Pope posed a threat to the Soviets because of his support for Solidarity and Polish nationalism, and more particularly from his alleged warning to the Soviet leadership that an invasion of Poland would cause him to lay down his crown and join the Polish resistance. While this claim has never been supported by any evidence, and has been consistently refuted by Vatican spokesmen,[31] the Pope's alleged threat to the Soviets was the heart of the NBC case. Like the earlier "TV Eye" program, NBC relied heavily on former Italian Security Minister Mazzola to support the plausibility of such risky (and foolish) action by the Soviets. And, as in Sterling's *Reader's Digest* article, the program stated that Agca had been recruited by the KGB before he ever left his hometown, and that his subsequent association with the Right in Turkey was only a cover for his real commitment to the Left. The mass of detail which showed that Agca had been assisted by this rightwing network of Turks in the two years before shooting the Pope was thus dismissed as irrelevant, because if Agca had already been recruited by the KGB, the rightwing network also must have been manipulated by the Soviets and their agents. Finally, the NBC program concluded with the interesting observation that a Soviet plot against the Pope was not without precedent, citing as examples the U.S. plots against Lumumba, Castro, and "possibly" Qaddafi!

One significant U.S. follow-up to the NBC program was the hearing held by the congressional Commission on Security and Cooperation in Europe on September 23, 1982, two days after the NBC broadcast. The Commission, which had been established to oversee Soviet compliance with the Helsinki Accords, heard Claire Sterling, Michael Ledeen, and Bulgarian émigré Atanas Slavov. The Commissioners were unanimous in their certainty that the Bulgarians and the Soviets were behind the Plot. Claire Sterling outlined for the Committee the version of the assassination plot which she had recently written for *Reader's Digest*. She implied that great significance lay in the fact that Solidarity and the Polish government ratified the Gdansk agreement on August 31, 1980, the same day that Agca left Bulgaria for Western Europe. She also told the Committee that no one from any of the U.S. intelligence agencies had discussed her findings with her.[32]

31. See Chapter 7, p. 200.
32. The hearing was apparently held at the urging of Commission member Representative Donald Ritter of Pennsylvania. A guest at the hearing was Senator Alfonse D'Amato of New York, who declared that (a) he had talked with the monsignor in the Vatican who had delivered the alleged message from the Pope to the Soviet Union; (b) the Vatican was

The most significant outcome of the efforts of Sterling and NBC was to frame the case in Italy itself. On October 5 Judge Martella flew to Washington, according to the *Washington Post*, "in hope of evaluating two recent U.S. media reports suggesting that Soviet Bloc intelligence agencies were involved." Martella told a *Post* reporter that, while no hard evidence existed linking the eastern Bloc to the plot, "he could not rule out the possibility." According to the *Post*, Martella "has asked the Justice Department to help him obtain meetings with persons familiar with the case including, possibly, the journalists responsible for the NBC and *Reader's Digest* articles."[33] He is known to have met with Arnaud de Borchgrave and to have been given a special viewing of the NBC-TV program on the Plot Against the Pope.

On October 29, according to Martella's Report, the interrogation of Agca was renewed. Martella asked Agca about the reports of several witnesses, supported by the Lowell Newton photograph, that Agca had been assisted by at least one other person in St. Peter's Square on the day of the shooting. Agca readily volunteered the information that "there was in fact another person . . . , namely the Bulgarian citizen Sotir Kolev" who had been introduced to him in Sofia "as an expert on terrorism in Europe." Shortly after several meetings with Kolev, Agca told Martella, his companion Oral Celik arrived in Sofia. His coming, according to Agca, was determined "by the opportunity to plan terrorist acts in Europe, using the 'Gray Wolves' in the interests of countries within the Soviet sphere such as Bulgaria." The most important such act, according to Agca, was a projected assassination of the Pope.

According to Martella's Report, on the day that Agca first named his Bulgarian contact, "Kolev," he placed him at the center of an elaborate conspiracy which would net him and his gang over a million dollars in exchange for killing the Pope. The money would be paid into Celik's bank account by Turkish businessman Bekir Celenk.[34] One-third of this

convinced that the Soviet Union was behind the assassination; (c) he had told this to the CIA on October 19, 1981; and (d) he had met with Claire Sterling immediately after his return from Italy "and began to compare some notes." ("The Assassination Attempt on Pope John Paul II," Hearing Before the Commission on Security and Cooperation in Europe, 97th Congress, 2nd Session [September 23, 1982], p. 12.) At the hearing Senator Patrick Leahy of Vermont said that, as a member of the Senate Intelligence Committee, he had been briefed by the CIA about the possible Soviet role in the papal assassination attempt on more than one occasion (p. 3), though no dates were given.

33. Robert J. McCartney, "Plodding Inquiry Studies Bulgarian Link," *Washington Post*, October 6, 1982.

34. Despite Agca's claim that it was actually paid and was thus presumably traceable,

sum would go to Musa Celebi's Western European network of Gray Wolves in exchange for the support they would provide Agca and his companions; and it was Celebi who supposedly telephoned Agca the go-ahead signal at the end of April 1981. Meanwhile "Kolev," according to plan, arrived in Rome at the beginning of May to supervise last-minute operations. Together he and Agca cased the Square, and "Kolev" made arrangements for Agca to stay at a guest house under the name of Ozgun. On the following day "Kolev" pointed out another Bulgarian—"Bayramic"—who was to assist Agca in escaping after the assassination.

The most significant step in Agca's identification of the Bulgarians came a week later. On November 8 Agca was shown a photograph album of 56 Bulgarians living in Rome since 1977. He was asked if any of the people in the photos were "Kolev" or "Bayramic." Agca immediately identified the first photograph as that of "Kolev," and the second as "Bayramic."[35] Agca then went on to identify the person in photograph number 20 as "Petrov," a military attaché at the Bulgarian Embassy. "I admit that I have not so far referred to this person in order not to worsen my case," Agca told Martella, saying that he had no cor-roborating evidence. But Agca then stated that he had known "Petrov" since November 1980, having been given the Embassy telephone number by Celenk in Sofia in August.[36]

this money has never been located in the course of four years of Italian official investiga-tions. During the Rome trial, also, Yalcin Ozbey, a member of the Gray Wolves and close friend of Agca, testified on September 20, 1985, that Celik had visited him in West Ger-many, and had not only failed to mention the receipt of any money, but even had to bor-row from Ozbey for current expenses.

35. Later, on June 28, 1983, Agca stated that, at the time of his identification of "Bayramic," he did not know that his real name was Antonov or that Antonov worked for Balkan Air. But when it was "recorded that the person I recognised as 'Bayramic' was Sergei Antonov, employed at the 'Balkan Air,' . . . not only did I declare falsely that I knew the real occupation of Bayramic, but also that I knew by heart the two telephone numbers of Balkan Air." Agca then went on to declare that he had learned these telephone numbers when Martella briefly stepped out of the room and he was able to consult a tele-phone directory. *Martella Report*, pp. 372-73(486-87).

36. When he first mentioned Celenk to Martella in May 1982, Agca had said that "he had not talked directly with Celenk" but had only seen him and had him identified at a distance. Subsequently, Agca read Mumcu's book *Arms Smuggling and Terrorism*, in which Celenk was a featured performer. The Turkish journalist Orsan Oymen points out that following his reading of this new source, Agca related episodes from Mumcu's book in the form "I was told by Celenk" that such-and-such had occurred! Martella never caught on to this process. See Orsan Oymen, "Behind the Scenes of the 'Agca Investiga-

With the insights gained from his visit to Washington and Agca's identification of Bulgarians,[37] Martella requested warrants for the arrest of Sergei Antonov ("Bayramic") and the military attaché Jelio Vassilev ("Petrov"). He also directed that proceedings be started against the diplomat Todor Aivazov ("Kolev"), who was protected by diplomatic immunity.

Although both Aivazov and Vassilev had already returned to Bulgaria, apparently as part of a routine rotation, Antonov was arrested at his office on November 25. His home was searched and a "guide to the Vatican" was confiscated. The next day the interrogation of the incredulous Antonov was begun, with Martella quizzing him about each of Agca's statements concerning "Bayramic": Did he like flowers? Did he collect miniature liquor bottles? Et cetera. Martella's investigation of Antonov and his alibi, which occupies much of the remaining 1,000 pages of his Report, reflects his belief that any contradictions in Antonov's testimony or any lapses in his memory after 18 months about where he was and what he was doing in May 1981 were indicative of Bulgarian guilt. Similarly, any shifts or contradictions in the testimonies of those Antonov claimed could vouch for his whereabouts at key times were seen by Martella as signs of connivance among the defense witnesses to get their story straight.

While Martella's investigation largely degenerated into mere alibi checking following the arrest of Antonov, the sensational news that the Soviet Bloc had been implicated in the papal assassination attempt shifted the locus of the case out of the investigators' offices and back to the mass media, which swung behind the new story with only marginal reservations. The shift in tone of western media coverage as a result of Agca's declarations and the arrest of Antonov is well illustrated by the changes made in the NBC program, "The Man Who Shot the Pope," rebroadcast in the one-hour slot before President Reagan's "State of the Union" message on January 25, 1983. Information about Agca's Turkish roots was almost entirely deleted, and the sole concern of the program was to present—with a supportive framework and completely uncritically—Agca's declarations that the Bulgarians had done it. What-

tion,' " *Milliyet*, November 1984.

37. We show in Chapter 5 that the photo albums were almost certainly shown to Agca prior to the identification parade of November 8, 1982. We will see, also, that the photos allegedly showing Bulgarians on the scene on May 13 were misidentified by Agca (the Lowell Newton photo of the fleeing person) or probably fabricated by a source not yet identified (the photo showing Antonov in the Square).

ever tentativeness the earlier program had contained the rebroadcast deleted. And where the original program had concluded with the somewhat startling point that a Soviet-backed conspiracy was conceivable because of earlier U.S. assassination plots against Castro and Lumumba, the rebroadcast dropped this point and concluded with a ringing warning that the failure of western governments, particularly the United States, to pursue the case aggressively wherever it might lead was tantamount to treason. "The Reagan administration," intoned Marvin Kalb, "is etching no profile in courage, allowing Italy to stand alone against the fury of the Soviet Union." For the Reagan administration, and particularly for the CIA, proof of Soviet guilt "could shatter hopes for détente, trade, and arms agreements." "The continuing investigation," concluded Kalb, "has the potential of a time bomb ticking away in a corner of East-West relations."[38]

The Baroque Era of the Bulgarian Connection

Once Agca had begun to talk about "Kolev" and the Bulgarian Connection, there suddenly seemed no end to the "Connections" which he could reveal. He claimed to have been sent by the Bulgarians on a surveillance mission to Malta and Tunisia to check out whether it would be feasible to assassinate their heads of state, Dom Mintoff and Habib Bourguiba. He spoke of spying in Switzerland and of plotting to kill Lech Walesa. His testimony also linked the plot to kill the Pope to ongoing investigations into Bulgarian state involvement with smuggling[39] and with the Red Brigades. Each of these alleged plots, complex in themselves and resting often on Agca's testimony alone, "confirmed" each other through repetition and through their sensational treatment by the mass media. The media also developed their own information from intelligence agencies and defectors to help forward the chorus of a Bulgarian Connection.[40] The cumulative effect of all this was to consolidate western belief in the truth of the Bulgarian Connection. Yet the support given by these tangential plots and scandals to the basic claims was only

38. "The Man Who Shot the Pope: A Study of Terrorism. Update." January 25, 1983, 8 p.m. to 9 p.m. Official transcript, pp. 61-62.

39. We take up this thread of investigation-propaganda in Chapter 3 and Appendix B.

40. See the discussion in Chapter 7 of the "Mantarov Connection" developed by the *New York Times*.

atmospheric, producing no real evidence to strengthen Judge Martella's case.

The "Plot" to Kill Lech Walesa. By far the most important of the secondary plots that emerged out of Agca's testimony was the alleged conspiracy to kill Lech Walesa. Agca first mentioned such a plot on November 8, 1982. But the issue apparently was not investigated in depth until December 29, 1982, when he was interrogated by magistrates Priore and Imposimato, who were conducting further inquiries into the case of the Red Brigades and one of their leaders, Agca's prison neighbor Giovanni Senzani. Once again Agca was shown the album of 56 photographs, and once again he identified his three Bulgarian co-conspirators. On this occasion, however, "Agca not only recognised the same photographs that he had identified before . . . , but he also stated that he recognised in photo no. 8 Mr. Ivan Tomov."[41] According to the Martella Report, Agca told the magistrates:[42]

During our meetings Ivan Tomov and Kolev expounded to us a plan to kill Walesa when he came to Italy. According to this plan I was supposed to take part in the murder of Walesa using a pistol or a remote-controlled plastic bomb. Ivan Tomov and Kolev told me that the choice of which method to use would depend on information that would certainly come from Italian trade unionists who were close to Walesa—people who were in contact with them and who could supply them with all the necessary details about Walesa's itinerary.

In a further interview on February 4, 1983, Agca again stated that he had plotted with the three Bulgarians indicted in the papal conspiracy and with the Bulgarian Dontchev ("Ivan Tomov" 's real name) to kill Walesa in January 1981. Again Agca repeated details of their preparations and of the spots chosen for the assassination. But now he stated that the plans were canceled "because [Dontchev] told us that he had learned from an Italian trade unionist whose name I don't know that the Italian Secret Service had by now received the 'information' of a possible assassination attempt against Walesa."[43] Martella questioned Agca

41. *Martella Report*, p. 132(181-82).
42. *Ibid.*, pp. 132-33(182-83).
43. *Ibid.*, pp. 358-59(467-68). The "Italian trade unionist" in question was undoubtedly Luigi Scricciolo. The "Scricciolo Affair" remains among the murkiest aspects of the Bulgarian Connection. Scricciolo had been arrested in February 1982 and charged with being an accessory in the kidnapping of General James Dozier, who had been held by the Red Brigades for six weeks, from mid-December 1981 to late January 1982, before being rescued by the Italian police. But while allegedly spying for Bulgaria, Scricciolo had worked closely with the AFL-CIO, arranging for Solidarity delegates to attend two meet-

on this subject again on February 11, and a week later sent a recommendation to the Attorney General of the Court of Appeal in Rome that indictments be issued in this alleged conspiracy. After some jurisdictional juggling, Martella's investigation into the conspiracy to murder Walesa was renewed in mid-April.[44]

Then, somewhat mysteriously, came Agca's "Retraction" of June 28, 1983. In that part of Agca's retraction concerning the Walesa plot, Agca maintained that he had never met Dontchev, and that the details which he gave to Judge Imposimato on December 29, 1982 concerning the plot had been learned from listening to Imposimato read portions of the testimony of an indicted trade unionist—Luigi Scricciolo—to Judge Priore. He also said that he was able to pick out Dontchev from the photo album because Imposimato showed him Dontchev's picture and said, "This is Ivan Tomov, Scricciolo's friend, do you recognise him?" While Agca continued to maintain that he and his papal co-conspirators discussed killing Walesa, he now said the plot never went anywhere.

On August 23 Martella charged Agca with slander against himself and the others. During his examination of September 15, 1983, Agca admitted that he had lied—"in order to make my declarations more credible."[45] But Martella persisted in pressing Agca on how he knew so many details, because none of them was contained in any of Scricciolo's interrogations prior to December 29; and so even if Judge Imposimato had read portions of these interrogations to Judge Priore in Agca's presence, Agca could not have learned the details to which he confessed at that time.[46]

There the matter has rested. Agca has maintained rather lamely that he was able to lie in such detail because his interrogators asked him questions in a yes-or-no fashion and he was able to make lucky guesses.

ings at the U.S. Embassy, one with a U.S. diplomat and a second with an assistant to AFL-CIO chief Lane Kirkland. (For a warm letter of solidarity to Scricciolo from AFL-CIO representative Irving Brown, see Christian Roulette, *La Filiere: Jean-Paul II, Antonov, Agca* (Paris: Editions du Sorbier, 1984), p. 265.) His later confessions of involvement with the Bulgarians in spying and in negotiations with the Red Brigades fed well into the ongoing Bulgarian Connection publicity. Scricciolo's involvement in the alleged Walesa plot remains obscure. He supposedly told investigators that he knew of such a plot, and Agca later claimed to have obtained many details about the plot from hearing Scricciolo's earlier testimony on the matter. While Scricciolo is still in jail and awaiting trial, it is significant that Martella dropped all charges against Agca, Scricciolo, and the Bulgarians for involvement in the Walesa plot.

44. *Martella Report*, p. 367(479).
45. *Ibid.*, p. 377(492-93).
46. Sterling, *op. cit.*, n. 1, pp. 242-43.

Claire Sterling maintains—still—that Agca was able to provide details of the alleged plot against Walesa because the plot was real and Agca's initial declarations were true. Others—including the authors—believe that Agca was able to provide his detailed description because he was coached while he was in prison, an argument which we develop in Chapter 5. As for Scricciolo, whether he was a Bulgarian spy, a double agent, or none of the above, his case and his declarations served to give credibility to Agca's primary claims: that he was hired by Bulgaria to kill the Pope.

The Case Starts to Unravel

The Walesa plot, and Agca's claims of Bulgarian sponsorship of trips hither and yon to scout out assassination possibilities, took a toll on the credibility of the Bulgarian Connection, although the western media succeeded in keeping these matters very low key. The most serious damage, however, resulted from a growing list of Agca's "retractions" of previously key claims in his story. The first retraction came in December 1982, after Aivazov and Vassilev held a press conference in Sofia to deny Agca's allegations. At this press conference it was obvious to the assembled reporters, based on distinctive physical characteristics, that Aivazov ("Kolev") could not have been the character shown running away from the Square in the Lowell Newton photograph of May 13, 1981. Three days after the press conference Agca recanted his claim that Kolev had been the person in the Square.

The most significant retraction concerned Agca's claim that he had visited Antonov's apartment just a few days before the assassination attempt, and that while there he had met Antonov's wife and young daughter. This touch added seeming veracity to Agca's story, because—if true—it showed that he was on very familiar terms with at least one of the alleged co-conspirators. On the other hand, Agca's claim seemed wildly improbable in the context of a carefully constructed plot, as it violated in the extreme the cardinal rule of "plausible deniability."

Antonov's defense team was able to assemble documentary evidence that Antonov's wife and daughter had left Rome several days before the time when Agca said that he had met them. Soon after news reports of the alibis of Mrs. Antonov and her daughter had appeared, Agca again adjusted his story. In an interview with Judge Martella on June 28, 1983, Agca admitted to having lied about three crucial points. First, he stated that he had never met Antonov's wife and daughter, as he had claimed earlier. Second, he now said that he had never visited Antonov's apartment at all. As in the case of his claims about Mrs. Antonov, Agca's apparent ability to describe Antonov's apartment had added weight to his more general claims. But a telling error in his description—his claim that Antonov's apartment was divided by a folding door, present in other apartments in the building, but which had been removed from Antonov's apartment before Agca's alleged visit—not only led to this particular retraction but also added strength to the charge that Agca had been coached. Finally, Agca admitted that he had never met the Bulgarian Dontchev, though he continued to maintain that he had discussed assassinating Lech Walesa with Antonov and the other Bulgarians. Once again, Agca's ability to describe Dontchev, whom he now admitted he had never met, raised questions about coaching.

Although Agca's retractions would seem on their face to be of great importance in assessing the truth of the Bulgarian Connection, Italian authorities and the mass media kept these facts (which would have called into serious question the Sterling-Henze party line) almost completely under wraps for more than a year. In late September 1983 an item by Henry Kamm appeared in the New York Times saying that "Italians May Charge Turk With Slander of Jailed Bulgarian."[47] The article noted that Antonov's lawyer had not been notified of the nature of the slander. After reviewing some of the apparent weaknesses in Agca's story, Kamm concluded that "It could not be learned whether these were the reasons for the reported decision to indict Mr. Agca for slander." In late November a small item in the Times, reporting that Antonov's lawyer was going to sue Agca for slander, quoted the attorney as saying he had been told that Martella's charge against Agca concerned the alleged plot against Walesa.[48] It was not until June 1984, nearly a year after the retraction took place, that the leaking of the Albano Report brought them into the public domain.[49]

Claire Sterling maintains that Agca's retraction was false, being prompted by the kidnapping of Emmanuela Orlandi, the daughter of a

47. New York Times, September 30, 1983.
48. "Pope's Attacker, Accused of Slandering Bulgarian, To Be Sued," New York Times [AP], November 26, 1983.
49. The New York Times, the original vehicle of this release, kept the retraction under cover for a much longer time; see Chapter 7, pp. 190-94.

Vatican official. This kidnapping took place on June 22, 1983, and was reported in the press four days later. Agca's retractions were made to Judge Martella on June 28, two days after the press reports. "The kidnapping may have convinced him," wrote Sterling, "that his Turkish or Bulgarian accomplices were trying to get him out of prison."[50] But Sterling's interpretation is not only far-fetched, it disregards some relevant facts.[51] First, demands for Agca's release were not made public until someone claiming to be one of the kidnappers called both the Vatican and ANSA, the Italian news agency, on July 6. The caller to ANSA said that "some days ago we had contact with a Vatican secretary, a message that the Vatican has hidden."[52] Thus Agca's retraction preceded, rather than followed, the kidnappers' announcement that Emmanuela was being held until Agca was released. Second, if Agca's retractions were made in order to influence his would-be liberators, he must have assumed that they had an informer in Judge Martella's office, for, as we noted above, these retractions were largely unknown for almost a year after they were made. Moreover, when he was given an opportunity for a brief exchange with the press just after Emmanuela's kidnapping, Agca repeatedly stated that he had been trained by the KGB and the "Bulgarian secret services" for his assassination attempt, and shouted that "I refuse any exchange."[53] Finally, while the Italian police received hundreds of hoax calls from people claiming to be her kidnappers, the police consistently credited the kidnapping to a group calling itself the "Turkish Anti-Christian Liberation Front." A call from the group to the Italian newspaper *Il Messaggero* demanded that Gray

---

50. "Agca . . . recanted part of his testimony about the purported plot on Mr. Walesa on June 28, 1983, as soon as he could after he found out about a kidnapping of the daughter of a Vatican employee." Claire Sterling, "Agca's Other Story: The Plot to Kill Walesa," *New York Times*, October 27, 1984.

51. For a fuller discussion, see Chapter 6, pp. 138-40.

52. "Caller: Have Girl; Agca Must Be Free," *Philadelphia Inquirer*, July 7, 1983. Another article said that the caller told Italian news agencies that he had contacted the Vatican after the Pope's first appeal for Emmanuela's release, which was made on July 3. ("Pope John Paul Pledges Support for Efforts to Find Missing Teenager," *Philadelphia Inquirer*, July 11, 1983.)

53. "Agca Asserts KGB Aided in Pope Plot," *New York Times*, July 9, 1983. As the *Washington Post* noted, both U.S. and Italian observers were convinced that Agca's informal press conference was "not accidental." (Sari Gilbert, "Hoax Calls Regarding Agca Bedevil Italian Officials," July 13, 1983.) The Italians' actions were denounced by both the Bulgarians and the Soviets. Agca's remarks—that he had been trained by the KGB, that he had been trained in Syria and Bulgaria, and that the Bulgarians and Antonov were guilty—were featured on all three U.S. television networks.

Wolves leader Celebi, as well as Agca, be released.[54] While the evidence is thin, it suggests that if the kidnappers had any real link at all with Agca—something which the police increasingly came to doubt—they were probably part of the Gray Wolves network.[55] Agca's impromptu press conference was but the first of a series of events following his June 28 retractions which served both to keep the alleged Bulgarian Connection before the public eye and to mask the growing weaknesses of the case. The publication in late 1983 of Sterling's *The Time of the Assassins* and of Henze's *The Plot to Kill the Pope*, which were received with generally respectful if not enthusiastic reviews, were given wide recognition and served to restate the case of the disinformationists.[56] A similar effect was achieved by the publicity given to Agca's two-hour reenactment of his supposed movements in and around St. Peter's Square on the day of the assassination attempt. This mini-drama, which occurred on October 18, was followed on November 7 by a similar exercise in which Agca was taken to the street on which the Bulgarian Aivazov had lived, in order to see if Agca could identify Aivazov's house. The fact that he could not do so did not detract from the public-relations effect of the exercise, which was to revive media interest in the alleged plot.[57] The Bulgarian Connection re-

54. "Call to Rome Paper is Latest Kidnap Clue," *Philadelphia Inquirer* [UPI], July 23, 1983.

55. Sari Gilbert of the *Washington Post* noted that DIGOS, the Italian anti-terrorist police, turned the case over to the homicide squad on July 11, and that the investigation was "now concentrating on the possibility that the demands regarding Agca are probably a cover-up for something else, ranging from murder to a secret romantic elopement" ("Hoax Calls Regarding Agca Bedevil Italian Officials," *Washington Post*, July 13, 1983). A month later, however, UPI reported that Italian magistrates were investigating the possibility that the KGB had organized the kidnapping to discredit the Pope." "Rome Said to Suspect KGB Role in Abduction," *New York Times*, August 11, 1983.

56. See, for example, Edward J. Epstein, "Did Agca Act Alone?" *New York Times Book Review*, January 15, 1984, pp. 6-7; Gordon Crovitz, "The Bulgarian Connection," *Wall Street Journal*, February 3, 1984, p. 20. A mass market version of the pre-confession Sterling-Henze line appeared in mid-1983, with the publication of *Pontiff*, by Gordon Thomas and Max Morgan-Witts (Garden City, New York: Doubleday and Company, 1983). *Pontiff* was serialized in a number of newspapers. As we have pointed out elsewhere, the use of evidence in this study is so appalling that none of its conclusions can be taken seriously. See "The Press, the K.G.B., and the Pope," *The Nation*, July 2, 1983, pp. 1, 14-17.

57. "Assassin Re-enacts His Steps Before '81 Shooting of Pope," *New York Times* [UPI], October 19, 1983; and "Assailant of Pope is Questioned," *New York Times* [UPI], November 7, 1983.

turned to the front pages again in late December, when the Pope visited Agca in prison. The 21-minute meeting received front-page coverage in both the *Times* and the *Post*, which reported that the Pope forgave Agca while the latter expressed his repentance. [58]

Downhill to the Trial. In December 1983 Judge Martella completed his two-year investigation and delivered his report on the case to state prosecutor Antonio Albano, who had the responsibility to decide whether there was sufficient evidence to bring Antonov and the other accused Bulgarians and Turks to trial. Prosecutor Albano's Report was filed with the court on May 8, 1984. The 78-page document declared that the evidence gathered by Judge Martella warranted bringing the defendants to trial, thus returning the case to Martella for a final determination of whether or not to proceed. The Albano Report was "leaked," and appeared first on June 10, 1984, in an extensive front-page article in the Sunday *New York Times*, authored by Claire Sterling herself. [59]

The immediate consequence of the Albano Report was to return the Bulgarian Connection to the headlines, now bolstered by official claims of Bulgarian guilt. Although primarily a rehash of earlier charges, the Report had two features worthy of mention. Most important, it discussed Agca's retractions of June 28, 1983, although it explained them away as a "signal" to Agca's sponsors. The Report also gave prominence to Agca's contention that the getaway plan called for the assassins to be driven from the Square to the Bulgarian Embassy by Antonov, where they were to be loaded onto a Transport Internationaux Routiers (TIR) truck, which would then be sealed by customs officials and driven across several national frontiers to Bulgaria. (Such trucks, once sealed, escape having their contents examined at each international border.) Albano's Report said that such a truck was in fact sealed at the Bulgarian Embassy on the very afternoon of the assassination attempt. [60]

58. Henry Kamm, "Pope Meets in Jail With His Attacker," *New York Times*, December 28, 1983; and John Winn Miller, "Pope Visits Assailant As 'Brother,' " *Washington Post*, December 28, 1983. None of the published accounts of the Pope's visit included any reference to what Agca later claimed transpired, which was that the two men discussed Agca's belief that he was Jesus Christ and the relation of the assassination attempt to the so-called third secret of the Miracle of Our Lady of Fatima.

59. For an analysis of Sterling's distorted summary of the Albano Report, and the Report itself, see Chapter 7, pp. 190-94.

60. While the presence of the truck on May 13 was consistent with the Bulgarian Connection hypothesis, the burden of evidence indicates that this was a coincidence unrelated to the events at the Square. The use of a TIR truck would be another violation of "plausi-

On October 26, 1984, Judge Martella finally issued his own report, which accompanied his decision that Antonov, Agca, and other Bulgarians and Turks should be brought to trial. In some respects this came as an anticlimax. The Martella Report contained little that was new. None of the problems in the case was resolved in the indictment, and no new evidence was advanced which removed the burden of the case from resting entirely on Agca's credibility. The first news accounts of the indictment were written without access to Martella's Report, so that they provided minimal information, but once again returned the prosecution's case to the headlines. The initial focus was on Martella's claim that Agca had been accompanied by a second gunman, Oral Celik, who fired one shot at the Pope, slightly wounding him. *Newsweek* announced that the indictment gave "new credence to the 'Bulgarian Connection,'" while the *New York Times* editorialized that "the existence of the plot no longer seems conjectural."[61]

In the months separating Martella's final Report from the beginning of the trial in May 1985, several developments raised issues that would come to the fore at the trial, and that presaged Agca's wild vacillations

ble deniability," which is characteristic of the entire Plot. The movement of TIR trucks is known to the Italian government, and the Bulgarian Embassy is surely under intelligence surveillance. This would make their use extraordinarily risky. On the other hand, as the police would know about TIR truck movements, this could have been the basis of a coached response. During the course of the trial, Agca suddenly abandoned the TIR truck sequence as the primary escape route, claiming instead that an auto getaway with Gray Wolves was the first option, with the TIR to be held in reserve.

Other problems with the truck as the escape vehicle are as follows: (1) the truck was loaded and sealed by Italian customs officials on a public street, not within the Bulgarian Embassy compound; (2) the Italian customs officials responsible for inspecting the truck have given sworn statements that when it was sealed nobody was secreted within it; (3) if Celik was somehow smuggled out of Italy to Bulgaria by this route, the Bulgarians unaccountably allowed him to resume his travels through Europe (he has been seen in a number of countries in recent years); (4) the trial evidence brought out the fact that the Bulgarians had requested that the truck be loaded and inspected on May 12, but that a one-day delay occurred by request of Italian customs; (5) a note found in Agca's possession on May 13, 1981, with details of his plans, mentions a train ticket and trip to Naples, but nothing about Bulgarians, cars, or trucks; and (6) if, as some have suggested, the Bulgarians intended (but failed) to kill Agca in St. Peter's Square, why would they arrange for a truck to convey him out of harm's way?

61. "The Pope Plot: A Second Gun," *Newsweek*, November 5, 1984, p. 39; "The Fingerprints on Agca's Gun," *New York Times*, editorial, October 30, 1984. Virtually alone in the mass media, Michael Dobbs of the *Washington Post* pointed out that the only plot convincingly argued in Martella's Report was a *Turkish* plot, and that any Bulgarian Connection still rested on Agca's word only. "Pope Investigation Focuses on Would-be Assassin's Accomplices," October 28, 1984.

on the witness stand. One was the discovery that Agca had written a letter to a military attaché at the U.S. Embassy in Rome claiming that he had accused the Bulgarians under instructions from the United States. The letter, which was written in August 1983, expressed distress that certain U.S. publications had called him a liar. "What is my guilt?" he asked. "You told me: 'Speak up!' and I began to speak."[62]

Two weeks later Agca's credibility again suffered damage when, in a taped television interview with a reporter from the Italian state-run network RAI, he still maintained that he had been trained by Bulgarian agents in Syria, but now denied that he had acted on anyone else's behalf in his attempt on the Pope.[63]

A final topic that made its appearance in the immediate pre-trial period soon came to have a substantial impact on the trial itself. On March 20, 1985, the business section of the *New York Times* carried an article on the interwoven scandals of Francesco Pazienza, an Italian former secret services employee and all-around "fixer" who had been jailed in New York City in connection with the collapse of the Banco Ambrosiano.[64] The article, the first to bring Pazienza to the notice of *Times* readers, noted toward the end that an Italian Parliamentary Commission had named Pazienza as the moving force behind "Super S" (a secret clique within Italian intelligence); that he had been a liaison between Super S and the Mafia; that he had "attempted to serve as a link between Italian officials and the incoming Reagan administration after the election of 1980"; and that his counterpart in this diplomatic work was none other than Michael Ledeen, a junior partner among the disin-

62. "1983 Agca Letter Faulted U.S.," *New York Times*, January 19, 1985. The letter also claimed that a former Soviet diplomat in Iran could provide testimony that Andropov had conspired to kill both the Pope and Lech Walesa; and that, as "the U.S. foreign policy is in a state of irresoluteness and bankruptcy . . . , to overcome the Soviet threat it should be said to the public that Andropov bears the responsibility for the assassination attempt against the Pope and the Kremlin should be made to change its leader." Agca's letter was published in the Italian newspaper *Repubblica* on January 18, 1985. The *Times* failed to note that Agca's claim to have had contact with a Soviet diplomat in Iran had been "retracted" in January 1984. See Sari Gilbert, "Agca Letter to Envoy Published in Rome," *Washington Post*, January 19, 1985.

63. "Agca Recalls Prison Visit by Pope," *New York Times*, February 5, 1985, and ABC Evening News, February 4, 1985. In NBC's Evening News on the same date, Marvin Kalb reported only Agca's claims that he had been trained to destabilize Turkish democracy and was then sent on a mission to kill the Pope.

64. E. J. Dionne, Jr., "New Hope for Clues in Italian Scandals," *New York Times*, March 25, 1985.

formationists seeking to link the Bulgarians and Soviets to the attempt on the Pope. We will return to Pazienza at length in another context;[65] here we note that readers of the *Times*'s business section were given a short (and extremely inadequate) preview of the role this major figure in modern Italian corruption would soon come to play in the trial of the Bulgarian Connection.

The Second Trial

The trial of Agca, Sergei Antonov, and their alleged co-conspirators, lasted the better part of a year, running from May 27, 1985, to March 29, 1986. Led by veteran Judge Severino Santiapichi, with another judge and six lay jurors, and state prosecutor Antonio Marini, the court did not rely very heavily on the findings of Investigating Judge Martella. It chose instead to cover the charges with a virtually fresh inquiry, focusing less intently on Bulgarian alibis and looking more closely at Agca as a witness, examining his Gray Wolves links, and even delving into possible abuses by the security services. Aside from the requirement of Italian law that all witnesses be heard, the thoroughness of the trial coverage appears to have resulted from skepticism by the court about the quality of the investigative phase of the case, and from the case's political sensitivity, which demanded the appearance of comprehensiveness to legitimate *any* outcome.

In some respects the trial was over in the first days of Agca's testimony, which demonstrated to the court and other observers that, while intelligent and resourceful, Agca was subject to delusions of grandeur and was highly unreliable as a witness. His reiterated claims to be Jesus Christ and to be in possession of the secrets of Fatima took the court aback. But equally devastating was his continuously changing testimony and his failure to provide any evidence or basis for confirmation of his central claims of Bulgarian involvement. It became evident that Martella had distilled out one version of Agca's claims, which corresponded closely to the one put up by Claire Sterling and Marvin Kalb in the summer and fall of 1982, and that Martella had failed to obtain independent evidence for these allegations or to examine seriously their internal inconsistencies.

The case against the Bulgarians disintegrated further as the parade of Turkish Gray Wolves passed through the court. None of them admitted

65. See Chapter 4, pp. 91-99.

to participation in the plot or knowledge of Bulgarian involvement, although several claimed to have heard rumors of the latter. A witness such as Abdullah Catli, who admitted sheltering Agca and buying a gun for him, had no apparent reason to deny Bulgarian participation in the plot if it had been real. Yet the trial failed to uncover a single witness to a Bulgarian contact with Agca. The $1.3 million allegedly paid by the Bulgarians through Celenk to Agca and his fellow conspirators has never been found.[66] The rented automobile allegedly used by the Bulgarians to move Agca around Rome has never been traced. And the photo of Antonov in the Square has been rejected by the Court as not authentic.

While the case against the Bulgarians fell apart in the Rome trial, the Gray Wolves connection was confirmed and strengthened. The trial evidence showed that Agca traveled within the Gray Wolves network all through Western Europe, up to the time of his coming to Rome. Some of his Gray Wolves comrades admitted to knowing what he was up to in the spring of 1981, although they all denied participating in the Plot.[67] However, he got money from the network, its members supplied him with the gun, and he had meetings and contacts with them even in the last, Italian phase of his travels. It has not been proved that any of his Gray Wolves comrades were with Agca in Rome on May 13, 1981, but we strongly suspect that one or more of them were present. Whatever the truth of the Gray Wolves' assassination-day presence and support, the trial left Agca within a Gray Wolves, not a Bulgarian, network and support system. The first conspiracy was clearly a Gray Wolves conspiracy.

The trial also strengthened the case for a "second conspiracy" and the coaching hypothesis. In the investigative phase of the case, conducted by Judge Martella, the lid had been kept tight on the role of the secret services, the conditions of Agca's imprisonment, and the evidence for inducements and pressures. That lid was partially removed during the trial. Sometimes this was inadvertent, as in Abdullah Catli's

66. In the middle of the trial Celenk was released by Bulgaria and allowed to return to Turkey, where he was arrested, interrogated, and held for various crimes. Celenk died shortly thereafter, while incarcerated. It is an interesting fact that while the Bulgarians were willing to free Celenk, the Turkish government would not permit him to go to Rome to testify on the Bulgarian Connection despite urgent requests from the Italian court.

67. On September 20, 1985, Yalcin Ozbey, when asked whether Agca had invited him to participate in the assassination attempt, refused to answer the question on the ground of possible self-incrimination.

and Yalcin Ozbey's revelation that the West German police had tried to bribe Celik and Ozbey to confirm Agca's claims. Sometimes it was more direct, such as Giovanni Pandico's detailed description of the circumstances by which Agca's confession was coerced and guided by the Mafia and secret services.[68] The great publicity given in Italy to Pazienza's and SISMI's abuses of power forced a closer look at the secret services role and led to new claims supporting the coaching hypothesis. None of this evidence was conclusive, but as we will see in Chapter 5, it had cumulative power vastly greater than Agca's implausible claims.

Before looking in more detail at the evidence showing the Bulgarian Connection to be a fake, however, we will examine the Turkish background of the "first conspiracy," and then look at the Italian context within which the second conspiracy could be forged.

68. See Chapter 5, pp. 102-12.

3. The First Conspiracy: Agca and the Gray Wolves

While it is possible that the Pope's would-be assassin was manipulated by some outside party, in our view Agca's motivation must be sought in his Turkish roots. In this chapter we will show that Agca was firmly based in Turkey's neofascist Right, and that he had long been active in the terrorist group called the Gray Wolves. These roots are quickly passed over by the "terrorism experts" who, claiming to see no reason why a *Turk* would want to kill the Pope, cast their gaze to the East to find the motivation for such a conspiracy. Yet an elementary acquaintance with the history and ideology of the Gray Wolves quickly reveals a world view which adequately supports—if it does not "rationally" explain—an attempt on the Pope's life. Just after the attempted assassination, for example, Agca's younger brother Adnan told a reporter from *Newsweek* that Agca wanted to kill the Pope "because of his conviction that the Christians have imperialist designs against the Muslim world and are doing injustices to the Islamic countries."[1] Such a view, as we shall see, was in accord with the mainstream of Turkish rightwing thought; and Agca's attempt to assassinate the Pope was but an extreme instance of the campaign of terror used by the Turkish Right against its enemies.

The Roots of Turkish Fascism

The chief vehicle for the rise of a neofascist Right in Turkey in the 1960s and 1970s was the Nationalist Action Party (NAP). The NAP was

1. "The Man With The Gun," *Newsweek*, May 25, 1981, p. 36.

formed in 1965, when Col. Alparslan Türkes and some other former army officers took over the Republican Peasants' Nation Party (RPNP), a largely moribund party of the traditional Right. Türkes was a charismatic former army officer who first came to national prominence in 1944 when he, along with some 30 others, was arrested for participation in an anticommunist demonstration, a first indication that the government of Turkey was about to drop its tacit alliance with Hitler and join the allies. Türkes again achieved prominence when he and other extreme rightwing military officers were exiled from Turkey following the 1960 military coup that eventually established Turkey's modern constitutional structure. The return of Türkes, and the other officers who had been exiled, in 1963, and Türkes's subsequent takeover of the Republican Peasants' Nation Party, signaled a resurgence of the Turkish Right; and the swift exit of the RPNP's traditional leadership left Türkes and his associates in undisputed control of the small party.[2]

The Pan-Turkism movement, to which Türkes and his colleagues were the heirs, had its roots in the late nineteenth century. At first the Pan-Turks had hoped to reunite all Turkic peoples in a single nation stretching from western China to parts of Spain.[3] As the map in Illustration 3.1 shows, Turkish nationalists considered the Turkish people a nation divided, separated by boundaries which ignored Turkic cultural and linguistic unity. While the pre-World War I Ottoman Empire included most of the Turkish people, many Turks were left out, and the Empire also included other nationalities and ethnic groups which were not Turkish. Thus Pan-Turkism developed in opposition to the Ottoman Empire; it sought, as did many nationalist movements of that era in southeastern Europe, an international realignment which would regroup their suppressed peoples into a single, homogeneous nation.

The breakup of the Ottoman Empire during the First World War, however, hardly satisfied these aspirations. The new nation of Turkey which emerged from the war and the Kemalist revolution was much reduced in scope and left the majority of the Turkic peoples outside of its boundaries. Moreover, rather than causing the breakup of the Russian Empire, the World War and the Russian Revolution reconfirmed

2. Jacob M. Landau, *Radical Politics in Turkey* (Leiden: Brill, 1974), pp. 193-217; and Charles Patmore, "Türkes: The Right's Chosen Leader," *New Statesman*, April 6, 1979, p. 478.

3. By "Turkic peoples" we follow the broad definition outlined by Charles W. Hostler in his *Turkism and the Soviets: The Turks of the World and Their Political Objectives* (New York: Praeger, 1957), pp. 4-83.

Illustration 3.1: Cover of *Bozkurt* showing extent of spread of Turkish people beyond the boundaries of Turkey.

the subjugation of the predominantly Turkish regions of Tsarist Russia, cementing them to the new Union of Soviet Socialist Republics and frustrating the hopes of Pan-Turks that these areas could be detached from the Soviet Union and aligned with an enlarged Turkish nation. Finally, the relatively cordial relations achieved by the new Soviet and Turkish revolutionary regimes in the 1920s resulted in the suppression of Pan-Turkish organizations and ideas within Turkey, while the enthusiastic nation-building projects of the Kemalist state served to deflect potential recruits to Pan-Turkism into the Turkish political mainstream.

There were several consequences of this realignment of national boundaries and political forces. First, Pan-Turkism henceforth focused even more sharply on the plight of the "Outer Turks," those peoples who spoke one of the Turkic languages or who shared the Turkish culture and were outside Turkey's new national boundaries. They were consistently numbered by Pan-Turkish writers at more than 50 percent of all Turkish peoples, and an exceedingly high priority was placed on Turkish reunification. Moreover, the most important or politically sensitive areas in which they were found were in Cyprus (the birthplace of Türkes) and in the Soviet Union. The Pan-Turkism movement referred to these latter peoples as "Captive Turks," and for both ideological as well as revanchist reasons the Pan-Turkism movement became strongly anticommunist and anti-Soviet between the World Wars. In fact, Pan-Turkism became increasingly aligned with the international fascist movement, and became subtly transformed. Where it had once based its definition of "Turkism" on a common language and culture shared by different peoples throughout what its more misty-eyed advocates called "Greater Turan,"[4] under the influence of the fascist movements of the 1930s it increasingly emphasized the common *racial* ties of the Turkish peoples and preached a doctrine of Turkish racial superiority akin to the Nazis' doctrine of Aryan supremacy.

Thus it was not surprising that the German invasion of the Soviet Union in 1941 was greeted with enthusiasm by Pan-Turkish organizations. Not only did it strike a blow at the ideological enemy; more im-

4. According to Jacob Landau, Pan-Turanism "has as its chief objective rapprochement and ultimately union among all people whose origins are purported to extend back to Turan, an undefined Shangri-La-like area in the steppes of Central Asia. . . . Turanism is consequently a far broader concept than Pan-Turkism, embracing such peoples as the Hungarians, Finns, and Estonians." The term came to be adopted by many Pan-Turkists, who used it to mean *Turkish Homeland* in a very broad sense. *Pan-Turkism in Turkey: A Study of Irredentism* (Hamden, Conn.: Archon Books, 1981), p. 1.

portantly, it promised an opportunity to dissolve the Soviet Empire and to unite with the Turkish motherland the Turkish peoples "held captive" within the Soviet Union. These hopes were also recognized by the Nazis. As German armies advanced into the Soviet Union, Germany's ambassador to Turkey, Franz von Papen, cabled a secret report to the Ministry of Foreign Affairs outlining the possibilities for enlisting the "Pan-Turanism Movement" against the Soviet Union. "Germany," concluded von Papen,[5]

is called upon to pay special attention to the drawing of details for the formation of a strong state organization in the southeast with the aim of keeping the Soviets constantly apprehensive of this state. This task cannot be fulfilled in a satisfactory manner by the Ukraine; its people are Slavs, and they could easily come to believe at any time . . . that their common concord lies with the U.S.S.R. As far as the Turks are concerned, this possibility is wholly excluded.

As for the Turks, many responded eagerly to German overtures and the possibilities created by the apparently impending defeat of the Soviet Union. One area expert notes that "the Pan-Turkist irredentists regarded as inevitable the defeat of the U.S.S.R. and considered possible the creation of a confederation of all the Turkish peoples of Soviet Russia and Chinese Turkestan under the Turkish Republic's leadership." In the autumn of 1942, anticipating the fall of Stalingrad, the Turkish Republic concentrated troops at the Caucasian border, "ready to exploit all the possibilities the German-Soviet war and a collapse of the U.S.S.R. could furnish for the realization of Pan-Turkish ideals."[6]

Beginning in late 1941, more than a hundred thousand Soviet Turks were recruited out of prisoner-of-war camps by the Nazis and enrolled into army units that fought alongside the Germans. In 1944 the Turkestan National Committee initiated the formation of the East Turkish Waffen Verband, an SS unit, which consisted of four regiments of Turks from the Soviet Union. But by this time the cause of Germany, and thus of the Pan-Turks, was all but lost; and with the defeat of Germany in 1945 most Turkish people were still outside Turkey proper. Pan-Turkish organizations and publications continued to be dominated by a strongly anticommunist, and especially anti-Soviet, ideology; and while they were later to resume their alignment with international fas-

5. Cited in Hostler, *op. cit.*, p. 174.
6. *Ibid.*, pp. 176-77.

cism, they also became aligned with the U.S.-led anti-Soviet camp in the emerging Cold War.[7] This was the inheritance that Türkes and his colleagues brought to the NAP in the mid-1960s. The party's structure served in turn as a vehicle to disseminate a Pan-Turkish world view, and it soon emerged as a force to be reckoned with in modern Turkish politics. The political program of the NAP was set almost exclusively by Türkes himself, whose writings and speeches combined a vision of a science-based, state-planned economy which would modernize Turkey with an archaic world view that was rooted in the legends of the gray wolf who led the Turkic peoples out of Asia to their homeland in Anatolia.

As with European fascism, Türkes's unwieldy ideological amalgam sought to appeal to the "little man" allegedly crushed between capitalist monopolies and a growing labor movement. It is important to understand this, if only because western terrorism "experts" have expressed skepticism that Agca could both be a rightist and make anti-capitalist statements, as he has done. A good example of the NAP's attitude toward capitalism can be found in this passage from one of its journals:[8]

Finance capital is by its nature and purpose not national. Banks, insurance companies, and financial trusts that are attached to it are the mortal enemies of the national economy. . . . Finance capital is concerned with weakening and destroying the national economy in all its aspects by robbing the banks, manipulating the stock exchange, and by various other swindles. . . . There is also a class of compradors which participates in these activities of this anti-national capital, reaping large profits and sharing in the crime. They are virtually traitors. Thus the struggle between the national and the anti-national economy is one between international capital and its accomplices against the nation.

Yet, continuing the parallel with National Socialism, none of this "little man" propaganda prevented the NAP from enlisting the support of wealthy businessmen. According to the prosecutor's indictment of the NAP in the spring of 1981, following the crackdown on the party in the wake of the military coup the previous fall, records seized at party

7. *Ibid.*, pp. 55, 179; and Jacob Landau, *op. cit.*, n. 4, Chapters 3 and 4.
8. *Yeniden Milli Mücadele*, 54 (February 9, 1971), cited in Feroz Ahmad, *The Turkish Experiment in Democracy: 1950-1975* (London: C. Hurst & Co., 1977), pp. 263-64.

headquarters showed that the NAP received funds from the Chairman of the Executive Committee of the Secretariat of Turkish Businessmen, the President of the Istanbul Chamber of Industrialists, the Chairman of the Union of Chambers, the President of the Istanbul Chamber of Industry, the President of the Executive Committee of the Istanbul Bank, and many others.[9]

Türkes's brand of Pan-Turkism was also addressed to ultra-patriots who believed that their nation was being humiliated by its weakness in relation to the Soviet Union and the capitalist powers of the West, particularly the United States. This point is also overlooked by those propagators of the Bulgarian Connection who profess to be mystified by Agca's various pronouncements against "imperialism." Perhaps the most important such instance was his handwritten message, allegedly found among his possessions upon his arrest in Rome, declaring that his assassination attempt was a protest against both the Soviet invasion of Afghanistan and the U.S.-supported counterinsurgency in El Salvador. Yet Pan-Turkish propaganda is rich in such denunciations.

As is readily apparent, the Pan-Turkish social and political milieu into which the young Mehmet Ali Agca was absorbed in the 1970s had a well-developed, distinctive fascist ideology. While still in high school, Agca became involved with the NAP's youth affiliate, the Gray Wolves. The Wolves were so-named not only to enhance their ferocious image, but also to emphasize the atavistic part of the NAP's heritage; and it is said that the young recruits would howl when assembled together. In the late 1960s the NAP had established dozens of training camps for young people throughout Turkey, and had built the movement's strength largely on the basis of its youth organizations.[10] The military coup of March 12, 1971, gave the NAP its chance: as the military government turned against the Left, the Gray Wolves became a dominant force in many schools and the universities.

The NAP also prospered on the national political scene. A parliamentary crisis in late 1974 left the small rightwing parties, including the NAP, holding the balance of power in parliament. Demirel, the leader of the conservative Justice Party, moved to form a "National Front" government which would combine the forces on the right under his

9. *Searchlight* (Great Britain), No. 75 (September 1981), p. 13.

10. A secret report, prepared by the Turkish Ministry of the Interior in 1970 but suppressed by Prime Minister Demirel of the Justice Party, listed 26 such camps allegedly organized between August 1968 and July 1970. The report was made public during the height of NAP activity in November 1978. *Searchlight*, No. 47 (May 1979), pp. 5-6.

leadership. According to a leading historian of modern Turkey:[11]

Newspapers which supported the Front parties popularized the slogan "Demirel in Parliament, Türkes in the street. . . . " As a manifestation of this "division of labor," by the beginning of 1975 rightwing violence in the street carried out by Action Party "commandos" had become almost a daily occurrence. The aim of this violence was to emphasize the so-called danger from the Left, and it gave the Nationalist Action Party an opportunity to exert a political influence totally out of proportion to its following in the country and its strength in the Assembly.

Two of the NAP's three parliamentary representatives were given cabinet posts in the National Front government: Türkes was made Deputy Prime Minister, while a second NAP deputy was made Minister of Customs and State Monopolies.[12] By 1977 the party was strong enough to win seven percent of the vote in the general elections, giving them 16 Members of Parliament. Skillfully using its parliamentary faction and its forces in the streets, the NAP gained control of the Ministry of Education, which in turn assisted the Gray Wolves terrorists who beat and murdered their opponents to gain hegemony in many schools.[13] And the

11. Feroz Ahmad, *op. cit.*, n. 8, p. 347.

12. A physical attack on Demirel occurred shortly after the formation of the Front. At the trial, his assailant was shown to have been associated with the NAP. If Demirel had been killed, Türkes would have assumed the post of Prime Minister. According to Feroz Ahmad, "There was much speculation as to what might have happened if Demirel had been killed. Some thought that the government, led by Türkes (a man with fascist leanings), might have declared a state of emergency . . . and established an openly fascist regime. . . . This conspiracy theory was made more plausible because Türkes was said to have a large following among junior officers in the armed forces, who were willing to support such a regime. During the summer of 1975, the author heard both stories constantly while in Turkey" (*ibid.*, pp. 351, 361). Ahmad also notes that "Türkes wanted to have martial law proclaimed" (p. 362), and nearly succeeded in doing so in June 1975. Just before a visit by Türkes to the city of Diyarbekir, a stronghold of Shia and Kurds who were strongly opposed to Türkes and the NAP's Sunni and Turkish chauvinism, NAP commandos "came to Diyarbekir 'like an occupation force,' . . . and shouted slogans in the streets: 'Flee, the Turks are coming.' " Ahmad reports that, in response to these provocations, there was a demonstration against Türkes "which became violent and almost led to the proclamation of martial law" (p. 362).

13. Sterling, Henze, and NBC-TV have dwelt on the fact that Agca mysteriously passed an entrance examination allowing him to enter Istanbul University. They hint that this is evidence that Agca was aided by some sinister (*i.e.*, Red) power. They never acknowledge the special position which the extreme Right had obtained in the educational field, which provided an institutional basis for easing favored candidates through the educational system in the late 1970s.

NAP used its control of the Customs Ministry to turn the endemic smuggling from Turkey to Europe to its own profit. Finally, the NAP deployed its small but politically crucial weight in the parliamentary balance of power to prevent the government from cracking down on the party's terrorist "commandos," the Gray Wolves.

At the time of the military coup of September 1980, there were some 1,700 Gray Wolves organizations in Turkey with approximately 200,000 registered members and about a million sympathizers. Immediately following the coup, the NAP was outlawed and Türkes was arrested.[14] In its indictment of the NAP, which was handed down in May 1981, the Turkish military government charged 220 members of the party and its affiliates with the responsibility for 694 murders. This was only a fraction of the killing attributed to the Turkish Right. Statistics for 1978, for example, recorded 3,319 fascist attacks, which resulted in 831 killed and 3,121 wounded.[15] Contrary to the impression advanced by Claire Sterling in *The Terror Network*, the overwhelming bulk of political and sectarian violence in the pre-martial law period was initiated by the Gray Wolves, who were protected by their friends in the military, police force, and government.

Agca As Terrorist: The Gray Wolves Connection

Although Agca's immersion in the world of the Gray Wolves has been inconvenient for supporters of the Bulgarian Connection hypothesis, the evidence connecting Agca to Turkey's neofascist Right is overwhelming. What is more, these connections never tapered off and may be traced right up to Agca's sojourn in Rome.[16] Where Sterling,

14. Diana Johnstone has suggested that the assassination attempt on the Pope might have been motivated in part by the NAP-Gray Wolves resentment at their betrayal by NATO and the West, for whom they had served as a destabilizing force, but who had then allowed them to be swept up along with the Left in the aftermath of the Turkish military coup. "Assassins: Goal of Turkish Terror is Confusion," *In These Times*, June 3-16, 1981.

15. *Searchlight* (Great Britain), No. 47 (May 1979), p. 6.

16. The trial provided solid proof of the Gray Wolves connection up to Agca's stay in Rome. It failed to clarify the question of which, if any, Gray Wolves were with him on May 13, 1981. The last authenticated contact was on May 9, when Omer Bagci delivered a gun to Agca in Milan. We believe that one or more Gray Wolves accompanied Agca at the assassination attempt, but hard evidence is lacking.

Henze, and Investigating Magistrate Martella saw Agca's relationship with the Gray Wolves as either bogus or ephemeral, the evidence points to a durable connection, providing organization, personnel, funding, and an ideological basis for the assassination conspiracy.

Agca's association with the Gray Wolves began when he was in high school. According to Rasit Kisacik, a Turkish journalist who has studied Agca's early years, he was often seen with Gray Wolves leaders while in high school; and when the police raided Agca's home in 1979, they found photographs showing the young Agca in the company of leaders of the Gray Wolves.[17] Moreover, the people Agca came to know among his hometown Gray Wolves activists aided him in many of his later terrorist activities. While in theory the Gray Wolves were directed by the NAP, in fact, according to Michael Dobbs of the *Washington Post*, "the command structure seems to have been a loose one, allowing plenty of room for semiautonomous factions and groups that did not necessarily take their orders from the top."[18] The loose network of Gray Wolves from Agca's home base, the Malatya region of eastern Turkey, seems to have functioned as one such semiautonomous group. Led by Oral Celik—apparently involved in the murder of Turkey's most prominent newspaper editor, Abdi Ipekci, and in the operation that broke Agca out of prison in 1979, and identified by Agca as the second gunman in the attack on the Pope[19]—the Malatya gang supported itself by smuggling and robbery. We find them present at each of the milestones on Agca's path from high school to St. Peter's Square.

In 1978 Agca enrolled in Istanbul University. He apparently spent little time in classes. Instead he hung out in rightwing cafés like the Marmora, which "advertised the politics of those who frequented it with a large mural of a gray wolf on one of the walls."[20] According to Feroz Ahmad, "students in the hostel where he lived remembered him as a well-known 'militant' who was allegedly seen shooting two students in the legs during an attack on a leftist hostel. His notoriety in terrorist cir-

17. Marvine Howe, "Turk's Hometown Puzzled by His Climb to Notoriety," *New York Times*, May 23, 1981.

18. Michael Dobbs, "Child of Turkish Slums Finds Way in Crime," *Washington Post*, October 14, 1984.

19. This identification was supported by Ozbey during the trial, but was denied by other Gray Wolves. Celik was a good friend of Agca, and Agca's motive in falsely implicating Celik is not clear.

20. R. W. Apple, Jr., "Trail of Mehmet Ali Agca: 6 Years of Neofascist Ties," *New York Times*, May 25, 1981.

cles was such that leftists tried to kill him on a number of occasions."[21]

On February 1, 1979, the Malatya gang assassinated Ipekci. Agca was arrested a few months later; and, although there now seems to be serious doubt whether Agca was indeed the gunman or just an accomplice, he quickly confessed to the crime. At his trial the following October Agca steadfastly denied any connection with the NAP or the Gray Wolves, claiming instead to "represent a new form of terror on my own." After several sessions of his trial, Agca threatened in court to name "the truly responsible parties" when the trial next convened. This clear signal that someone had better get him out was delivered within days after the formation of a new, conservative government, dependent on NAP votes for its parliamentary majority; and a few days later some Gray Wolves led by Oral Celik smuggled Agca, disguised as a soldier, through eight checkpoints and out of prison.

Agca's first act upon escaping from prison was to send a letter to *Milliyet*, Ipekci's newspaper, threatening to kill the Pope, who was about to visit Turkey. Once again we stumble on an event which presents inconvenient facts for Sterling and company, for on its face Agca's act supports the probability that he (and the Malatya gang) needed no KGB hand to guide them toward a papal assassination. In his letter to *Milliyet* Agca stated:[22]

Fearing the creation of a new political and military power in the Middle East by Turkey along with its brother Arab states, western imperialism has . . . dispatched to Turkey in the guise of religious leader the crusade commander John Paul. Unless this untimely and meaningless visit is postponed, I shall certainly shoot the Pope.

Was this letter written at the direction of Agca's KGB controller, as Sterling and Henze maintain, as a devilishly clever cover for Agca's KGB links? Was it written, as Agca himself later maintained, as a diversion to throw his pursuers off the scent? While we cannot say with certainty, the fact that the contents of the letter accord perfectly with the ideological views of the Gray Wolves and the NAP strongly suggests that the letter simply speaks for itself;[23] and while Agca and the Malatya

21. Feroz Ahmad, "Agca: The Making of A Terrorist," *Boston Globe*, June 7, 1981.
22. Sinan Fisek, "Attacker Named As Escaped Assassin," *London Times*, May 14, 1981. A slightly different translation may be found in Claire Sterling, *The Time of the Assassins* (New York: Holt, Rinehart and Winston, 1983), p. 19.
23. For evidence of NAP press hostility to the Pope's visit in 1979, see Chapter 6, p. 156, n. 90.

gang failed to carry out their threat to kill the heavily guarded Pope during his visit to Turkey, such an act was on their agenda. At this point Agca's life as a fugitive began. Wanted by Turkish authorities and Interpol, Agca nevertheless moved with apparent ease through some dozen countries in the 18 months separating his prison escape from his rendezvous with the Pope in May 1981. Throughout this time Agca was rarely outside the Gray Wolves network and was frequently in contact with the Malatya gang. After murdering the informer who had earlier tipped off the police to his whereabouts, Agca was taken by the Gray Wolves to Iran to hide out. Some months later he returned to Turkey and, aided by a false passport provided him by Gray Wolves members, he was smuggled into Bulgaria and through that country, arriving in Western Europe in the fall of 1980. Agca thus narrowly escaped the military coup which forced many Gray Wolves underground or into exile abroad. The Malatya gang soon followed Agca to Western Europe, where they sought shelter among the Gray Wolves network in the large Turkish immigrant communities of Switzerland and West Germany.

In fleeing from Turkey Agca was not abandoning the Gray Wolves network so much as seeking the shelter of its extèrior branches. The NAP and the Gray Wolves had recruited for many years among the millions of Turkish men who left their country to work in Switzerland, West Germany, or other European countries for one or more years before returning home.[24] When a 1976 Turkish court decision made it illegal for the Gray Wolves and the NAP to maintain foreign affiliates, the Western European branches were reorganized into the Federation of Turkish Idealist Associations or into Turkish "cultural" clubs, but they secretly maintained their ties to the NAP. The Federation claimed 50,000 members in Europe at the time of the military coup in September 1980, with 129 chapters, including 87 in West Germany. The West German police estimated that at least 26,000 Turkish workers in West Germany were members of neofascist organizations.[25]

24. For a vivid account of this great migration, see John Berger and Jean Mohr, *A Seventh Man* (London: Penguin Books, 1975).

25. Another report estimated that there were 200 conservative Islamic centers in West Germany; and the *New York Times* cited "recent documentation by West Germany's labor federation [which] pointed out strong anti-Western, anti-Semitic, and anti-Christian currents in the Islamic centers' publications" (John Tagliabue, "Militant Views Among Turks Trouble Bonn," May 21, 1981). The de facto political alliances between the NAP and Islamic fundamentalism in Turkey were probably operative in Western Europe as well.

This network of rightwing Turkish organizations sheltered Agca between the time he left Turkey and the day he shot the Pope. Simply to list the confirmed links which have emerged at Agca's trial in Rome and in collateral trials in other Gray Wolves centers in Western Europe reinforces this conclusion:

1. Agca came to Western Europe with a passport provided by Gray Wolves leader Abdullah Catli. Catli had obtained the passport with the help of a customs official who was a member of the Gray Wolves.

2. Agca was sheltered by Catli and other Gray Wolves in Olten, Switzerland, a major Gray Wolves smuggling center.[26] One of Agca's companions in Olten, Mehmet Sener, was sentenced in Switzerland to a five-year prison term for drug smuggling. Catli and Oral Celik were wanted for questioning at Sener's trial.

3. Yalcin Ozbey, who was brought in to testify in Rome, was jailed in Bochum, West Germany on drug smuggling charges. Before the murder of Ipekci in 1979, Ozbey and Agca had a joint bank account. Another Gray Wolves friend of Agca, Rifat Yildirim, was caught with heroin in Frankfurt.

4. Musa Celebi, one of the top leaders of the Gray Wolves in Western Europe, had numerous contacts with Agca in 1980 and 1981, giving him money and meeting with him in Zurich only six weeks before the assassination attempt.

5. Agca's gun was purchased for him by Catli, and was delivered to him in Milan only four days before the assassination attempt by the Olten Gray Wolves leader Omer Bagci and two other Gray Wolves.

6. At the time of the Pope's visit to the Netherlands in May 1985, another Gray Wolves member, Arslan Samet, was arrested at the Dutch border while carrying a Browning revolver stolen at the same time as the one used by Agca in St. Peter's Square.

7. Numerous phone calls between Agca and Gray Wolves leaders in West Germany and Switzerland were intercepted by the police in the months before the assassination attempt.

In short, the available evidence shows that Agca was a Gray Wolves

---

26. For the Gray Wolves in Switzerland, see "Türkische Mafia Und Die Grauen Wolfe in Der Schweiz," *Informationstelle Türkei* (Postfach 2151, 4001 Basel, 1985). This useful volume includes analyses and excerpts from Turkish and Swiss newspapers on the criminal activities of many of the Gray Wolves mentioned above. Much useful information also emerged during the 1985 sessions of the trial, as Ozbey, Catli, and other Gray Wolves were called by Judge Santiapichi and testified about Agca's connections to the Gray Wolves in Switzerland.

militant, and up to May 13, 1981, all his contacts led straight to the
Gray Wolves.

Agca As An "International Terrorist"

Sterling, Henze, and some members of the Italian judiciary[27] have portrayed Agca as a "pure" or "international" terrorist, who rises above
mere political loyalties and dedicates his life to random political violence. We may usefully pause to examine the "proofs" that Agca was
an apolitical international terrorist, for the fallacies they embody are not
only relevant to evaluating the Gray Wolves linkage, they also illuminate the quality of the Sterling-Henze-Kalb evidence for the Bulgarian
Connection.

Agca's Gray Wolves affiliation as "cover." The Sterling-Henze school
has suggested that the Soviets and the Bulgarians recruited Agca early
and had him serve in the Gray Wolves as a "cover." Thus his threat to
kill the Pope in 1979 was an attempt to provide a later basis for the claim
that he was a Turkish fascist, when in fact he was already under KGB
discipline.

One problem with this line of argument is the absence of the faintest
trace of supporting evidence. Another is that many of Agca's Gray
Wolves comrades would have had to be similarly manipulated. A third
problem is that the alleged Soviet motive to kill the Pope—the threat of
Poland's Solidarity—did not exist in earlier years, nor at the time when
Agca made the threat in 1979. A further problem is that the assassination threat can be explained on grounds of Gray Wolves-NAP ideology
without resort to hypothetical scenarios. *Anything* can be proved by this
form of pseudoscientific reasoning.

Agca was not a card-carrying member of the Gray Wolves. Sterling and
Henze claim that Agca never obtained an official Gray Wolves membership card. It may be noted that this line of proof is diametrically opposed
to that made in the previous point. If Agca were a KGB recruit and they
wanted to tar him with the brush of Turkish fascism to cover up a later
terrorist act, the KGB would have made sure that Agca did the necessary paperwork. Indeed, the absence of a membership card undermines

27. See Chapter 5, pp. 113-15.

the argument that Agca was controlled by the KGB while a Gray Wolves activist. Apart from this contradiction, however, the record of durable linkages and a longstanding political commitment must be persuasive to nonpseudoscientists, barring credible alternative evidence.

The motive behind Agca's confessions. Apart from their unwillingness to give proper weight to Agca's Gray Wolves connections, Sterling and company ignore three motivations for Agca's confessions implicating the Bulgarians that render them worthless as evidence:

Loyalty: By claiming he was an "international terrorist," Agca took the blame and kept the heat off his Gray Wolves comrades for many months. He had done the same thing in Turkey by "confessing" to the Ipekci murder in 1979. In the case of the Bulgarian Connection, Agca should certainly have little objection to channeling ultimate guilt from his best friends to the Communists, a longstanding Gray Wolves foe.[28]

Self-Preservation: By accommodating his captors he made life much easier for himself. We describe later the probable "deal" struck, and the inducements and threats that made it worth his while to finger the Evil Empire.

Publicity: Agca had long sought fame and recognition. According to Turkish journalist Ismail Kovaci, "Agca suffers both from jealousy and delusions of self-grandeur. For him, terrorism represented his way of leaving his mark on the world."[29] Michael Dobbs of the *Washington Post* states:[30]

Many who encountered Agca both in Turkey and in Italy, have spoken of his "Carlos Complex"—his image of himself as a top-flight international terrorist with the whole world hanging breathlessly on his every word. His desire for personal publicity seems unquenchable. At one point in the Italian investigation, he

28. One theory of Gray Wolves involvement, expounded by Orsan Oymen, is that the Gray Wolves in Western Europe were not keen on the assassination attempt, which was a preoccupation of Agca's (held over from the Pope's visit to Turkey in 1979). Agca persuaded his comrades to support him by promising that if caught he would blame the Soviet Bloc for the Plot, not the Gray Wolves. Agca did implicate the Bulgarians and Soviets immediately, although along with others, and eventually he came through with a full-scale "confession." It is interesting to note that Celebi held a press conference in Bonn on May 21, 1981, in which he proclaimed that Agca had nothing to do with the Gray Wolves and that the assassination plot had been organized and sponsored by the KGB. See Orsan Oymen, "Behind the Scenes of the 'Agca Investigation,' " *Milliyet*, November 1984.

29. Michael Dobbs, "Child of Turkish Slums . . . ," *Washington Post*, October 14, 1984.

30. *Ibid.*

abruptly clammed up when the magistrates refused his demand that journalists be present as he "confessed."

Having exhausted his ability to derive eminence from shooting the Pope, Agca's deal to implicate the Bulgarians opened up new avenues to attain star status and TV recognition. So did the trial, where he could reveal his special role as the Son of God.

Agca says just what Claire Sterling says an international terrorist ought to say. Since deciding to cooperate with the Italian authorities, Agca has played the international terrorist card aggressively. Perhaps too aggressively. Although until the 1985 trial he only claimed to have had contact with low-level Bulgarian functionaries, he kept saying with great decisiveness that the KGB was involved. He could not know this from any direct experience, but he learned the "model" into which his mentors and captors wanted him to fit, and he kept helping them out. During the trial, he suddenly trotted out a Sofia meeting with the Soviet Deputy Ambassador, to the consternation of the prosecution and a chorus of derision from the defense and the press. Agca's caricature of the Sterling vision of the terrorist-for-hire (by the KGB) is so close to the original that some of the Italian magistrates have been impressed by the excellent fit![31]

In the real world, coached witnesses say what their coaches want them to say. In a world of disinformation and internalized propaganda, the courts and press marvel at the conformity of the "confession" to the forecasts of the coaches!

The Smuggling Versus CIA Connection

Money was the lifeblood of the NAP and the Gray Wolves networks: money for guns, money for bribes, and money to maintain the party's organizational apparatus. As one former Gray Wolves member testified,[32] the Western European network of the Gray Wolves

31. See the comments of Magistrate Rosario Priore in Chapter 4 below.

32. *Die Tageszeitung* (a West Berlin daily), September 4, 1980. The witness, Ali Yurturslan, was later used as a source on the NBC program, "The Man Who Shot the Pope — A Study in Terrorism," but any information he had given NBC about Gray Wolves smuggling was not used.

sends large quantities of money back to Turkey. Not only money, but weapons and equipment. Guns from France, West Germany, Belgium, and Bulgaria are smuggled by sea into Turkey. . . . One of the Nationalist Action Party's greatest sources of funds is drug smuggling. Heroin and hashish are smuggled out of Turkey and into Europe, and the NAP even markets much of the drugs in Europe itself. The profits go to buying guns in Turkey.

A British survey of the NAP's participation in drug smuggling states:[33]

The first indications of their involvement came in 1973 when Kudret Bayhan, a NAP member of the Turkish senate, was detained in France with a consignment of heroin. Also arrested with Bayhan were two other members of the NAP's executive committee. In 1976 another NAP senator with a car [trunk] loaded with the drug was arrested on the border between Italy and Yugoslavia. Three years later Italian police at Trieste arrested nineteen Turkish right wingers transporting a total of £2 million [about $5 million] worth of heroin. Some of them admitted to police investigators that the heroin was destined for the United States, where it was to be traded for arms with underworld contacts.

While it is dangerous to place much confidence in any of Agca's declarations, Turkish military prosecutors who reopened the Ipekci murder case have accepted as plausible Agca's assertion that while in Istanbul he supported himself through a black market smuggling operation organized by the Malatya gang.

Although much of the smuggling to and from Turkey was carried out by sea, some of it also crossed the Bulgarian land bridge separating Turkey from Western Europe. Given the vast flow of Turks and others traversing Bulgaria on their way to and from Western Europe in the 1970s, it was virtually impossible for Bulgaria to control its borders against smuggling. Even with apparently serious efforts to control the drug trade it is a notable fact that many of the biggest complainers (e.g., the United States and Italy) have been unable to curb the traffic in their own countries.

Some credible Italian and Turkish investigators have claimed that Bulgaria tolerates and even participates in some facets of smuggling, such as the arms trade, in order to earn hard currency. But this alleged participation and acquiescence has never been proved to extend to drugs, and the Bulgarian government's claims of serious efforts to con-

33. "The Heroin Trail and Gray Wolves Guns," *Searchlight* (Great Britain), No. 65 (November 1980), p. 7. See also Feroz Ahmad, *op. cit.*, n. 21.

trol that form of smuggling have been given credence by the U.S. Customs Service (see Appendix B).

It is dangerous to make the leap from the existence of smuggling to state direction and control of smuggling, and even more dangerous to then claim state responsibility for all the crimes of the smugglers. Moreover, we now know that the Turkey-Bulgaria-Italy smuggling route was run at least in part by officials from Italy's military intelligence agency (SISMI);[34] and in reporting on March 23, 1983, that the three top CIA officials in Rome were in "deep trouble," NBC News suggested that one source of their problems was "that they might have been using a guns and drug smuggling route between Sofia, Bulgaria and Milan, Italy to run their own agents into Eastern Europe. . . . " In short, it would appear that, as with all lucrative but illegal trades, the smugglers' highway between Turkey and Western Europe was lined with money and accommodated the intelligence agents of many nations as well as the smugglers themselves.

Sterling, Henze, and Martella saw the root of the Bulgarian Connection in the drug and arms smuggling activities of what they call the "Turkish Mafia." The main linkages are those between the Turkish Mafia and those Bulgarian state officials who tolerated, protected, and/or helped organize the smuggling. In Sterling's view, Agca was a relatively low-level employee of this Mafia, and while in Bulgaria he was on the payroll of Abuzer Ugurlu, the "Godfather" of the Turkish Mafia. Ugurlu, in turn, worked with or for another Godfather, the Turkish businessman Bekir Celenk. According to Sterling and company, it was through Celenk and Ugurlu that the Bulgarians directed the Turkish smuggling operations, and through them that the smugglers received Bulgarian protection. And according to Agca (and then Martella), it was Celenk who offered to pay Agca more than a million dollars to kill the Pope.

The weaknesses of this linkage of Agca and the assassination attempt to the Bulgarians via the smuggling connection are severe. First, once again much of this story rests on the credibility of Agca, the sole source of many crucial details. Furthermore, we know that Agca had read Ugur Mumcu's *Arms Smuggling and Terrorism*, and there is reason to believe that many of the details Agca gave his interrogators about such well-

34. "La P-2, les service italiens, le trafic drogues/armes: l'attentat contre le pape et la CIA," *Le Monde du Renseignement*, October-December 1983, pp. 43-44.

known smugglers as Abuzer Ugurlu and Bekir Celenk were taken from this book.[35]

Second, while the smuggling trade between Turkey and Bulgaria has been significant, it has involved the principals in a business relationship with reciprocal benefits. The assumption that the Bulgarians *control* the Turkish Mafia participating in that trade is unproven and implausible.[36] So is the assumption that the NAP is a simple instrument of the Turkish Mafia. Michael Dobbs presents evidence that Ugurlu was dependent on the NAP for protection, rather than the other way around. Dobbs notes that "to carry out this large-scale smuggling operation, Ugurlu . . . needed agents in the Turkish customs ministry," and points out that "it is now known that key customs posts were infiltrated by supporters of the [NAP] . . . during the late 1970s."[37] Particularly between 1975 and 1978, when they participated in the National Front government, the NAP placed many of its supporters in key positions in the customs ministry and at border crossing points. Needing funds to carry out party activities, the NAP was in a position to deal profitably with the smugglers and was increasingly able to take over the business itself. According to Orsan Oymen, "My opinion is that . . . it was the Gray Wolves who were in a position to ask favors from the Mafia. They were the ones with the political influence at the time, because of their control over the customs ministry."[38] Finally, Ugur Mumcu, the leading authority on the Turkish-Bulgarian drug connection, does not accept the notion that Ugurlu, the Turkish Mafia, and the Gray Wolves were instruments of Bulgarian political policy merely by virtue of their mutually profitable business linkages.[39]

A third important weakness of the smuggling-based model is its neglect of the anticommunism of the NAP and Gray Wolves and their links to the United States and CIA. If these are given their proper weight, not only is the idea that the Gray Wolves were up for hire by the communist powers seen as foolish, but questions are also raised about the possibility of a CIA root for the assassination attempt.

35. See Chapter 2, p. 27, n.36.
36. See Appendix B.
37. "Child of Turkish Slums," *Washington Post*, October 14, 1984.
38. Quoted by Michael Dobbs, *ibid.*
39. Ugur Mumcu, *Papa, Mafya, Agca* (Istanbul: Tekin Yayinevi, 1984), pp. 198-211. Michael Dobbs points out that Mumcu believes that Ugurlu also worked for Turkey's intelligence agency, MIT. "Agca Makes His Way From Sofia to St. Peter's," *Washington Post*, October 15, 1984.

While the Bulgarians had links to the Turkish Mafia via the smuggling trade, the United States had established a far more powerful position in the heart of Turkish society, notably in its army and intelligence services. The huge Turkish loans of 1947-48 and the integration of Turkey into the U.S.-dominated NATO made the U.S.-Turkish relationship one of patron and client by the early 1950s.[40] Between 1950 and 1979 the United States provided a further $5.8 billion in military aid.[41] The arms supply and training programs helped integrate the Turkish military, police, and intelligence services into those of the United States. Under the Military Assistance Program and the International Military Education and Training Program, 19,193 Turks received U.S. training between 1950 and 1979. U.S. trainees in client states have been instrumental in leading counterrevolutionary coups that have served their patron's interests.[42] The patron is also often effectively an occupying power, organizing the military and police, manipulating the political environment, and building its own bridges to serviceable (usually rightwing) groups within the state.

The most likely avenue linking the CIA to the Turkish Right runs through Turkey's "Counter-Guerrilla," a branch of the Turkish General Staff's Department of Special Warfare, which was created sometime in the 1960s. One study of Turkey's Counter-Guerrilla notes that it was headquartered in the same Ankara building that housed the U.S. military mission, and that the training of officers assigned to this unit "begins in the U.S. and then continues inside Turkey under the direction of CIA officers and military 'advisers.' " During the 1960s, according to the same study, the CIA assisted the Turkish intelligence organization MIT in drawing up plans for the mass arrest of opposition figures; and the same work claims that this plan was put into operation following the 1971 coup.[43] Another study, by former Turkish military prosecutor and

40. By the end of Fiscal Year 1950 the Turks had received $150 million in economic aid, plus over $200 million in military aid, along with over 1,200 U.S. military advisers. Joyce and Gabriel Kolko, *The Limits of Power* (New York: Harper & Row, 1972), p. 413.

41. Michael T. Klare and Cynthia Arnson, *Supplying Repression: U.S. Support for Authoritarian Regimes Abroad* (Washington: Institute for Policy Studies, 1981), p. 81.

42. See Edward S. Herman, *The Real Terror Network* (Boston: South End Press, 1982), pp. 121-32.

43. Jurgen Roth and Kamil Taylan, *Die Türkei—Republik Unter Wolfen* [Turkey: A Republic Ruled by Wolves], (Bornheim, West Germany: Lamur Verlag, 1981). Excerpts from this study were translated in *CounterSpy*, Vol. VI, No. 2 (February-April 1982), pp. 23 and 25, and some of it was reprinted in "Türkische Mafia Und Die Grauen Wolfe in

Supreme Court Justice Emin Deger, states that there was a close, working collaboration between the NAP armed commandos, or *Bozkurts*, and the Counter-Guerrilla units. There was also a close tie between the Counter-Guerrilla and the CIA. Deger charged further that the CIA, acting through MIT and the Counter-Guerrilla, promoted rightwing terrorist actions to destabilize the Turkish government and to prepare the way for the military coup of 1971.[44] It also seems quite clear that the United States and the CIA were very anxious to oust the Demirel government in 1971, and assisted in the coup of that year. According to former U.S. diplomat Robert Fresco, Demirel's government had simply become incapable of containing the growing anti-U.S. radicalism in Turkey.[45] Turkish writer Ismail Cem argues, in his *March 12 From the Perspective of History*, that the failure of the Demirel government to deal with the "Hashish Question"—*i.e.*, to curb hashish and heroin production in eastern Turkey—as well as its failure to check radicalism, prompted U.S. support for the coup.[46]

Within this broad framework of overwhelming U.S. influence in Turkey and its apparent willingness to use it to manipulate Turkish politics, there are indications that the United States, and particularly the CIA, exercised influence in the rightwing political sectors that included the Gray Wolves. The CIA-Gray Wolves Connection starts with the "Captive Turks," those peoples of Turkic origin who lived in the Soviet Union and were the objects of much of the Pan-Turkish propaganda and solicitude. These Captive Turks provided a target of opportunity for U.S. intelligence in the post-World War II years similar to the Byelorussians, Ukrainians, and others who joined forces with the Nazis against the Soviet Union and later enlisted in the shadowy East European networks of the CIA. These latter operations have recently received a great deal of publicity, particularly as a result of the work of John Loftus and

Der Schweiz", *op. cit.*, n. 26.

44. Emin Deger, *CIA, Counter-Guerrilla, and Turkey*, cited in S. Benhabib, "Right-Wing Groups Behind Political Violence in Turkey," *MERIP Reports*, No. 77 (May 1979), p. 17. Deger bases part of his argument on what he calls the "Dickson Report," a document which was apparently the product of U.S. military intelligence in Turkey and which argues, according to Deger, "the common goals of imperialism with the Justice Party" (p. 138). The authenticity of this document has been disputed (see Claire Sterling, *The Terror Network* (New York: Holt, Rinehart and Winston, 1981), p. 333), but no evidence has ever been published by those who claim it is a forgery.

45. Robert M. Fresco, "A Problem of Visibility," *The Nation*, September 14, 1980.

46. Ismail Cem, *Tarih Acisindan 12 Mart* (Istanbul: CEM, 1977).

his book, *The Belarus Secret*. Loftus discovered that a secret division of the U.S. State Department had recruited the leadership of a Byelorussian military unit which had governed that region of the Soviet Union while it was under Nazi occupation. This "Belarus Brigade" had participated zealously in massacres of Jews, and had retreated westward with the defeated German Army, even engaging U.S. military forces in combat. Loftus found that the State Department's secret Office of Policy Coordination had recruited the Byelorussians, thinking that they were gaining a working intelligence apparatus and the nucleus of a possible guerrilla operation within the Soviet Union.[47] While no evidence has come to light of a similar U.S. operation directed toward the tattered remnants of those units of Soviet Turks that had fought alongside the Germans against the Soviet Union, there is no reason to suppose that the U.S. motivations and practices toward pro-Nazi East Europeans that have been exposed by Loftus were not also operative in the U.S. approach to Turks.

The best-known link between the CIA and the modern-day Pan-Turkish movement is that provided by Ruzi Nazar. Nazar is a Turkoman who was born near Tashkent in the Soviet Union and deserted the Red Army to join the Nazis during World War II. After the war Nazar was recruited by the CIA, and according to Turkish journalist Ugur Mumcu, he "was successful in penetrating Turkish fascist circles in the days when Agca worked as a hired gun" for the NAP.[48] In the 1950s Nazar

47. John Loftus, *The Belarus Secret* (New York: Alfred A. Knopf, 1982). Some indication of the Pentagon's interest in the "Captive Turks" is given in the prefatory material in Charles W. Hostler's *Turkism and the Soviets*. Hostler was a member of the U.S. Military Mission to Turkey from 1948 to 1950; and, while a member of the U.S. Air Force, conducted this study on Turkish peoples within the U.S.S.R. In his Introduction he notes that, "My aim is to consider the political potentiality of the Turkish world. . . . In the case of a Third World War—or intensification of the Cold War—or in case of internal troubles involving disintegration of Soviet power, Turkish nationalism (especially the Pan-Turkish variety of Turkish nationalism) will influence the policies of the Turkish Republic and the action of the politically developed Turkish peoples of the Soviet Union." (*Ibid.*, pp. 2-3.) The Turkish military government's 945-page indictment of the NAP in May 1981 included a letter from the party's West European leader, Enver Altayli, to Türkes, in which Altayli listed his West German intelligence contacts. Among them was a Dr. Mehmet Kengerli, who was described as a former Nazi SS officer born in Azerbaijan. Marvine Howe, "Turks Say Suspect in Papal Attack is Tied to Rightist Web of Intrigue," *New York Times*, May 18, 1981.

48. Mumcu was interviewed and some of his work summarized in the *Atlanta Constitution*, January 30, 1983. Mumcu claims to have received information about Nazar's CIA links from a Turkish general who maintained close ties with Nazar.

had worked as a part-time contributor to the Voice of America, and it was perhaps through this work that he met Paul Henze, who was then working for the CIA at Radio Free Europe. Nazar apparently joined Henze when the latter was sent by the CIA to the U.S. Embassy in Turkey in 1959. But by the time that Henze had become Chief of Station in 1974, Nazar's cover had been blown and his usefulness in Turkey had come to an end. Nazar was then transferred to the U.S. Embassy in Bonn where, according to Mumcu, his assignment was to penetrate Gray Wolves organizations for the CIA, while maintaining his close ties to Col. Türkes and the NAP.[49] Nazar was still active in these functions in the 1980s. His continuing extreme rightwing orientation is evidenced by the fact that he is a leading member of the Munich-based Anti-Bolshevik Bloc of Nations (ABN), and represented that organization at the World Anticommunist League Convention in Dallas in September 1985.[50]

In sum, the links of the CIA to the NAP and Gray Wolves were easily as impressive as any NAP-Gray Wolves connections to the Bulgarians.[51] While the NAP was admittedly ambivalent toward the capitalist West, it shared with the West an unmitigated hostility toward the Soviets that makes a CIA connection to the assassination attempt more politically credible than a Bulgarian Connection. Finally, there is a matter of results. If we look for the source of the Plot in the real beneficiaries, the Plot turned out very well for the United States and badly for the Soviets. Nonetheless, we do not believe that the CIA was behind the Plot. In our view, the origin of the shooting lies in the Gray Wolves' ideology and Agca's need to attain hero status by a political act. The benefits to the West accrued from the "second conspiracy"—the induced confession in Rome—and not by the shooting per se.

49. In his book *Papa, Mafya, Agca*, Mumcu reproduces a long letter from the West German Gray Wolves leader Enver Altayli to Türkes, which indicates clearly that a friendly and cooperative relationship existed between Altayli and Ruzi Nazar, and that Altayli obtained information from Nazar (pp. 145-46). Nazar also had a direct and cordial relationship with Türkes (p. 144). Mumcu also reports that while still in Turkey in the early 1970s, Nazar helped Türkes's daughter obtain a job in a U.S. airlines agency. See his *Agca Dosyasi* (Istanbul: Tekin Yayinevi, 1984), pp. 28-29.

50. Martin A. Lee and Kevin Coogan, "The Agca Con," *Village Voice*, December 24, 1985, p. 23.

51. The Soviet author Iona Andronov has put up a CIA-based model that is somewhat more credible than that of Claire Sterling. See Appendix D.

Final Note

Mehmet Ali Agca was a Turkish fascist, linked closely to the Gray Wolves and working with them every step on the way to Rome. This was amply reconfirmed at the 1985-86 trial, which highlighted the complex web of associations linking Agca to other Gray Wolves activists. At the same time, the trial produced not a shred of evidence, independent of Agca's own testimony, that he had had any contact with a Bulgarian in Sofia, Rome, or elsewhere. Thus, when Agca entered Bulgaria through a border customs station controlled by the Gray Wolves, or when he procured a passport issued in the name of NAP militant Faruk Ozgun, obtained with the help of Abdullah Catli and a customs official also in the Gray Wolves, there is no reason not to take these events at face value: One of Turkey's most notorious terrorists had boarded the "underground railroad" long used by the Gray Wolves to get their drugs, guns, money, and militants back and forth between Turkey and Western Europe.

4. The Rome-Washington Connection

The creation and institutionalization of the Bulgarian Connection must be situated in the political environment of the late 1970s and early 1980s. In the late seventies, anti-détente forces within the United States waged a furious battle against the second Strategic Arms Limitation Treaty (SALT II) and any further pursuit of understandings and rapprochement between the great powers. Aided by the Iranian hostage crisis, they were sufficiently powerful and well mobilized to be able to kill SALT II and help usher in the New Cold War.

In Italy, also, the strengthening of the Communist Party in the mid-1970s and the threat of its participation in government had aroused great fears in U.S. officials and Italian conservatives. A landmark in the erosion of that threat was the murder of moderate Christian Democratic leader Aldo Moro in 1978.[1] The recession of the late 1970s and early

1. Although Moro was murdered by the Red Brigades, the ultimate source of his death is in dispute. As noted in the text below, Moro was number one on the hit list of an aborted rightwing conspiracy of 1966, Plan Solo. Contacts with the Red Brigades were made by a variety of political interests: Libya, George Habash's Popular Front for the Liberation of Palestine, the CIA, and Israel (which sought a relationship with the Red Brigades in the hopes that destabilization in Italy would make the United States more dependent on Israel as its Mediterranean area ally). (See Luciano Violante, "Politica della sicurezza, relazioni internazionali e terrorismo," in Gianfranco Pasquino, editor, *La Prova Delle Armi* (Istituto Carlo Cattaneo, Bologna: Societa Editrice Il Mulino, 1984), p. 110, note 54.) Violante declares ironically that "the only services to which the Red Brigades seem to have been impenetrable are the Italian ones" (p. 112), but this is not firmly established. It is an interesting fact that the Italian establishment refused to ransom Moro, although they paid lavishly to obtain the release of a lesser Christian Democratic functionary, Ciro Cirillo. The Italian security services were remarkably ineffective in locating the kidnapped Moro, missing important leads. Diana Johnstone notes that "General Musumeci interpreted the clear tip to Moro's whereabouts, 'Gradoli,' as the village of

1980s, the Soviet invasion of Afghanistan, the new wave of terrorism, and the New Cold War environment in the United States strengthened the Right and Center and weakened the Communist Party and Italian popular movements. With the coming into power of Reagan, the ruling Italian parties joined the New Cold War with enthusiasm and competed energetically for honors as the local favorite.

The New Cold War and the "Antiterrorism" Offensive

In the United States the forces opposing détente have had an important institutional representative in the Committee on the Present Danger (CPD) and its follow-on Coalition for a Democratic Majority (CDM). The CPD has had high-level representation in both political parties.[2] Among the intellectual weapons used by the CPD and its allies, "international terrorism" and the "Soviet Threat" rank supreme. By the mid-1970s, the so-called "Vietnam Syndrome" had weakened the force of traditional anticommunist appeals in rallying support for U.S. intervention abroad. Terrorist and Soviet threats are well suited to reinvigorate that traditional appeal, and they have been used regularly by the CPD to justify a more aggresssive stance toward the Soviet Union (and all of its alleged proxies and sympathizers).

A major problem for the CPD faction has been credibility: What can the media and public be induced to swallow in the way of evidence of

Gradoli in Viterbo province, and dispatched police there in vain. Moro was actually being held right in Rome, in the via Gradoli, as was discovered too late. Musumeci led another wild goose chase to a frozen mountain lake on a false tip that, when published, was interpreted by the Red Brigades as a signal from the authorities that Moro's death was accepted." ("Latest scandal leads to Reagan administration," *In These Times*, December 5-11, 1984.) Given the damaging effect of the death of Moro on the Communist Party and the Left in general, a rightist role in channeling the Red Brigades actions is a plausible, even if unproven, hypothesis. Further support to the hypothesis is given by other Red Brigades actions that have been immensely convenient to the Italian Right, such as their latest crime, the March 27, 1985 murder of economist Ezio Tarantelli, killed by the Red Brigades allegedly because of his interest in weakening a protective wage-price mechanism. But not only was Tarantelli an implausible target, his murder swung popular support toward the very things the Red Brigades claimed to be opposing. Are they dumb fanatics or serving a hidden agenda?

2. Carter's National Security Adviser, Zbigniew Brzezinski, was a member of the CPD. Brzezinski's chief of propaganda was Paul Henze, a long-time CIA officer and one of the leading exponents of the Bulgarian Connection. See Chapter 6.

the Soviet Threat? In the late 1970s the claim of Soviet military superiority and U.S. "unilateral disarmament" made substantial headway, and a further turn to the right yielded a further enhancement of media and public gullibility. A continuing difficulty, however, was that—aside from remote Afghanistan—the failure of the Soviet Union to send troops beyond its borders made the Soviet Threat too abstract for some Americans and many Europeans. Something closer to home was needed.

A substantial contribution to solving this dilemma came from the State of Israel. Israel was under international attack in the late 1970s for its policies of forcibly displacing Arabs and installing Jewish settlers on the West Bank, its violation of the civil rights of non-Jews, and its refusal to recognize any Palestinian right of self-determination. In 1979 even the Carter administration assailed Israel for its violations of Arab rights, and 59 well-known U.S. Jews petitioned Prime Minister Menachem Begin to reconsider his policy of expropriation and resettlement.

The Israeli solution to this problem was to step up the propaganda war. This had two features. One was to identify the Palestinians as "terrorists." This served to dehumanize them and make it possible to deal with them as "two-legged animals" (Begin), which is to say, on the basis of force alone. The second theme of the invigorated propaganda campaign was to claim that the PLO was a tool of the Soviet Union, and that the Soviets were engaged in a worldwide campaign to destabilize the democracies. This second theme was well designed to appeal to U.S. conservatives and to fit in with the Reagan presidential campaign and programs. Israel would be a front-line defender of democracy against "Soviet-sponsored terrorism." The forcible Israeli settlement of the West Bank and refusal to deal with the Palestinians would be accepted as part of the unified struggle against "international terrorism," rather than as a denial of basic human rights.

An important focal point of this refurbished, two-tiered propaganda campaign was the first meeting of the Jonathan Institute, held under Israeli auspices in Jerusalem from July 2-5, 1979. The Jonathan Institute is a virtual arm of the Israeli government,[3] and representation at the July 1979 conference included a very large contingent from the Israeli state,

---

3. For a brief account of the Institute, see "The Jonathan Institute," *CovertAction Information Bulletin*, Number 22 (Fall 1984), p. 5. The Institute has met twice since its original meeting, once in Washington and again in Israel.

especially from the defense and intelligence establishments.[4] The U.S. contingent was virtually a Who's Who of the CPD and CDM, including Richard Pipes, Norman Podhoretz, Midge Decter, Senator Henry Jackson, Ben Wattenberg, George Will, and Bayard Rustin. Also present from the United States were Claire Sterling and Vice-President-to-be George Bush. CIA and other U.S. intelligence representation was substantial: Bush, former Director of the CIA; Ray Cline, former CIA Deputy Director for Intelligence; and Major-General George Keegan, Jr., former chief of Air Force intelligence. Present from Great Britain were Brian Crozier and Robert Moss, both long-time assets of the CIA and British intelligence.

The conference opened with an address by Israeli Prime Minister Begin, who urged the conference members to get out and disseminate the "Soviet terrorism" message. While the conference was still in session, Ian Black of the *Jerusalem Post* noted that "The Conference organizers expect the event to initiate a major anti-terrorist offensive."[5] The participants were well situated to implement this offensive. Many were important politicians, and a large contingent were media pundits with direct access to a mass audience. Throughout the West the conference propaganda theme resounded, immediately and repetitively. In France, Jacques Soustelle, former leader of the OAS secret army (pardoned in 1968 for his treasonous activity during the Algerian war), a conference participant and newspaper correspondent, summed it all up in *L'Aurore*: The conference had "confirmed" that the Soviets "pull all the strings" behind "international terrorism." "Toujours le 'K.G.B.' " was the paper's caption. The same point was made to a receptive western press by Will, Wattenberg, Sterling, Crozier, and Moss. The Jonathan Institute conference sponsors issued a compendium of world press coverage some time later, noting in the introduction:

The Western press . . . responded to the challenge. As these pages show, the Conference's message penetrated into many of the leading newspapers and journals in the United States, Western Europe, South America and elsewhere. That the Conference had finally exposed what speaker Robert Moss, Editor of the *Economist Foreign Report*, called the "Conspiracy of Silence" was no better demonstrated than in the television documentary called *The Russian Connec-*

4. Four former chiefs of Israeli military intelligence participated in the conference. Our account of the conference draws on the valuable M.A. Thesis in International Relations by Philip Paull, "International Terrorism: The Propaganda War," San Francisco State University, June 1982.
5. Quoted in *ibid.*, p.19.

tion. Jointly produced by the American Public Broadcasting Service and the Canadian Broadcasting Corporation, it was shown nationally in the United States and Canada on September 25, 1979.

On November 2, 1980, the last Sunday before the U.S. presidential election that brought Reagan to power, the *New York Times Magazine* carried an article by Robert Moss entitled "Terror: a Soviet Export." (This is the same Moss who had previously been exposed as the author of a CIA-funded attack on Allende, 10,000 copies of which were bought by the Pinochet government.) This article, so strategically placed and timed, symbolizes the power of the rightwing syndicate that met in July 1979, and the alliance between that syndicate and the mass media. It also served to usher in the Reagan-Haig propaganda campaign and its focus on "international terrorism."

Reagan, Haig, Weinberger, and company faced a problem similar to that of Begin. They came into office determined to reestablish clear U.S. military superiority over the Soviet Union. As spelled out in the Pentagon's Five-Year Plan, the objective was to allow the United States to operate without constraint over the entire globe—even to destabilize and roll back the Soviet Empire.[6] An arms race would also be useful in impoverishing the Soviet Union, as the poorer country would have to spend to painful excess to keep only modestly behind the wealthier and more technologically advanced one. While this strategy is clear,[7] the cooperative western media have not allowed this reality to interfere with their uncritical transmission of official U.S. claims of Soviet prowess,

6. A summary of this Five-Year Plan was provided by Richard Halloran, "Pentagon Draws Up First Strategy For Fighting a Long Nuclear War," *New York Times*, May 30, 1982.

7. Halloran says, "As a peacetime complement to military strategy, the guidance document asserts that the United States and its allies should, in effect, declare economic and technical war on the Soviet Union. It says that the United States should develop weapons that 'are difficult for the Soviets to counter, impose disproportionate costs, open up new areas of major military competition and obsolesce previous Soviet investment.' " Halloran continues: "At the other end of the scale, the plan says that 'we must revitalize and enhance special-operations forces to project United States power where the use of conventional forces would be premature, inappropriate or infeasible,' particularly in Eastern Europe. Special operations is a euphemism for guerrillas, saboteurs, commandos and similar unconventional forces. . . . Further, 'to exploit political, economic and military weaknesses within the Warsaw Pact and to disrupt enemy rear operations, special-operations forces will conduct operations in Eastern Europe and in the northern and southern NATO regions,' the document says. Particular attention would be given to eroding support within the Soviet sphere of Eastern Europe." *Ibid.*

bargaining chip strategies, and the genuine interest of the Reagan administration in arms control and reducing nuclear arms to zero.[8]

Nevertheless, the contradiction between the Reagan arms buildup and the assertions of benign purposes is so immense that a larger infusion of propaganda has been required. In fact, it has been necessary to stir up a serious quantum of fear and irrationality to bridge the Reagan credibility gap. The public had to be convinced that the Reagan policies were designed to contend with something truly threatening and evil. The theme of Soviet sponsorship of international terrorism has served this need effectively. The way in which the Reagan administration took advantage of the Soviet downing of the Korean airliner, using it as a propaganda instrument to dehumanize the enemy, is an object lesson in both the uses of propaganda and the perceived importance of placing the Soviets in a bad light.[9] To be able to pin the attempted assassination of the Pope on the Soviet Union would be an even more important propaganda coup. Accomplishing this useful end was a challenge to western intelligence, media, and political institutions, but it was one which they met with remarkable success.

The Italian Context: The Fascist Tradition and the Postwar Rehabilitation of the Right

Western commentators have typically assumed that Italian authorities investigated the Bulgarian Connection reluctantly, embarrassed by its international implications, and that they pursued the case with the integrity and fair play characteristic of the Free World. That the very existence of the Bulgarian Connection might possibly be *explained* by its

8. The *New York Times*, having published the excellent summary by Halloran cited in the previous note, then proceeded to ignore its implications in its editorials over the next several years.

9. For a discussion of the treatment of Korean Air Line flight 007 as a model propaganda exercise, see Edward S. Herman, "Gatekeeper Versus Propaganda Models: A Case Study," in Peter Golding, Graham Murdock, and Philip Schlesinger, eds., *Communicating Politics: Essays in Memory of Philip Elliott* (Leicester: University of Leicester Press, 1986)

Italian context—by conservative vested interests, political infighting, and Cold War politics—is a point that never arises in the western media. This reflects a potent propaganda system at work.

In reality, Italy has been periodically torn by major political scandals ever since its defeat in the Second World War. An important feature of postwar Italy was the continued and virtually unimpaired power of the industrial, financial, military, and intelligence elite that had worked for Mussolini. The rehabilitation of the Mussolini-era elite was part of a worldwide phenomenon, by which U.S. and allied occupying armies systematically supported the very forces which had collaborated with fascism—whether in Korea or Thailand, Italy or Germany.[10] Thus, in the Italian case, the prime aim of the U.S. occupying authorities was to contain and defeat the leftwing forces that had achieved great strength as antifascist partisans.[11] U.S. protection of Klaus Barbie was in no way an exception:[12] The U.S. occupying authorities in Italy went to great pains to protect Prince Junio Valerio Borghese, a noted fascist collaborator with the Nazis,[13] and most senior fascist politicians and military and se-cret police figures were quickly returned to positions of power under al-lied pressure.

This antidemocratic underpinning to the superimposed democratic framework was strengthened by the Cold War. Fascist forces gained greater confidence as they came to understand their serviceability to Washington as protectors of the Free World. As Italy was seen in Washington as an especially vulnerable area, given its large Communist Party and powerful working class movement, the United States did not hesitate to bolster the power of these Mussolini-era holdovers in the in-terest of containing the Left.

10. See Noam Chomsky, "Containing the Anti-Fascist Resistance: From Death Camps to Death Squads," in his *Turning the Tide: U.S. Intervention in Central America and the Struggle for Peace* (Boston: South End Press, 1985).

11. See Gabriel Kolko, *The Politics of War* (New York: Random House, 1968), pp. 60-63; Joyce and Gabriel Kolko, *The Limits of Power* (New York: Harper and Row, 1972), pp. 147-51; Basil Davidson, *Scenes From The Anti-Nazi War* (New York: Monthly Re-view Press, 1980); and Roberto Faenza and Marco Fini, *Gli americani in Italia* (Milan: Feltrinelli, 1976).

12. See Magnus Linklater, Isabel Hinton and Neal Ascherson, *The Fourth Reich: Klaus Barbie and the Neo-Fascist Connection* (London: Hodder and Stoughton, 1984).

13. On the roles of James Angleton (OSS, later CIA) and Ellery Stone, head of the Al-lied Control Commission, in the protection of Borghese, see Faenza and Fini, *op. cit.*, n. 11, p. 327. See also, Francoise Hervet, "Knights of Darkness: The Sovereign Military Order of Malta," *CovertAction Information Bulletin*, Number 25 (Winter 1986), pp. 30-31.

U.S. Penetration and Manipulation. With its military occupation of Italy during and immediately after World War II, the United States was not only the major force reshaping the Italian political economy, it established a patron-client relationship that persists up to the present. This relationship was based on U.S. economic and military power, an aggressive use of that power, and the willingness of the Italian elite to enter into a profitable though subordinate relationship with an external protector.

As in 1922, when Mussolini seized control of the Italian state, the threat of the Left in postwar Italy was the overriding concern of U.S. authorities, and they were prepared to go far to keep the Left out of power.[14] Enormous resources were poured into Italy to manipulate the postwar elections. A Marshall Plan subsidy of some $227 million was voted by Congress just prior to the Italian elections of April 18, 1948. Much of this money was transmitted secretly to the Christian Democratic Party and to the split-off trade unions organized under U.S. sponsorship.[15] In the mid-1970s the Pike Committee of the U.S. House of Representatives estimated that $65 million had been invested in Italian elections in the period 1948-68. Ten million dollars was pumped into the election of 1972.[16] Former CIA officer Victor Marchetti estimated CIA outlays were $20-30 million *a year* in the 1950s, dropping to a mere $10 million a year in the 1960s. These funds were also used to subsidize newspapers, anticommunist labor unions, Catholic groups, and favored political parties (mainly the Christian Democrats).[17]

A second thrust of U.S. policy was the buildup of the Right. According to one study of the U.S. penetration of Italy:[18]

14. U.S. officials and leading businessmen had greeted enthusiastically Mussolini's march on Rome and overthrow of a democratic order, regarding it as a defeat for Bolshevism *and reformism* and a return to "stability." For the magnate and Secretary of the Treasury Andrew Mellon, Mussolini was "a very upstanding chap . . . making a new nation out of Italy." According to Judge Elbert Gary, Chairman of U.S. Steel, "a master hand has, indeed, strongly grasped the helm of the Italian state." For details see David F. Schwartz, "'A Fine Young Revolution': The United States and the Fascist Revolution in Italy, 1919-1925," *Radical History Review*, 33 (1985), pp. 117-38.

15. Faenza and Fini, *op. cit.*, n. 11, pp. 267-304, especially p. 298.

16. *CIA: The Pike Report* (Nottingham: Spokesman Books, 1977), p. 193.

17. "The CIA in Italy: An Interview with Victor Marchetti," in Philip Agee and Louis Wolf, eds., *Dirty Work: The CIA in Western Europe* (Secaucus, N.J.: Lyle Stuart, 1978), pp. 168-69.

18. "The CIA Collects Fascists," Faenza and Fini, *op. cit.*, n. 11, p. 262.

The link between American strategic services and armed reactionary groups was established in 1944 when James Angleton was invited to Rome by the OSS to direct the "Special Operations" section and then the Strategic Services Unit. His relations with the movements of the Right and with the clandestine formations always had a double objective: on the one hand, to receive anticommunist information and, on the other, to utilize certain men and certain groups in special operations. . . . It is certain that many of the initiatives taken by the Italian extreme Right in those years found aid, connivance and especially legitimation from these services.

A National Security Council report of March 1968 stressed the U.S. undertaking "to help out the clandestine anticommunist [*i.e.*, extreme Right and fascist] movement with funds and military assistance." It contended that the Italian army affords "no serious guarantee against Tito's [sic!] armies . . . [which] makes it necessary that all forces anticommunist in sentiment should be taken into consideration."[19] Following the victory of the Right in the elections of April 1948, a new, secret antisubversive police force was established under the Ministry of Interior, with U.S. advisers. This was filled largely from the old fascist secret police of Mussolini. At the same time, the fascist party Italian Social Movement (MSI) began a massive expansion program, with the assistance of U.S. intelligence officials.[20] MSI had significant backing from business interests in both Italy and the United States, and probably received financial support from the U.S. government.[21] The honorary chairman of MSI was Prince Junio Valerio Borghese, the long-time fascist leader, who had been protected by the United States at the end of the war. General Vito Miceli, another MSI leader, received an $800,000 U.S. subsidy through U.S. Ambassador Graham Martin in 1972.[22] MSI official Luigi Turchi was a guest of honor at the Nixon White House in 1972.[23]

19. "The Importance of Recognizing Anticommunist Revolutionary [sic] Forces," NSC Document No. 740454, March 12, 1968, quoted in Stuart Christie, *Stefano delle Chiaie: Portrait of a Black Terrorist* (London: Refract Publications, 1984), p. 10.

20. Christie, *op. cit.*, n. 19, pp. 10-12.

21. *La Strage di Stato: Controinchiesta* (Rome: Edizioni Samona e Savelli, 1970), pp. 115 ff.

22. Diana Johnstone, "The 'fright story' of Claire Sterling's tales of terrorism," *In These Times*, May 20-26, 1981, p. 10; *CIA: The Pike Report, op. cit.*, n. 16, p. 195.

23. Christie, *op. cit.*, n. 19, pp. 44-45.

A third strand of U.S. containment policy was the buildup and strengthening of Italy's military and intelligence services, manned by the proper anticommunist cadres. In 1949, in the framework of Italy's joining NATO, the Information Service of the Armed Forces (SIFAR)[24] was organized under the guidance of U.S. intelligence. The close relationship between Italy's joining NATO and the reorganization of the Italian intelligence services is enlightening. According to the most recent study of the Italian secret services, by Giuseppe De Lutiis:[25]

Between the two events there is a strict temporal succession: March 30 the reconstitution of the services being decided, and then the signing of the Atlantic alliance on April 4. On August 1, Parliament ratified the adhesion of Italy to the Pact, on August 24, NATO became operational and on September 1, SIFAR started. . . .

According to Gianni Flamini, SIFAR was essentially established by the CIA, and served as a "docile referent" of all the American services—the Central Intelligence Agency, the Defense Intelligence Agency, and the National Security Agency—as well as the West German secret service, the *Bundesnachrichtdienst* (BND).[26] Flamini states:[27]

In substance, SIFAR was also a kind of pied-à-terre for American espionage agencies, an instrument used to collect information useful to Washington, to control the loyalty to NATO of the Italian armed forces, to interfere in political life, and to orient the selection of military officers in favor of the interests of American strategy and American big industry.

The dependent status of Italy's intelligence services is spelled out more precisely by Massimo Caprara:[28]

24. This name was later changed, becoming SID. SID in turn was eventually divided into SISDE, concerned with internal security affairs, and SISMI, the service with responsibility for external intelligence matters.

25. Giuseppe De Lutiis, *Storia dei servizi segreti in Italia* (Rome: Editori Reuniti, 1985), pp. 46-47.

26. Gianni Flamini, *Il partito del golpe: Le strategie della tensione e del terrore dal primo centrosinistra organico al sequestro Moro*, I (Ferrara: Italo Bovolenta, 1981), pp. 5-7.

27. *Ibid.*, p. 7.

28. Massimo Caprara, "I setti diavoli custodi," *Il Mondo*, June 20, 1974, quoted in De Lutiis, *op. cit.*, n. 25, p. 46.

On the basis of the NATO accords, SID [the later name of SIFAR] was obliged to pass information and to receive instructions from a central office attached to the CIA. . . . The code name of the receiving office in the USA was Brenno. In strictly military matters, the relations with the USA were conducted with the ONI [Office of Naval Investigations], with OSI [Office of Special Investigations (Air Force)], and with the DIA [Defense Intelligence Agency], which depended, in turn, on the Defense Department and which also collected information in technical and scientific fields. . . .

De Lutiis points out that the obligations of the secret services go beyond this, as they rely on U.S. facilities in the fields of espionage and telecommunications, including NSA interception and decoding of signals, and the secret services are parties to a 1947 western intelligence agency information pooling system in which their unequal status was fixed by prior agreement.[29]

SIFAR was the instrument of a "permanent project of anticommunist offensive called in code Demagnetize, a version analogous to a similar project under way in France."[30] The main features of this project, according to Flamini,[31] were

political, psychological and paramilitary operations aiming to reduce the presence of the Italian communist party. . . . The ultimate objective of the plan is to reduce the strength of the communist parties, their material resources, their influence in the French and Italian governments and particularly in the trade unions, in order to reduce as much as possible the danger that communism poses in France and Italy, in accord with the interests of the United States in these two countries.

The extreme rightwing orientation of SIFAR is indicated by the fact that in 1952 its project Demagnetize was directed by Giovanni De Lorenzo (head of SIFAR) and, from U.S. intelligence, Vernon Walters. Walters has been a central figure in U.S. destabilization efforts abroad. He was active in Brazil in the coup of 1964, and close to Pinochet and the head of the secret police, Manuel Contreras, in Chile. De Lorenzo, a man of the extreme Right and a friend of Borghese,[32] was a principal planner and organizer of two attempted fascist coups in postwar Italy. De Lorenzo also became head of the Italian carabinieri, the largest

29. Ibid., p. 47.
30. Roberto Faenza, Il malaffare (Milan: Mondadori, 1978), p. 313, quoted in Flamini, op. cit., n. 26, p. 10.
31. Ibid.
32. De Lutiis, op. cit., n. 25, p.105.

paramilitary police force in Europe, which was quickly integrated into the defense plans of NATO.[33] Both SIFAR and the carabinieri were loaded up with individuals of the Right. A fourth thread of U.S. policy in Italy was preparing organizations and contingency plans specifically oriented to contesting a victory of the Left, even if brought about by strictly democratic processes. Marchetti noted in 1974 that "the CIA has emergency plans," and he thought that the possibility of a coup d'état along the lines of that of the Greek Colonels in 1967 was a likely CIA scenario. The military and intelligence structures put in place in Italy, as in Greece and Chile, were well suited to such contingency plans. NATO, for example, strongly encouraged the development of secret military and paramilitary organizations under the rubric of Civil Emergency Planning, with forces and plans that would go into action in defense of the Free World in the event of a Soviet (or Yugoslav!) invasion or internal political upheavals. The workings of this protective model were on full display in Greece in 1967, when the fascist Colonels' takeover put into effect the NATO contingency "Plan Prometheus" in toppling the democratically elected government. The forces implementing this plan were elite members of the U.S.-trained and NATO-controlled Mountain Assault Brigade.[34] It should be noted that this coup, using NATO forces, was not in response to a Soviet invasion or any internal Communist threat—it merely facilitated the preservation in power of a government that would be strongly responsive to U.S. and NATO orders, and removed the threat of one coming to power that would be somewhat more independent.

The buildup of NATO military and paramilitary forces to combat the threat from the Left was actually part of a larger U.S. strategic plan. The 1960s was the age of maturation of the U.S. "insurance policy" strategy of building up security forces in client states, training them in counterinsurgency methods, indoctrinating them on the Communist threat, and then sending them home to protect "freedom."[35] Although this was

33. *Ibid.*, pp. 25-28; Terracini et al., *Le instituzioni militari e l'ordinamento costituzionale* (Rome: Editori Riuniti, 1974), p. 54. SIFAR had an economic research section (REI) that worked closely with Italian industry, serving as an informational link and coordinator of activities between intelligence agencies and business. The head of the research unit stressed the role of intelligence in facilitating economic policy—for example, its service in combating Communist attempts to exploit austerity measures. See Flamini, *op. cit.*, n. 26, p. 17.

34. Christie, *op. cit.*, n. 19, p. 39.

35. See especially, Miles Wolpin, *Military Aid and Counterrevolution in the Third World* (Boston: Lexington, 1972). The concept of an "insurance policy" strategy is based on a speech by U.S. General Robert W. Porter, who described our investment in the Latin

all done under the facade of "protecting democracy,"[36] this pretense was one of the great hypocrisies of modern times. In the wake of this strategy came a series of counterrevolutions, led by U.S.-trained military and security service personnel, that left Latin America covered with neofascist National Security States, and institutionalized torture and death squads.[37] Fascists are reliable anticommunists, and where anticommunism is the paramount value, there will be little hesitancy in mobilizing them to do the dirty work and to rule or share the rule of threatened clients.

In Italy, the formation of NATO led to the development of auxiliary forces, recruited from the fascist underground, who could act under official cover as part of a military backup force. Under this program, special training was given by the Italian armed forces in western Sardinia to members of Stefano delle Chiaie's extreme rightwing organization, which authored many of the most important terrorist outrages of later years in Italy.[38] Some 200 cadres of the extreme Right were also sent by the Italian intelligence agency SID for training in the Colonels' Greece in 1968.[39] Thus NATO contributed to the strengthening of both official and unofficial forces looking toward an authoritarian solution to political problems and willing to collaborate with rightwing terrorism in achieving that end.

The "Party of the Coup." This phrase has been used in Italy to refer to a loose alliance of extreme rightwing activists, intellectuals, industrialists, and military and secret services personnel who were determined to counter the rise of the Left by seeking a "law and order" or fascist government. They worked toward a coup by enlisting and organizing sympathetic persons in power for an actual coup attempt, and by encouraging and using strategies of terrorism and disruption to pro-

military establishment as a form of insurance policy against investment losses. See Jan Black, *United States Penetration of Brazil* (Philadelphia: University of Pennsylvania, 1977), p. 228.

36. Secretary of Defense Robert McNamara testified before Congress on April 9, 1962, that one of the great merits of U.S. military training programs was that "Each of these men will receive an exposure to democracy at work." Cited in Black, *op. cit.*, n. 35, p. 160.

37. See Edward S. Herman, *The Real Terror Network: Terrorism in Fact and Propaganda* (Boston: South End Press, 1982), Chapter 3.

38. Christie, *op. cit.*, n. 19, p. 141.

39. De Lutiis, *op. cit.*, n. 25, p. 191.

vide the conditions justifying the termination of democratic government.

The "party" came into existence in response to the political and organizational advance of the Left in the early 1960s, the subsequent formation of a Center-Left government in 1964, and the increasing possibility that the Communist Party itself might share in the exercise of national political power. A landmark event in the coalescence of this loosely knit group was a 1965 meeting organized in Rome by the Pollio Institute, an independent foundation linked to the military and the Christian Democratic government. The meeting was chaired by an active-duty general and the president of the Milan Court of Appeals, and was attended by leaders of the security forces, rightist politicians, and a number of individuals who later achieved notoriety as fascist terrorists (Stefano delle Chiaie, Mario Merlino). The dominant themes of the meeting were the Communist threat and the need for a global mobilization to counter this threat. The use of subversive and violent methods was openly discussed. It was proposed that organizing work be done among the most conservative constituencies: state functionaries, professionals, teachers, small industrialists, etc.; that there be "pressure actions" (*azioni di pressione*) undertaken by armed groups; and that clandestine destabilizing actions be carried out. All this was to be coordinated by a top level council,[40] which continued to function for some years. Many of the participants in the meeting were eventually recruited into the secret services and played a role in later coup attempts and terrorist acts.[41]

There were numerous coup plans and at least one genuine but aborted attempt at a coup by the forces of the Right between 1964 and 1974. In 1964 a plan was drawn up by General De Lorenzo (head of the carabinieri and SIFAR) and some 20 other senior military officials for a coup that would have involved the assassination of Premier Aldo Moro and his replacement by a rightwing Christian Democrat. This coup plan, code named "Plan Solo," was called off at the last moment as a result of a political compromise between the socialists and rightwing Christian Democrats.[42] A rightwing coup was actually begun in 1970, using the

40. Franco Ferraresi, "La Destra Eversiva," in Ferraresi, ed., *La destra radicale* (Milan: Feltrinelli, 1984), pp. 57-61.

41. The well-known Italian fascist Guido Giannettini attended the 1965 conference and subsequently worked for both the Italian and German secret services. De Lutiis, *op. cit.*, n. 25, pp. 95-107; Christie, *op. cit.*, n. 19, pp. 139-40.

42. Christie, *op. cit.*, n. 19, p. 24. Plan Solo was so named because its instrumentality

code name "Tora, Tora" (although in later years it was usually referred to as "the Borghese coup"). Fascist leader Junio Valerio Borghese and Stefano delle Chiaie led an occupation of the buildings of the Ministry of Interior in Rome on December 7, 1970. For reasons still not clear, the coup was called off, and for three months the matter was hushed up by the Italian secret services.[43] After the story broke, Borghese and delle Chiaie, forewarned as usual, were able to escape to Spain, still under friendly fascist rule.[44]

De Lorenzo was in the forefront of another effort to build for a coup d'état, helping to organize a putchist group known as the "Rose of the Winds." His carabinieri were purged of any dissidents from hardline anticommunism, and a further effort was made to make all of the secret services into politicized, ideologically rightwing agencies. Within the armed forces a secret organization of anticommunist officers was established. At the top of this Rose of the Winds conspiracy was a group of 87 officers representing every military and secret services branch. SIFAR was given the job of collecting dossiers on Italian "subversives" who were to be neutralized in a coup. This conspiracy was uncovered in 1974. According to one of the plotters, Roberto Cavallero, "when trouble erupts in the country—rioting, trade union pressure, violence, etc.—the Organization goes into action to conjure up the option of a return to order. When these troubles do not erupt (of themselves), they are contrived by the far Right . . . directed and financed by members of the Organization."[45]

It should be reiterated that De Lorenzo, a major force in organizing the Rose of the Winds, and a man of the extreme Right, came into prominence and authority as head of SIFAR, a CIA-dominated organization. A later head of SID, the successor organization to SIFAR, General Vito Miceli, was also of the extreme Right, and was a conduit for U.S. funds in Italy. Both De Lorenzo and Miceli, upon leaving the "public service," became leaders of MSI, the Italian fascist party. It is also worthy of note that Miceli, when acknowledging the existence of

was solely the carabinieri, a military force controlled by De Lorenzo and, as noted, integrated into NATO. De Lutiis, *op. cit.*, n. 25, p. 85.

43. At the time, it was rumored in Italy that the coup had been called off because the promised U.S. support failed to materialize. Among the documents seized after Borghese's flight was a draft plan to send a special ambassador to the United States to ask for a loan and offer to send Italian troops to Vietnam. Ferraresi, *op. cit.*, n. 40, p. 102.

44. De Lutiis, *op. cit.*, n. 25, pp. 103-5.

45. Quoted in Christie, *op. cit.*, n. 19, p. 36.

the secret Rose of the Winds conspiracy, stated to the investigating magistrates that the organization was established "at the request of the Americans and NATO . . ."[46] Cavallero also claimed that the Rose of the Winds secret parallel group was under the direction of "Italian and American secret service members, as well as some agents of multinational corporations."[47]

Propaganda Due (P-2). In a scandal that broke in 1981, shortly after the attempted assassination of the Pope, Italians became aware of the immense power of P-2. In a sense, P-2 merely extended the Rose of the Winds conspiratorial structure beyond the military and secret services to the entire administrative apparatus of the Italian state. As a later official investigation put it, P-2 had established a "state within a state."

The immediate effect of the scandal was the resignation of several cabinet ministers and high civil servants whose membership in P-2 had been revealed. This was quickly followed by the fall of the Forlani government in June 1981. It was not until July 12, 1984, however, that the Italian Parliament completed its extensive investigation of P-2 and issued its 170-page final report. The *Report of the Parliamentary Commission of Inquiry on the Masonic Lodge P-2*,[48] which went completely unnoticed in the U.S. mass media, describes one of the most comprehensive attempts to undermine and control a western democracy since World War II. It reveals a far-reaching rightwing conspiracy which permeated the higher echelons of Italian political life, including all those institutions which took responsibility for creating and then investigating the Bulgarian Connection.

Licio Gelli, the head of P-2, was a lifelong supporter of fascist causes. As a youth he fought for Franco in the Spanish Civil War, and he served Mussolini loyally during World War II. Soon after the war, following disclosures that he had been involved in the torture and murder of Italian partisans, Gelli fled to Argentina. There he became intimately involved with fascists, including José López Rega, the founder of the AAA Anticommunist League, whose members gained notoriety as torturers and executioners in the "secret war" of the early 1970s. Gelli remained in Argentina for 20 years before returning to Italy as an Argentinian consul.

46. *Ibid.*
47. De Lutiis, *op. cit.*, n. 25, p. 111.
48. All quotations in this section not otherwise attributed are to this Report.

Upon his return to Italy, Gelli was initiated into Freemasonry. In Italy, as in many other countries, freemasonry long served as a secret, anti-clerical organization, generally drawing its members from the middle class and the technocratic strata. Gelli's sponsor recommended him as "someone in a position to make a notable contribution to the order in terms of recruitment of qualified [*i.e.*, important] persons." In 1971 Gelli was made organizing secretary of Loggia Propaganda, which henceforth was known as "the Gelli-P-2 Group." In his new role Gelli was permitted to initiate new members, a privilege previously permitted only to Venerable Grand Masters. He immediately began to recruit "a great number" of generals and colonels in the Italian military. At the same time, going against the longstanding tradition of Italian masonry that excluded political discussions, Gelli began to politicize P-2 lodge meetings. According to an agenda in the possession of the Parliamentary Commission, for example, one meeting considered "the political and economic situation in Italy, the threat of the Communist Party now in accord with clericalism aiming at the conquest of power," and "our position in the event of a coming to power of the clerico-communists."

During the initial phase of Gelli's conspiracy, he recruited with an eye to the possibility that P-2 would have to organize political action against a seizure of power by the Left. For this reason he placed particular emphasis, during the late 1960s and early 1970s, on recruiting military and intelligence personnel. By 1974 Gelli had recruited a total of 195 military officers, of whom 92 held the rank of general or colonel. The Report of the Parliamentary Commission concluded that Gelli's recruitment of Italian military personnel constituted "a map of military power at the highest level with persons who often assumed a role in events of particular significance in the recent history of our country, as well as in relation with events of a subversive character." The Report also noted that Gelli was able to manipulate the P-2 military membership to advance "the political objectives of Gelli and P-2, objectives hardly compatible with services on behalf of democratic institutions since they responded to directives from centers of power extraneous, if not hostile, to such institutions." Gelli also "played a direct role in promotions in the military service," according to the Report, which claimed that "The penetration of P-2 into circles at the top of the military hierarchy ended in creating a situation in which entrance into the [P-2] lodge constituted a sort of obligatory passage in order to rise to higher levels of responsibility." High officers also pressured their subordinates to join P-2 if they wanted to make higher rank or achieve their preferred posts. Gelli was equally successful in recruiting among the intelligence services. The Parliamentary Report points out that the heads of all three secret services in Italy—General Grassini of SISDE, General Santovito of SISMI, and Prefect Peolosi of CESIS—were members of P-2. The Report also states flatly that Gelli himself was a *member* of the Italian secret services. Gelli's influence in the highest circles of Italian intelligence was similar to the role he played with the Italian military: These intelligence organizations and their leaders, often acting at the behest of Licio Gelli, were "involved with subversive groups and organizations, inciting and aiding them in their criminal projects" in support of Gelli's political objectives.

The major shift to the left in Italy, which was marked by the elections of 1975 and 1976, suggested the real possibility of an eventual accession to power of the Communist Party. This produced a fundamental shift in Gelli's P-2 strategy. According to the Parliamentary Commission, where Gelli had earlier fostered destabilization, he now aimed at political *stabilization*.[49] This would be achieved through penetrating the highest reaches of not only the military and intelligence agencies, but also the top echelons of all levels of Italian life. Gelli's new objective was to obtain a position of outright control—behind the scenes—so that even if the Communist Party came to power it would make no real difference in the basic structures of Italian political life.

With his new strategy, Gelli successfully "penetrated into the most important sectors of the institutions of the State." By 1979, P-2 membership had grown to at least 953, and the Parliamentary Report notes that Gelli's "new members came from the most sensitive quarters and highest levels of national life, . . . amounting to an extended, authoritative, and capillary apparatus of persons which Gelli, in his capacity as Venerable Master of P-2, could dispose at will." P-2 membership rolls included three cabinet ministers; 43 generals; eight admirals, including the head of the armed forces; the heads of the three intelligence services; 43 Military Policemen; the police chiefs of Italy's four main cities; the mayors of Brescia and Pavia; the editor of Italy's leading newspaper,

49. The Parliamentary Commission implied that the shift in strategy was more complete than it was in fact. A new two-track strategy is more plausible and more compatible with subsequent events. It is noteworthy, for example, that a December 1985 Bologna court indictment named Gelli as one of the organizers of the Bologna bombing of 1980.

the *Corriere della Sera*; 36 members of Parliament and members of numerous state agencies.[50] The number of P-2 members in the state administration totalled 422. Especially important in the view of the Parliamentary Commission was P-2 infiltration into the Italian Treasury and those institutions involved in foreign trade. P-2 also penetrated the prestigious Bank of Italy, an institution with important overseas connections.[51]

The "silent coup" also targeted Italy's mass media. One of Gelli's most important successes was the takeover of the Rizzoli publishing group. Rizzoli controlled the leading Italian newspaper, the *Corriere della Sera* of Milan,[52] whose daily sales of 500,000 were the highest in all Italy. At its zenith the Rizzoli publishing group was printing one in four Italian newspapers. The Gelli-P-2 Group also acquired control or important influence over many local newspapers, including *Il Mattino*, *Sport Sud*, *Il Piccolo*, *Eco di Padova*, *Il Giornale di Sicilia*, *Alto Adige*, and *Il Lavoro*. Gelli and P-2 used this influence within the media, according to the Parliamentary Report, for the "coordination of the entire provincial and local press, so as to control public opinion throughout the country."

Gelli's influence over the *Corriere della Sera* and other newspapers, his intimate ties with the Italian secret services, and his influence in almost every major Italian institution, revealed "the general line of an alarming, comprehensive plan for the penetration and conditioning of national life."

50. A partial list of P-2 membership in the Italian state sector in 1979 is as follows: Interior Ministry: 19 members; Ministry of Foreign Affairs: 4; Ministry of Public Works: 4; Ministry of Public Instruction: 32; Ministry of State: 21; Treasury: 67; Ministry of Health: 3; Ministry of Industry and Commerce: 13; Finance Ministry: 52; Ministry of Justice, including Magistratura: 21; Ministry of Cultural Affairs: 4; Ministry of Scientific and Technological Research: 3; Ministry of Transportation: 2.

51. Other major banks targeted for the establishment of strategic P-2 contacts in the international banking and business community were the Banca Nacionale del Lavoro, the Monte dei Paschi di Siena, the Banca Toscana, the Istituto Centrale delle casse rurali et artigiani, the Interbanca, the Banca di Roma, and the Banco Ambrosiano.

52. *Corriere della Sera* had fallen under the control of Banco Ambrosiano, whose president, Roberto Calvi, was a P-2 member and major financier of P-2 projects. Upon P-2's acquisition of the *Corriere*, its editor, Piero Ottone, a thorn in the side of both the Socialist and Christian Democratic Parties in Italy for many years, was replaced by his deputy, Franco Di Bella. When the P-2 house of cards fell in 1981, the records showed that Di Bella had been a member of the P-2 lodge since October 10, 1978. Calvi, of course, was the leading figure in the Vatican banking scandal of the late 1970s, and millions of dollars passed through his hands to rightwing dictators in Latin America.

As for the "Bulgarian Connection," would the members of the anticommunist brotherhood of P-2 be capable of concocting a case against the arch-enemy that would involve falsifying evidence? Were they in a position to do this by their reach into the police, secret services, the press, the judiciary, political parties, and the state apparatus? These questions were not explored in the western media; the quality of the Italian police-security establishment, with its deep roots in Italian fascist history, is off the western agenda.

The "Strategy of Tension". The "strategy of tension" was a rightwing creation, put into extensive practice beginning in the late 1960s by the "party of the coup."[53] The strategy was based on the idea that terrorist acts, if carried out by secret agents in a political environment where the acts would be attributed to the Left, would be serviceable to rightwing and fascist ends. The point was to make people very apprehensive and insecure, to put them in a mood to support a regime of law and order. This would be facilitated if the police, courts, and press regularly failed to identify correctly the perpetrators of violence, and allowed themselves to be manipulated into false attributions of its source.

Many of the proponents and implementers of the strategy were open fascists, aiming explicitly for a totalitarian solution. (The journalist Guido Giannettini, for example, who was employed by the Italian secret services, called himself a "nazi-fascist," not just a plain fascist.[54]) Mussolini's coup of 1922 and the Greek fascist takeover of 1967 were models for this "party." The Parliamentary Report on P-2 comments:

P-2 contributed to the so-called strategy of tension, that was pursued by rightwing extremist groups in Italy during those years when the purpose was to destabilize Italian politics, creating a situation that such groups might be able to ex-

53. The expression "strategy of tension" has been widely used in the Italian media to describe the attempt by rightwing forces to stop the leftward trend in Italian politics by the use of force. While there is little dispute about the reality of the actions carried out in support of this political objective, there is debate over the degree of explicit planning and organization of the whole process, and the exact composition of the forces involved. P-2 contributed to a centralizing tendency in the implementation of the strategy, but much of it seems to have been informal and loosely coordinated.

54. Christie, *op. cit.*, n. 19, p. vii. Giannettini was greatly appreciated by the U.S. military establishment. In November 1961 he was brought to the United States to conduct a three-day seminar on "The Techniques and Prospects of a Coup d'État in Europe" at the U.S. Naval Academy in Annapolis, Maryland. Christie, *ibid.*, p. 26; De Lutiis, *op. cit.*, n. 25, p. 164.

ploit in their own interest to bring about an authoritarian solution to Italy's problems . . . to condition political and public opinion that changes were demanded and radical solutions possible . . . with the overthrow of the democratic republic a real alternative among various possible outcomes.

The strategy of tension was implemented through a series of massacres, frameups, and abortive coup attempts. Prior to 1969 there had been numerous fascist attacks on Communists, unionists, and demonstrators, but no major terrorist attacks. The new strategy of massacre began in April 1969 with bomb explosions at the University of Padua and a Milan industrial fair. On August 8, 1969, bombs were placed in ten trains moving out of major stations, injuring ten people. Then in Milan on December 12, 1969, a bomb was placed in a bank on market day in the crowded Piazza Fontana. Sixteen people died and 90 more were injured. A bomb placed in another bank in the center of Milan was discovered before it could go off. Three bombs were set off in Rome, one of which injured 13 people. Subsequently, there were other massacres by the instruments of the party of the coup: The most notorious and "productive" were the December 17, 1973 rocket attack on a Pan Am plane at Rome's Fiumicano airport, killing 32; the May 28, 1974 bombing at an antifascist rally in Brescia, killing eight and injuring 102; the August 4, 1974 bombing of the Rome-Munich Italicus train near Bologna, killing 12 and injuring 48; and the Bologna station bombing of August 2, 1980, which left 85 dead and 200 injured.

The evidence is overwhelming that these terrorist acts were carried out by fascists in collusion with members of the security services.[55] But

55. It is a cliché of the U.S. Right, uncontested in the United States, that Italian terrorism is a predominantly leftwing phenomenon. This is based on major fabrications. A favorite author cited by the U.S. Right to authenticate their position is Dr. Vittorfranco S. Pisano, whose study, "Terrorism and Security: The Italian Experience," was published as a Report of the Senate Subcommittee on Security and Terrorism in November 1984. Pisano states that neofascist terror is not even a close runner-up to Red terror in Italy. Among other reasons for this is the alleged fact that "the terrorist right lacks the supportive structure available to its leftist counterpart" (p. 35). This chapter demonstrates that Pisano's assertion is a fabrication: The "terrorist right" in Italy has had the support not only of P-2, with its extensive institutional ramifications, but also the Italian intelligence services, carabinieri, and officers of the regular armed forces, who are in turn linked in various supportive ways to the CIA and NATO (see below).

It is also interesting that Pisano carefully avoids breaking down terrorist incidents in Italy by allocation to the Left and Right. He does give an appendix table showing terrorist incidents by year, 1968-82 (p. 63). The grand total of deaths by terror shown on his table is 334. The terrorist deaths allocable to neofascists based on the incidents mentioned on this page alone, which hardly exhausts the neofascist total, amounts to 151 or 45% of

in accordance with the logic of the strategy of tension, they were blamed on the Left. The Piazza Fontana bombing, for example, was immediately blamed on the anarchists, a diverse and weak group that was an easy victim of a well-managed conspiracy of the Right. The police, secret services, judiciary, and press all played their roles in this frameup. The local anarchist leader Giuseppi Pinelli died in police custody, an alleged "suicide." Although the evidence was soon clear that the Piazza Fontana bombing was a rightist strategy of tension action,[56] it has never been possible to bring the perpetrators (or the police who murdered Pinelli) to justice.

The main reason for this is that *the strategy of tension was implemented and protected by important elements of the state apparatus.* Franco Ferraresi points out, for example, that in a judicial investigation at Arezzo of the Italicus bombing, it was disclosed that "some fascists" among the accused actually worked for the police or secret services. It was also disclosed that they received valuable information on the progress of the investigation being carried out against them, and that Gelli had connections with key officials in the repressive apparatus of Arezzo.[57] Ferraresi adds that "Not by chance, in the course of the investigation the accused [spoke] repeatedly of the links between SID, the P-2 lodge, MSI [the Italian neofascist party], and elements of the Right in Arezzo."[58]

The Italian Intelligence Services and Rightwing Terrorism

Given the importance of the Italian secret services in the development of the Bulgarian Connection case, and the assertions by Albano and Martella that these services were apolitical and quite trustworthy,[59] it

the grand total. If we added in other clearly neofascist killings, we would well exceed half the total deaths by terrorism. It is clear why Pisano fails to make any count by political class of terrorist.

56. See Christie, *op. cit.*, n. 19, pp. 61-63, and the text below.

57. Gelli's connections included "magistrates (one of whom, the Attorney Marsili, was his son-in-law), an assistant chief of police and the leader of the CC [carabinieri], not to mention the national leadership of SID which was partly involved also (Gen. Miceli) in the Borghese affair. . . and in the Rose of the Winds plan." Ferraresi, *op. cit.*, n. 40, p. 107.

58. *Ibid.*

59. See especially the remark of Albano cited in Chapter 7, p. 191; also the discussion of Martella's views in Chapter 5, pp. 117-18.

may be useful to provide further and more detailed evidence of the security services' involvement in rightwing terrorism. In this connection, we should note first the virtual unanimity of informed Italian opinion of the *generality* of such involvement. Luciano Violante, a member of the Italian Parliament and former Magistrate of the Court of Turin, has stated that "One cannot say that there has been a single important episode of black [*i.e.*, rightwing] terrorism that does not involve in some way or another men who are either directly or indirectly connected to the services."[60] Stefano Rodota, also a member of Parliament and Professor of Law at the University of Rome, has said the same thing: "Traces, some heavy, some light, of direct actions or of involvement of the services are evident in all the judicial decisions that relate to the more serious acts of terrorism (especially black): the massacre of the Piazza Fontana; of the Piazza Della Loggia; of the Italicus train; of the Bologna station; the Rose of Winds affair; the Borghese coup."[61] As noted above, the Arezzo investigations revealed that a number of the suspects worked for the carabinieri, police, and secret services. An internal document of the intelligence agency SID indicates that Stefano delle Chiaie himself—mastermind of the Bologna bombing and an associate of Klaus Barbie—was "an informer of the Rome central police" with contacts also in the Ministry of Interior.[62]

Experts on Italian terrorism have also noted the *frequent failure of the security services to disclose or do anything about advance knowledge of terrorist actions*. From the beginning of the implementation of the strategy of tension in the late 1960s, the secret services successfully infiltrated both right and left groups that were later accused of crimes, but failed to prevent any terrorist acts. According to Giovanni Tamburino, Magistrate of Padua and a member of the Superior Council of Magistrates, "Those close to the victims of the massacre which occurred on August 2, 1980 in the station in Bologna lamented the fact that the services, despite having prior warning of the disaster, did not act on this knowledge, nor did they pass the information on to the magistrate after the massacre had taken place."[63]

60. Luciano Violante, "Politica della sicurezza, relazioni internationali e terrorismo," in Gianfranco Pasquino, ed., *La prova Delle Armi* (Istituto Cattaneo, Bologna: Societa Editrice Il Mulino, 1984), p. 100.
61. Stefano Rodota, "La riposta dello stato al terrorismo: gli apparati," in Pasquino, ed., *op. cit.*, n. 60, p. 82.
62. Linklater, *et al.*, *op. cit.*, n. 12, p. 207.
63. Giovanni Tamburino, "Le stragi e il loro contesto," in Paolo Corsini and Laura Novati, eds., *L'Eversione Nera: Cronache Di Un Decennio, 1974-1984* (Milan: Franco Angeli, 1985), p. 142.

A related feature of secret services involvement in rightwing terrorism has been their *protection of the terrorists and refusal to cooperate with the judicial system*. Five days after the Piazza Fontana bombing, for example, SID circulated a note to its branch offices stating flatly that delle Chiaie had organized the attack, and that his man Mario Merlino, who had infiltrated the anarchists, had actually planted the bomb. But SID failed to pass this information on to the magistrates in charge of the case.[64] A powerful statement of the same point was made by Rosario Minna, Magistrate of the Court of Florence, in a recent volume on terrorism in Italy. According to Minna:[65]

The classic example . . . of a web which indissolubly links together both the bottom and the top of the Italian power structure in its relations with black terrorism concerns the help given by the Italian secret services to the accused in the trial for the massacre of Piazza Fontana. Giannettini was helped financially when he escaped abroad; worse still, after the Magistrate of Milan had requested the arrest of Pozzan, . . . the Italian services took Pozzan to Spain, where they handed him over to delle Chiaie in Madrid, at a time when delle Chiaie himself was a fugitive from justice, wanted for the very same massacre of Piazza Fontana. So far, there has been no news of administrative or political sanctions against those officials who betrayed the state by these critical actions. Therefore, it is practically impossible that it was a matter of personal and improvised initiative on the part of a captain or general.

The network protecting terrorists in Italy extended far. In the Italicus case, the neofascist party MSI actually funded the terrorist killers. Admiral Birindelli, a past president of MSI,[66] apparently not liking this support of deadly terrorist actions, reported the MSI role to the carabinieri within several weeks of the massacre. This important information took seven years to reach the magistrates in charge of the case.[67] In attempting to understand why this delay occurred, we need only recall that the carabinieri as well as the secret services were heavily infiltrated by P-2, and the head of the carabinieri to whom Birindelli gave his information was a P-2 member.

64. Linklater, *et al.*, *op. cit.*, n. 12, p. 207.
65. Rosario Minna, "Il terrorismo di destra," in Donatella della Porta, ed., *Terrorismi in Italia* (Istituto Cattaneo, Bologna: Societa Editrice Il Mulino, 1984), p. 57.
66. And also a former Mediterranean NATO commander.
67. Ferraresi, *op. cit.*, n. 40, p. 107.

Stefano delle Chiaie was a principal in many major terrorist attacks in Italy between 1969 and 1980. He is almost certainly responsible for more deaths by violence than Carlos the Jackal. We have seen, however, that delle Chiaie attended the Pollia Institute Conference of 1965, was an informer for the Italian police, and was used by the secret services as a friendly vehicle to help spirit wanted criminals out of the country. Delle Chiaie also had ties with Federico D'Amato, the head of the Italian internal security service SISDE.[68] It is frequently pointed out in Italy that delle Chiaie has a charmed life. In 1984 the new head of SISDE, Vicente Parisi, updated the Italian Parliament on the Bologna massacre. Journalist Maurizio De Luca summarizes his remarks as follows:[69]

He spoke inevitably about delle Chiaie, and the nearly legendary impossibility of capturing him. It is known that delle Chiaie has traveled, and still does, in South and Central America quite undisturbed. Parisi explicitly said that the fascist leader is evidently given great protection first of all by the South American secret services. This implies that somebody else, more powerful, allows this protection. Who? Somebody asked Parisi openly, is it a superpower? In other words, are there American interests protecting delle Chiaie? Parisi, expressing himself very cautiously, seemed to imply so. He pointed out that the American secret service had given very inadequate help to their Italian counterparts in attempting to capture delle Chiaie. Given this situation, the committee overseeing the secret services decided to write to Craxi to take an official stand toward the nations who protect delle Chiaie, starting with the South American nations.

This interesting exchange was not reported in the mainstream U. S. press. Martin Lee and Kevin Coogan point out that the U.S. Customs Service was apparently aware of the fact that delle Chiaie had entered Miami on a plane from South America on September 9, 1982, traveling with Abdullah Catli, a leader of the Gray Wolves and friend of Agca.[70] He was not apprehended, and the Italian government was not informed of his whereabouts.

If Carlos the Jackal could be shown to be an informer for the Bulgarians or KGB, used by them as an intermediary and in other business relations, and allowed to move about freely in their territory and client

68. De Lutiis, *op. cit.*, n. 25, pp. 98-100.
69. "Operazione Primula Nera," *L'Espresso*, August 5, 1984.
70. Quoted in Martin A. Lee and Kevin Coogan, "The Agca Con," *Village Voice*, December 24, 1985. Pazienza told Lee and Coogan that customs officers informed him that "delle Chiaie enters and leaves the United States as he likes."

states, politicians and press in the West would shriek with indignation and pound tables over eastern Bloc "support of terrorists." Delle Chiaie, however, has been a "strategy of tension" activist and a sub rosa western "asset." The West accommodates well to his differences from Carlos.[71]

Corruption Unlimited: SISMI, Pazienza, and Company

The abuses of the secret services recounted above had deep structural roots in Italian society and in the American-NATO connection, and they continued into the period of the genesis and implementation of the Bulgarian Connection. On July 29, 1985, the Criminal Court of Rome issued a 184-page report and "Sentenza" (hereafter, Judgment) against Francesco Pazienza, Pietro Musumeci, Giuseppi Belmonte, and others for crimes committed while serving as high officials and agents of SISMI.[72] They were found guilty of embezzlement and corruption, but many of their crimes have larger implications and bear on the Bulgarian Connection case. They show an intelligence service out of control, carrying out fraudulent and illegal acts, and manipulated for personal and political purposes.

Among the crimes enumerated in the Judgment, we may note the following:

71. British Prime Minister Margaret Thatcher illustrates well the western pattern of discrimination and hypocrisy. Speaking before the American Bar Association in July 1985, Mrs. Thatcher stated that "We need action—action to which all countries are committed until the terrorist knows that he has no haven and no escape." Two weeks earlier, Mrs. Thatcher had ignored an impassioned plea from Prime Minister Craxi for her aid in obtaining the deportation of Italian rightwing terrorists, who had found a safe haven in England. The particular case arousing Craxi's ire involved Roberto Fiore, a leading member of the Armed Revolutionary Nuclei, convicted in 1984 of subversive conspiracy, attempted murder, armed robbery, and six counts of arson. The Home Office has rejected Italian appeals for Fiore's extradition on the ground that European Community Law requires that it be shown "that his personal conduct was such as to constitute a present threat to one of the fundamental interests of society." Apparently a rightwing terrorist does not meet this standard by his terrorist record alone. Are we to presume that Carlos would also be safe in England on this ground? See Mark Hollingsworth, "Fascist prosecutes journalist," *New Statesman*, November 15, 1985, p. 5.

72. Criminal Court of Rome, *Judgment in the Matter of Francesco Pazienza, et al.*, July 29, 1985, signed by Francesco Amato, President of the Court.

Forgery. Pazienza arranged for the forgery of a document carrying the signatures of Licio Gelli and others, which was planted in the May 8, 1981 issue of *Agenzia Repubblica.*[73] He either forged or passed along fraudulent papers supposedly showing that the then President of Italy, Pertini, had been on the Soviet payroll![74] Articles secretly subsidized by SISMI smearing various other individuals were planted in the press.[75] One forgery described in the Judgment was of "Letters of Information" about terrorist plans, allegedly obtained from a secret source that was paid a large sum of money for the information. The court concluded that the Letters were fabricated and the source did not exist, and that the purpose of the entire process was to allow Musumeci, Belmonte, and Santovito to divert large sums to their own pockets.[76]

Political manipulation. Pazienza attempted to split the Communist Party by supporting a hard line pro-Soviet faction within the PCI. He engaged in this effort as an agent of SISMI, although he sought external (mainly American) financing to advance the project.[77] Santovito acknowledged to a Parliamentary Commission on P-2 that SISMI had worked hard to try to pin some link to the Bulgarians on the PCI.[78] Numerous other efforts to enhance or denigrate favored or disfavored politicians, movements, or countries are recounted in the Judgment. (One of them, the "Billygate Affair," we discuss below.)

Improper dealings with terrorists. The Judgment describes in detail how, after the Red Brigades had kidnapped the Christian Democratic politician Ciro Cirillo, Pazienza used his contacts with the Mafia to negotiate a deal that was extremely generous to both the Mafia intermediaries and the Red Brigades. The Court felt that the mode of dealing with the terrorists was highly inappropriate, and that in this kind of operation Pazienza was doing things "of incredible danger to society. . . ."[79] The Court concluded that "An operation which began as an attempt

73. *Ibid.*, p. 102.
74. *Ibid.*, p. 103.
75. *Ibid.*, pp. 99-102.
76. *Ibid.*, pp. 119-73. Bruno Di Murro declared to the court that the "Pazienza group" took sums amounting to about one billion two hundred million lire from the coffers of SISMI between October 1980 and May 1981. *Ibid.*, p. 169.
77. *Ibid.*, p. 108.
78. Italian Parliamentary Committee of Investigation into the P-2 Masonic Lodge, Documentation Vol. 3, Tome XIX, March 2, 1982, p. 202.
79. Judgment, p. 26.

to find the kidnapped man and to single out his captors . . . turned into an operation characterized by the payment of a very heavy ransom to a terroristic group which would take advantage of it to carry on further their aggression against the state.''[80]

Protection of criminals and terrorists. The Court charged Pazienza with using a SISMI plane to transport a man wanted for crimes out of the country.[81] SISMI officials were also charged with giving investigating bodies information which they knew to be untrue about terrorists allegedly involved in the Bologna bombing, thereby diverting the investigation away from the real terrorists.[82]

In early December 1985, magistrates in Bologna issued 16 arrest warrants, accusing both Licio Gelli and former SISMI officials Pazienza, Belmonte, and Musumeci of "subversive association with the aim of terrorism" in connection with the Bologna bombing of 1980. Initial newspaper reports indicate that the secret service officials were being charged not merely with covering up the massacre, but with involvement in its overall planning.[83]

Disinformation. In early 1981, from information provided by Pazienza and an "external collaborator," two reports were prepared by SISMI tying the drug and arms traffic to Arabs and Bulgaria. The Judgment implies that these reports were fabricated, intended to divert attention away from SISMI's ongoing abuses by providing evidence of energetic secret service activity. It is possible that the "external collaborator" in this case was Michael Ledeen (see below). It is also noteworthy that the Bulgarians are already being introduced as villains in these pre-May 13, 1981 reports.

The Ledeen-Pazienza Connection. The Judgment devotes considerable space to the coordinated operations of Pazienza and Michael Ledeen. Pazienza was an operator of international scope, with significant relationships and mutual service extending especially to France and the United States. The Judgment alleges that Pazienza was on the payroll of the French secret services.[84] (It was well-known that he was a close

80. *Ibid.*, p. 18.
81. *Ibid.*, p. 25.
82. *Ibid.*, pp. 147-68.
83. See the series of articles in *La Repubblica*, December 12-13, 1985.
84. "From a reading of the quoted documents one can deduce the superior position that

friend of its head, Comte Alexandre de Marenches.) He had also established a relationship with Alexander Haig, which added to his authority in Italy (see further below).

Pazienza was also a good friend of Licio Gelli, and provided his private yacht to help Gelli flee after his escape from prison. He was also a close associate of Roberto Calvi, the murdered head of Banco Ambrosiano. Before his death Calvi had swindled more than a billion dollars through a complex chain of bank transactions that deeply involved P-2 and the Vatican Bank. Pazienza helped Calvi try to extricate himself from his difficulties, then to take refuge as the Banco Ambrosiano crisis reached its peak. He also introduced Calvi to Flavio Carboni, the last man known to have seen Calvi alive.[85]

At the time of Agca's assassination attempt, SISMI was headed by General Giuseppe Santovito, a P-2 member and Pazienza's patron. During Santovito's tenure Pazienza was a SISMI operative with extraordinary powers. In fact, the Judgment suggests that Pazienza even controlled Santovito.[86] Pazienza was not only Santovito's top aide, he was also the dominant individual in a small group of secret service "plumbers" called "Super S," made up of P-2 members, which used the resources of SISMI, and was answerable only to Santovito.[87]

Michael Ledeen enters the picture as a rightwing journalist, longtime associate of Claire Sterling,[88] friend of Alexander Haig, and the "Italy expert" in the Reagan transition team of 1980-81.[89] In tandem with Pazienza, Ledeen was well placed to help forward Reagan's political aims in Italy at the time of the assassination attempt against the Pope. At least as early as 1980 Ledeen became a friend of and collaborator with Pazienza. Perhaps through Pazienza's influence Ledeen worked for

Pazienza—already on the payroll of the French secret military service and connected with centers of foreign powers [the U.S. State Department is mentioned specifically]—had managed to acquire in the security organization." Judgment, p. 37.

85. On Pazienza and Calvi, see Rupert Cornwell, *God's Banker* (New York: Dodd, Mead, 1984).

86. Judgment, pp. 30-33.

87. *Ibid.*, pp. 34-40. Valuable details are also given in Sandro Acciari and Pietro Calderoni, "C'ero io, c'era Pazienza, c'era . . . ," *L'Espresso*, November 11, 1984; and Diana Johnstone, "Latest scandal leads to Reagan administration," *In These Times*, December 5-11, 1984.

88. See Chapter 6, p. 160.

89. During the early years of the Reagan administration he was also a consultant to the State Department and Pentagon. "Italian Officials Finger Ledeen, CIA," *CovertAction Information Bulletin*, Number 22 (Fall 1984), p. 41.

SISMI and was placed on its payroll.[90] He had the coded identification, Z-3.[91] Ledeen received at least $120,000 plus expenses from SISMI in 1980-81, some of which he funneled into a Bermuda bank account.[92] He received the money for various services: what he vaguely calls "risk assessment," helping train Italian intelligence agents,[93] and providing analyses of terrorism and the Soviet threat. The Italian press reported that Ledeen actually sold old U.S. intelligence reports to SISMI at stiff prices, which Santovito then passed on to Italian officials as the products of secret and original SISMI investigations. According to Diana Johnstone, Italian journalists to whom these secret reports were leaked were not fooled, and "found them an unconvincing rehash of old gossip, such as the notion that the Italian Communist Party was really run by a secret 'parallel' hierarchy commanded by Moscow."[94] The documents did further the echo-chamber effect, however, providing Italian intelligence service "confirmation" of the truths that U.S. disinformationists were purveying widely.

An important collaboration between Ledeen and Pazienza involved the so-called "Billygate" affair. Italian investigators had already shown that SISMI, Pazienza, and Michael Ledeen, working through Super S, lured President Jimmy Carter's brother Billy into a compromising relationship with Qaddafi during the 1980 presidential campaign. According to the Italian newspaper *La Repubblica*, prosecuting Judge Domenico Sica had evidence "that SISMI was the architect of the scandal over Billy Carter," and that the material in the case "was gathered mostly by Pazienza and by his American friend Michael Ledeen." The indictment against Pazienza explicitly mentioned Michael Ledeen as a co-conspirator in the illegal activities attributed to Pazienza. *La Repubblica* went on to say:[95]

Pazienza availed himself of SISMI both for the use of some secret agents and for

90. This point was confirmed by Santovito, the head of SISMI. Judgment, p. 110.
91. *Ibid.*, p. 39.
92. Jonathan Kwitny, "Tale of Intrigue: Why an Italian Spy Got Closely Involved In the Billygate Affair," *Wall Street Journal*, August 8, 1985.
93. The Judgment describes an "Operation Training Camps," in which Ledeen received 300 million lire for organizing training camps on antiguerrilla-anticommunist warfare. Pazienza claimed that part of the sum was his, but Ledeen kept the entire amount for himself. Judgment, p. 109.
94. Diana Johnstone, "A method to Agca's madness?," *In These Times*, July 10-23, 1985.
95. Quoted in Johnstone, *ibid.*

the expenses of organizing the scandalous plan. It seems that the organizers got a huge payoff for "Billygate." Moreover, Santovito and Pazienza got great advantages in return from American officials, in fact may have been helped in other obscure affairs. The "Billygate" operation did not come under SISMI's institutionally mandated task, and for that reason Judge Sica brought charges of pursuing private interest through official activities.

SISMI provided the tape recorder and hired a photographer to take pictures of Billy Carter with a Libyan representative.[96] As the enterprise was strictly in aid of Reagan's election campaign, the Court did not consider this a proper use of Italian secret service resources.

After Reagan's election Ledeen and his friend Pazienza became more powerful in Italy. Umberto D'Amato, a high police official in Italy, claims that in the uncertain conditions prevailing during the Reagan transition, "there was an interregnum during which relations between Italy and the United States were carried on in the persons of the duo Pazienza-Ledeen."[97] The influential position of the Ledeen-Pazienza team is suggested by their role as intermediaries between Italian politicians and high officials wanting to make contact with officials of the new Reagan administration. Even the Italian Foreign Minister Emilio Colombo used their services in making arrangements for a visit. The head of the Christian Democratic Party, Flaminio Piccoli, testified before a Parliamentary Committee that during a visit to Washington, after several days of futile attempts to visit Secretary of State Haig, General Santovito suggested that he seek out Pazienza. Jonathan Kwitny reports that "Mr. Piccoli testified that one phone call from Mr. Pazienza to a contact persuaded Mr. Haig to postpone a trip to Camp David to help President Reagan with a major speech, and grant Mr. Piccoli a 43-minute meeting."[98]

In August 1981, following the P-2 scandal of the previous spring, General Santovito was dismissed as head of SISMI, and Pazienza's role in SISMI was greatly reduced. Pazienza claims that he resigned from SISMI in March 1981, more than a month before the attack on the Pope.[99] He also alleges that the successor to Santovito, General Nino

96. Judgment, pp. 81-86.

97. Quoted in Sandro Acciari and Pietro Calderoni, "C'ero io, c'era Pazienza. C'era . . . ," *L'Espresso*, November 11, 1984.

98. Jonathan Kwitny, "Tales of Intrigue: How an Italian Ex-Spy Who Also Helped U.S. Landed in Prison Here," *Wall Street Journal*, August 7, 1985. For corroborating evidence of this account, see Judgment, p. 86.

99. The P-2 scandal originated in the discovery of Gelli's list of secret members of P-2

Lugaresi, and other members of SISMI, were the ones who actually coached Agca. According to Pazienza, Michael Ledeen had worked with Col. Sportelli and the SISMI chief of station in New York, Col. Marcello Campione, both of whom remained after the departure of Santovito. Pazienza claims that not only did the successor team coach Agca, they also collaborated with Ledeen in questioning the former Czech General and disinformationist Jan Sejna, whose fabrications were channeled from Ledeen to Claire Sterling.[100]

Thus, there was no general housecleaning of SISMI, and there is no reason to believe that the fundamental character of SISMI was altered. In fact, several of the remaining SISMI officials were subsequently arrested for involvement in the drug trade. Furthermore, while Pazienza has attempted to shift some of the accusations against SISMI and himself to his former colleagues and successors, his own role in the Bulgarian Connection is still far from clear. Soon after his exit from SISMI, Pazienza and former high SISMI official Pietro Musumeci organized a security consulting firm, which was quickly employed by Roberto Calvi and his Banco Ambrosiano. Pazienza then became very active in helping Calvi manage the bank's investments in and contacts with the Italian political parties. This gave him fresh resources, including closer relations with Socialist Party head Bettino Craxi, who visited Pazienza at the latter's house. Craxi's Socialist Party had been heavily financed by illegal contributions from Calvi's bank from 1975, and Craxi had been Calvi's stout defender when Banco Ambrosiano's misdeeds began to be uncovered in the late 1970s.[101]

Pazienza's Mafia ties were also important. Following the kidnapping of the Christian Democratic official Ciro Cirillo by the Red Brigades in 1981, Pazienza was brought in by the police to negotiate for Cirillo's ransom. Pazienza was able to negotiate Cirillo's release through his contacts with Raeffele Cutolo, the leader of the Naples Camorra (Mafia). According to the June 16, 1985 statement of former Cutolo as-

in a police raid of March 17, 1981. It is possible that pressure on P-2 members and their close associates began shortly after that date, although Santovito did not leave SISMI until August 1981.

Pazienza's claims were spelled out in a letter from him to Christian Roulette, which was introduced by Roulette into the trial record in January 1986. The contents of the letter are summarized by Diana Johnstone in "Bulgarian Connection: Finger-pointing in the pontiff plot labyrinth," *In These Times*, January 29-February 4, 1986.

100. See Chapter 6, pp. 135-36.

101. Cornwell, *op. cit.*, n. 85, pp. 114, 141.

sociate Giovanni Pandico,[102] when Cutolo was threatened with a transfer
out of Ascoli Piceno prison in 1982—with the implication that Cutolo
might be killed during the transfer—Cutolo contacted Pazienza and
Musumeci to help extricate him from his fix. Pandico claimed that
Musumeci visited Ascoli Piceno prison in late February or early March
1982,[103] and struck a deal: Cutolo would stay in Ascoli Piceno, but he
would help persuade Agca to implicate the Bulgarians and Soviets in the
plot to assassinate the Pope.

Ledeen, Pazienza, SISMI, and the Bulgarian Connection

As we have seen, recent investigations of the Italian secret services in
general, and SISMI and the Ledeen-Pazienza-SISMI connection in particular, have uncovered a wide variety of suggestive facts and relationships that bear on the emergence of the Bulgarian Connection. First, it is
clear that SISMI and other Italian intelligence agencies have long been
infiltrated and even dominated by P-2 members and the extreme Right.
These groups have been associated for many years with attempts to sub-
vert Italian democracy, to weaken and destroy the Left by means of a
"strategy of tension," and, if need be, to organize a coup to install a
government of law and order. It is apparent that agencies like SISMI
have been thoroughly politicized and have spent considerable effort pursuing covert political strategies.

Second, there is substantial evidence that SISMI had little scruple in
serving up forged documents, disseminating them, and planting them on
its political enemies. On May 19, 1981, only six days after the assassination attempt on the Pope, SISMI circulated a secret report within the
government claiming that the shooting of the Pope had been decided
upon and announced at a meeting of Warsaw Pact military leaders in
Rumania by Soviet Minister of Defense Marshal Ustinov in November
1980. This fabricated document is now part of the evidence in the case
against Pazienza and others and has been impounded by the Italian
courts.[104] An associate of Pazienza's, Francesco Mazzola, then Italian

102. Pietro Calderoni, "Cella con Servizi," *L'Espresso*, June 23, 1985. This was
based on an exclusive interview with Pandico.
103. Pandico told Calderoni the visit took place on March 1, but in his trial testimony
Pandico changed this to sometime in February.
104. See discussion and citations in *Report of the International Commission of Study
and Information on "The Antonov Affair"* (Brussels: International Association of Demo-

Under Secretary for Security, was the first Italian official to refer publicly to a "Bulgarian Connection."[105] In short, Italian intelligence had fabricated a KGB plot and was already disseminating it long before Agca made his first serious claims of Bulgarian involvement.[106]

Third, SISMI was honeycombed with corruption in the 1970s and early 1980s. In addition to the matters dealt with in the Judgment, Pazienza was deeply involved in the Banco Ambrosiano scandal. He is now wanted in Italy for, among other things, arranging a $3 million loan to an Italian construction company, whose top official used $2 million for personal ends, with Pazienza drawing a $250,000 finder's fee. We have mentioned Pazienza's numerous Mafia contacts. Santovito and several of his associates were eventually arrested and convicted for active participation in the drug and arms traffic. Some of these transactions even involved cooperation with the Turkish Gray Wolves to transport contraband goods across Bulgaria.[107] This relationship between SISMI and the Gray Wolves may have helped induce Agca to cooperate in the manufacture of the Bulgarian Connection.

Finally, SISMI was exceedingly amenable to serving as an errand boy for U.S. officials. We have mentioned the longstanding dependency on the CIA, reflecting the larger and deeper dependency of the Italian elite on U.S. power. The Billygate case, with Ledeen, Pazienza, and SISMI working together in the service of the Reagan election campaign, and manipulating the Italian media and political environment with money and the resources of an important intelligence agency, is suggestive. "Billygate" was a model of what can be done in the way of setting somebody up for a media coup, using the power available to U.S. agents and their Italian allies. It takes little imagination to contemplate the possibility that this duo or their numerous associates in the Italian intelligence agencies and police might have worked out a way to take advantage of Agca's presence in jail and his visit to Bulgaria.

cratic Lawyers, 1985), pp. 20-21. If this document were not a forgery, we may be sure that it would have been introduced into evidence by Martella and his colleagues much earlier.

105. He made his statement in an interview on Thames Television, T.V. Eye, on September 3, 1981. A consultant to the producers of the program was Paul Henze. Two days after the broadcast Henze delivered his report on the Bulgarian Connection to *Reader's Digest*, which then proceeded to hire Claire Sterling to investigate the "Connection."

106. As we note elsewhere in the text, Agca mentioned the Bulgarians very early, but superficially and along with a large number of other implausible claims.

107. "La P-2, les service italiens, le trafic drogues/armes: l'attentat contre le pape et la CIA," *Le Monde du Renseignement*, October-December 1983, pp. 43-45

Craxi and the Politics of the Bulgarian Connection

There is intense hostility and conflict between the Italian Communist Party and the Socialist Party and Christian Democrats. It is obvious that a successful linking of the Bulgarians and Soviet Union to the assassination attempt against the Pope would be a severe blow to the Communist Party and the Left. Socialist Minister of Defense Lagorio stated to the Italian Parliament that the attempted assassination attempt by Bulgaria was a "declaration of war." And the conservative press in Italy has produced a steady outpouring of the Sterling-Jonathan Institute line that the Soviet Union is the base of all terrorism. The western media have not commented on the fact that Lagorio's statement about a declaration of war was based on a belated confession by a long-imprisoned murderer, and that this assertion of guilt was made before any court had reached such a conclusion. Coming from a high official of the government, the statement shows both the high political stakes involved and the dubiousness of the Italian political scene for a fair investigation and trial.

Socialist Party leader Bettino Craxi has been either unable or unwilling to carry out any extensive programs of social reform. In place of these, he has built his political strategy on anti-Soviet rhetoric, militarization within the New Cold War framework, and associated service to the Reagan administration.[108] Craxi therefore had a large vested interest in the initiation, pursuit, and successful outcome of the case against the Bulgarians. The Christian Democrats, P-2, and reactionary elements in the police and security forces had a parallel interest. Thus the political elements with a stake in bringing and winning the case were formidable and have commanded powerful business, financial, and press support in Italy. They also received strong support from the Reagan administration, which gained enormous benefits from the Connection.

---

108. See Diana Johnstone, *The Politics of Euromissiles: Europe's Role in America's World* (London: Verso, 1984), Chapter 4.

5. Darkness in Rome: The Western System of Induced Confession

In his novel *Darkness at Noon*, Arthur Koestler imagines the way in which confessions were induced in the Soviet staged trials of the 1930s. Isolating the prisoner, persuading him of the hopelessness of his position, and convincing him that he could best contribute to his own and the national welfare by a properly directed confession yielded the desired results. With the incarceration and isolation of Agca, the subsequent pressures for cooperation, and the resultant confessions channeled to mutual advantage, the West produced an analogous result in Rome. Although the case against the Bulgarians was finally lost, the analogy still holds for a four-year travesty of justice that produced a huge propaganda windfall to its sponsors.[1]

Throughout the period immediately preceding Agca's naming of Bulgarians, the Reagan administration and the powerful right wing of Italy were striving to put into effect the message of the Jonathan Institute conference of July 1979: Tie the Soviet Union to "international terrorism." Agca's confessions and Martella's mindless pursuit of the case served well both the Reagan-Jonathan Institute objectives and those of P-2 and Bettino Craxi and his political allies in Italy.

1. The Bulgarian Sergei Antonov, although now released, was incarcerated for more than three years. He also seems to have collapsed mentally and physically from the stress of the accusations and confinement.

How Agca Was Coached

We believe that Agca was coached to implicate the Bulgarians. Coaching, as we use the term here, involved three elements. One was identifying for Agca the preferred villains. The second was inducing him, by offering benefits and/or threatening him with damage, to name them as his collaborators. The third ingredient was to supply Agca with the information necessary to allow him to formulate a plausible scenario of a conspiracy and to name specific co-conspirators. The direct and circumstantial evidence that all three of these things were done in the Bulgarian Connection case is now compelling.[2]

Many individuals with an interest in pinning the plot on the Bulgarians had access to Agca in prison, and they had an extended opportunity to bribe and threaten him. We saw in the previous chapter that the Italian secret services were dominated by P-2 members in 1981 and had a long history of subservience to U.S. intelligence. They also had a well-documented history of planting fabricated evidence on the Left. Both SISMI and the Interior Ministry were spreading concocted tales of Soviet and Bulgarian involvement in the assassination attempt long before Agca named any Bulgarians. The intelligence services not only had access to Agca in prison, they also had longstanding relations with the Mafia, whose incarcerated leaders dominated the Ascoli Piceno prison in which Agca was held.

There is also evidence that some people within the Vatican were eager to make Agca talk. The western press accepted the Sterling-Henze line that the Soviets sought to quell the Solidarity movement in Poland by removing its papal support. Unmentioned was the possible papal motivation for getting the imprisoned Agca to implicate the Soviets in order to strengthen Polish resistance to martial law and to weaken Soviet influence in Poland and elsewhere. The first book on the assassination attempt, *The Drama of May 13*, was published in West Germany by a Vatican priest, who claimed that the KGB had trained Agca in the Soviet Union and had ordered the shooting.[2] Suleyman Yetkin, an old Turkish comrade of Agca's from Malatya residing in West Germany, was paid a substantial sum of money in several installments by Dr.

---

2. The author, Vendelin Sluganov, got this "information" from the intelligence report forged by SISMI and released on May 19, 1981, mentioned in the previous chapter.

Hoemeyer, Secretary General of the Union of Catholic Bishops, to persuade Agca to say that he had been hired by the KGB.[3]

Orsan Oymen, the West German correspondent of the Turkish paper *Milliyet*, and its specialist in the assassination attempt, was told by Padre Ginno, a Vatican librarian, that "Our Church took advantage of the assault against the Pope. It suggested in a secret manner the KGB thesis to the press, and then stepped aside." The Vatican also had an agent within the prison: Father Mariano Santini, the Catholic chaplain in Ascoli Piceno. Santini had regular access to Agca in prison, and Padre Ginno suggested to Oymen that Santini was a key figure in getting Agca to talk. Giovanni Pandico, the chief state witness in the trial of the Mafia in Naples, also gives Santini a prominent place in his account of how Agca was induced to talk. Cardinal Silvio Oddi acknowledged to Oymen that Agca wrote a letter on September 24, 1982—just weeks before he named the Bulgarians, and immediately after the publication of Sterling's *Reader's Digest* article—in which he complained to Vatican authorities that the prison chaplain was putting pressure on him and that he feared for his life.[4] In short, not only did P-2 and the Italian secret services have a political interest in getting Agca to talk and have direct access to him, so did agents of the Vatican, who were actively using their influence in this direction from the time of the shooting.

Agca's motives are equally clear. There is solid evidence that he was induced to talk by the classic method of carrot and stick. After his first trial, he was taken to Ascoli Piceno prison, where he was supposed to be kept in solitary confinement for a full year. Isolated and harassed in various ways by prison officials, Agca complained about these pressures, both physical and psychological, to his family and to prison authorities. Following a softening up period, but long before the expiration of his term of solitary confinement, he was provided with a comfortable cell with TV, radio, and private bath. On December 29, 1981, officials of Italian intelligence visited him. Shortly thereafter Agca was visited for

3. This plan was eventually called off in March 1982, shortly after the meeting which, according to Giovanni Pandico, took place between Musumeci and Agca in February or early March 1982, as described in the text. Orsan Oymen, who reported these arrangements between Hoemeyer and Yetkin, was shown a letter of March 1982 calling off the visit to the prison. See Orsan Oymen, "Behind the Scenes of the 'Agca Investigation,' " *Milliyet*, November 1984.

4. *Ibid.* During the trial, Judge Santiapichi commented to Santini that Agca seemed to use an "ecclesiastically tinged" version of Italian. Santini denied having given Agca instructions in the Italian language, but in his final defense statement on March 8, 1966, Antonov's counsel Giuseppi Consolo claimed that Santini visited Agca more than 90 times.

the first time by Investigating Magistrate Ilario Martella. On February 2, 1982, Agca told his lawyer that he had been offered a deal by the intelligence services for talking—a reduction of his prison sentence to ten years or less.[5] It was also reported in the Italian press that Agca was threatened with a loss of his privileges and with being released into the general Italian prison population if he failed to cooperate. The implication was that this might result in assassination for the assailant of the Pope.[6] Martella himself acknowledged in his final Report that he had held out to Agca the possibility of having his sentence commuted by presidential pardon if he cooperated with the investigation.[7] Thus a period of using the stick, and a continuing threat of further applications of the stick, were combined with positive inducements to talk.

There is some dispute over the number and significance of intelligence services visits to Agca in prison. Judge Martella and Prosecutor Albano both claimed only a single visit in which nothing of great interest occurred. On the other hand, an Italian police report in August 1982 stated that the secret services conducted "interviews" (plural) with Agca for the purpose of trying to determine whether or not there were "international connections" (*i.e.*, a Bulgarian Connection) underlying the plot. The Italian press also reported multiple visits by the secret services to Ascoli Piceno prison and to Agca in particular. The interview of December 29, 1981, lasted five hours, according to one of the officers involved. The Albano and Martella Reports stress that Agca said little that was useful on December 29, 1981, and that Agca could hardly have been coached by officials who knew so little themselves. This misses the complexity of coaching, which is not limited to the supply of details. At the meeting of December 29, Agca was almost surely shown who the secret services wanted to cast in the role of villains and what he would have to do to get back into the limelight and improve his personal condition as a prisoner. These are important elements of coaching.

The actual decision to "confess" and the more detailed mechanics of making a proper confession undoubtedly came later. According to the

5. Diana Johnstone, "Latest scandal leads to Reagan administration," *In These Times*, December 5-11, 1984.

6. The secret services "visited Agca and warned him that once his solitary confinement was over, 'the authorities could no longer guarantee his safety.' Days before he was due to be moved to the main wing of the prison Agca began to reveal the 'Bulgarian Connection.' " Tana de Zulueta and Peter Godwin, "Face To Face With The Colonel Accused Of Plotting To Kill the Pope," *Sunday Times* (London), May 26, 1983, p. 50.

7. Martella Report, pp. 464-65(622-23).

statement of Giovanni Pandico, Agca was finally induced to talk by Raeffele Cutolo, the Naples Mafia chief, who was an inmate of Ascoli Piceno prison at the same time as Agca. Cutolo had been persuaded to do this by General Giuseppi Musumeci, a P-2 member and formerly second in command of SISMI.[8] In Pandico's account, Musumeci, Cutolo, a prison chaplain, and a prison official explained to Agca that he could expect trouble in prison if he failed to cooperate. It was also suggested to him that it might be possible to arrange for getting him out in six or seven years, if he did what was required of him. It was at this point, also, according to Pandico, that Agca was given detailed instructions on the lines of a preliminary confession.[9]

As a rightwinger and anticommunist it should not have been too difficult to persuade Agca that by implicating the Bulgarians he was contributing to a useful crusade against a common enemy. Many Agca observers have noted that Agca will tell his interrogators what they want to hear, as long as this is not damaging to his own interests. Agca will, in fact, tell his interrogators *more* than they want to hear because of his longstanding propensity to spin out mythical tales in which he is the hero. Orsan Oymen noted that "During my previous conversations with friends of Agca I had noticed some things which suggested signs of Agca's being obsessed with a mania for concocting stories. For instance, when Suleyman from Malatya told me about Mehmet Ali's years at high school, he claimed that his schoolmate had a liking for ad-

8. Pandico's claims have been denied by Cutolo, Musumeci, Pazienza, and others. Pandico's statement has not been corroborated, but the denials, by people in serious trouble on whom the Italian state has leverage, are of dubious credibility. There is no evident reason why Pandico would create a false scenario for this set of events, and his claims are plausible. Pazienza has suggested that Pandico's story was part of a plot by other elements of SISMI to shift the blame for the second conspiracy to him. According to Pazienza, it was these other elements in SISMI who coached Agca (see below). Pazienza's accusations are quite detailed and are possibly true, although he has lied on many matters and lacks credibility. Furthermore, Pandico's naming of Musumeci and Pazienza occurred only a week after his mother was injured in an attack presumably by the Mafia, and would seem to be aimed at damaging the Mafia, not as part of a SISMI-Mafia plot to cover themselves at the expense of Pazienza. Surprisingly, Pandico's claims were given indirect support by Claire Sterling, who asserted that she was told by an Italian judge that Cutolo had tried to "scare Agca to death" in order to ingratiate himself with the Italian prison authorities. Claire Sterling, "Silenzio so spara," *Panorama*, April 23, 1984.

9. Pietro Calderoni, "Cell With Services," *L'Espresso*, June 23, 1985; Bruno Rubino, "Pazienza? The Bulgarian Trail Is His Idea," *L'Epoca*, July 1, 1985. Both of these articles are interviews with Pandico.

venture and spy novels, invented all sorts of scenarios, and believed them himself."[10]

Agca would also be amenable to fingering the Bulgarians because this provided him with another opportunity to make a mark on the world. Self-aggrandizement and public recognition—what Mumcu and others call his "Carlos complex"—are apparently among Agca's driving emotional needs. Agca was referred to half-affectionately by some of his Gray Wolves colleagues as the "Emperor." The Emperor likes to be in the limelight, and enjoyed the notoriety of shooting the Pope. In fact, this appears to have been one of the motivating forces for the assassination attempt itself. Moving once again to center stage by his confession implicating the Bulgarians and KGB, Agca was pleased with the renewed attention and was eager to provide his new collaborators with what they wanted. Playing his new role, he repeated in rote fashion, and like a bad actor, all the formulas of the Sterling school of "international terrorism."

In our view of what actually transpired in Italy, Agca would not have required much direct coaching. Having been shown his options, and the usefulness and personal advantage of cooperation, he would understand that his captors were deeply interested in proving a Bulgarian involvement in the assassination attempt. This had already been made clear in the interviews of the secret services and in the drift of Martella's interrogations. By September 1982 Sterling's *Reader's Digest* article and the NBC-TV spectacular on the Plot had made their mark, and the Sterling model of a Bulgarian Connection had surely reached Agca through the media as well as via interrogations. Here was a ready-made opportunity to move back to center stage!

Pandico claimed that Musumeci came to Ascoli Piceno with a set of note cards on which were written the motivations that Agca was supposed to offer as the basis for his confession, as well as the details on what he was to say about Bulgarian and Soviet involvement. A year and a half before Pandico's statement, another Mafia member turned informer, Giuseppi Cilleri, had already been cited in the Italian press as claiming that Francesco Pazienza had been a "frequent visitor" to Ascoli Piceno prison and that he had personally given Agca instructions in preparation for the photo identification of Bulgarians.[11] Whether by such means, or by judiciously informative questioning combined with

10. Oymen, *op. cit.*, n. 3.
11. Calderoni, *op. cit.*, n. 9. The account of Cilleri's testimony was given in an article on Agca in *L'Espresso*, December 25, 1983.

access to the Sterling-Kalb version of the Plot, Agca was provided with enough detail to make a plausible first approximation case. He was eventually shown pictures of individuals and apartments, with identification sufficient to allow him to provide "surprising details."[12] Then, with generous access to journalistic accounts of the case and related issues,[13] and by the intelligent use of further questions by the secret services and magistrates,[14] Agca could provide new claims and more "surprising details" without requiring explicit coaching.

A curiosity in the case, which strongly supports the coaching hypothesis, is the long time that it took for Agca to name the Bulgarians. Arrested in May 1981, Agca did not begin to name his Bulgarian accomplices until October and November of 1982, a lapse of 17 to 18 months. This was the *period of opportunity*, during which the coincidence of interest between Agca and his captors could be made to yield a congenial confession. Agca failed to provide a single Bulgarian name until some six months after he had agreed to cooperate with the Italian authorities, which was in April 1982. Neither Sterling nor Martella has provided a satisfactory explanation for Agca's long delay in implicating the Bulgarians.[15] Our conclusion is that he did not confess earlier about Bulgarian participation because he had nothing to confess. He had to be softened up in prison and then induced to say the right things.

To recapitulate the reasons for believing that Agca was coached:

● A large array of political factions in Italy, extending from P-2 through the Craxi socialists, and including important people within the Vatican, had a strong political stake in getting Agca to implicate the Bulgarians and Soviet Union.

12. We discuss below the evidence that the photo identification parade was pre-arranged.

13. "Every single fact that Agca describes about the workings of the Turkish Mafia and its links with Bulgaria was contained in a series of newspaper articles which Agca read in jail." De Zulueta and Godwin, *op. cit.*, n. 6, p. 50.

14. "When asked by Martella in Bulgaria whether he had any salient physical features, Vassilev said that he had a mole on his left cheek. In a *subsequent* confession, as Vassilev points out, 'Agca described my mole in *the very same words* which I used in describing it here.' " *Ibid.*, pp. 48, 50. In his final defense summary on March 7, 1986, Antonov's attorney Consolo pointed out that Agca originally described Aivazov as speaking Italian "quite well." The proprietor of the boarding house in Rome where Agca stayed subsequently testified that the individual who reserved a room for Agca, alleged by Agca to have been Aivazov, spoke "perfect" Italian. Shortly thereafter Agca changed his account: Aivazov spoke "perfect" Italian. Agca was supposedly not privy to the secret testimony of the boarding house proprietor. This pattern occurred with great frequency.

15. We discuss Sterling's attempts at an explanation in Chapters 2 and 6.

● The Reagan administration was also anxious to demonstrate the depth of Soviet evil in the early 1980s, and its propaganda instruments were in the forefront in pressing each and every propaganda opportunity. Agca's visit to Sofia provided such an opportunity to Sterling, Henze, and company. The power of the U.S. media, and the links of the U.S. government, intelligence agencies, and business community to their counterparts in Italy are capable of affecting Italian political choices.

● Agca was perfectly positioned to be manipulated. He was in prison for life and easily subjected to inducements and threats by his captors.

● Agca was also readily manipulable by virtue of his personal characteristics and politics. He liked to make up stories and to be at the center of attention. He also had durable ties to the anticommunist extreme Right of Turkey.

● The possibilities of manipulating Agca were recognized by all parties from the start, and both SISMI and the Vatican "jumped the gun"—the former fabricated a Soviet plot within a week of the assassination attempt, while Vatican interests proposed that Agca be induced to talk long before he had claimed any Bulgarian involvement.

● All of the Italian intelligence services were headed by P-2 members and were broadly infiltrated by P-2 at the time of the assassination attempt. This provided the opportunity to disseminate disinformation on Bulgarian-KGB involvement and then coach Agca to claim the reality of the disinformation scenario. In early 1981 Francesco Pazienza was a SISMI agent, and he and Michael Ledeen had been in an alliance of convenience to serve Reagan in the Billygate affair. Italy has a longstanding rightwing and intelligence tradition of planting fabricated evidence on the Left.

● Despite his "solitary confinement," Agca had numerous visitors, many without the knowledge or approval of Investigating Magistrate Martella. As noted earlier, officials of the Italian intelligence services visited Agca on December 29, 1981, already probing into "international connections" and almost surely telling Agca who the security services were interested in implicating in the Plot and the advantages that would accrue to him by "cooperating." The Italian press has claimed that Agca was also visited by other SISMI officials, including Lieutenant Colonel Giuseppi Belmonte and Francesco Pazienza.[16] Agca himself told the court in June 1985 that he had been visited by Pazienza. We

16. Johnstone, *op. cit.*, n. 5.

also know that he was visited by U.S. and Turkish intelligence officials, by a Turkish journalist, and by others. His prison conditions were ludicrously porous for a condemned criminal who the Investigating Magistrate was relying upon for new information.

● Agca was in a prison cell next to that of Dr. Giovanni Senzani, a "penitent" member of the Red Brigades, who stood to benefit by cooperating with SISMI and the prison authorities. Senzani was in regular contact with Agca and supposedly taught him Italian.

● Agca was also frequently attended to by Father Mariano Santini, a Catholic prison chaplain who was later jailed for serving as a prison emissary of the Mafia. Why would Agca, a non-Catholic, require the aid of a Catholic chaplain? As we noted earlier, a Vatican official described Santini as a Vatican instrument in inducing Agca to talk, and Agca himself complained to the Vatican and elsewhere of pressure from Santini.

● Former mafioso Pandico has described in detail the pressures applied to Agca by Pandico's former boss Cutolo. Cutolo, an inmate in the Ascoli Piceno prison at the same time as Agca, was in a position to threaten him. Pazienza has denied his or Musumeci's involvement, claiming that other elements in SISMI, also linked to Michael Ledeen, actually did coach Agca, but have tried to shift the blame on to him. Pazienza named names and provided many details, although he is not noted for reliability. But as Diana Johnstone points out: "With Pazienza's denials and counter-accusations, the controversy is boiling down to a question of *who* within SISMI invented the Bulgarian Connection and whether they were prompted by American colleagues."[17]

● Following his period of isolation and harassment, but while still theoretically in solitary confinement, Agca had a TV set and radio, and received newspapers and private communications from outside the prison. According to Prosecutor Albano's Report, when in June 1983 Agca withdrew his assertion that he had visited Antonov's apartment and met his wife and daughter, he stated that he had obtained his description of Antonov's apartment—its layout, furnishings, etc.—from newspapers.[18] The prosecutor also conceded that Agca's feat in produc-

17. Diana Johnstone, "Bulgarian Connection: Finger-pointing in the pontiff plot labyrinth," *In These Times*, January 29-February 4, 1986.

18. Agca got useful materials for his confessions from Turkish books and magazine articles, as well as radio, TV, newspapers, and coaches. The role of Celenk in Agca's plot scenario escalated sharply after he read a book by Mumcu on arms smuggling in which Celenk was a key figure. See note 36 in Chapter 2. See also note 13 above.

ing the telephone numbers of various Bulgarians had been accomplished by his looking them up in a telephone book "inadvertently" provided to him. Agca repeated these declarations during the trial, telling the court that he had found the details of his "confessions" in the newspapers. While these admissions demonstrate the breakdown of controls over Agca's sources of information bearing on the case, they do not prove coaching. The Bulgarians, and Antonov's defense counsel, claim, however, that a thoroughgoing search of press coverage shows that at the time he provided the details on Antonov's apartment, *no Italian or Turkish newspaper had yet produced a single word about Antonov's flat in Rome.* This defense claim is in accord with common sense. Why would any paper have provided details of Antonov's apartment before Agca's claims made those details an issue? Such descriptions only followed his confession and the first investigative visit to Antonov's flat on June 11, 1983.[19]

● Former Minister of Defense Lagorio stated before the Italian Parliament that Agca identified his Bulgarian accomplices in September 1982 from a photo album that had been prepared by the secret services. Albano's Report placed the photo identification on November 8, 1982, and Martella also stated that on November 8 Agca picked out the Bulgarians "without being informed in any way of the names or positions of the people involved."[20] The contradiction between Lagorio and Albano-Martella has never been explained, but lends credence to the supposition that Agca was shown the photo album before November 8.

There are several other features of the photo album display which suggest bias, coaching, or both. One is that the album contained exclusively pictures of Bulgarians—56 in all—which means that if Agca had picked three persons at random he would still have named three Bulgarians. Second, prior to his initial photo identification session Agca had "confessed" to knowing only two Bulgarian officials, "Kolev" and "Bayramic." He identified these two as being photos number one and number two in the album, an amazing coincidence. (The odds against any two of 56 photos occupying places number one and two in the album by chance are 1,540 to one). Another noteworthy feature of the photo identification is that at his second session he picked out as "Petrov" the only person in the album dressed in military uniform.[21] It

19. Boyan Traikov, *Mystification, Dr. Martella!* (Sofia: Sofia Press, 1984), p. 28.

20. Quoted in Michael Dobbs, "A Communist Plot to Kill the Pope—Or a Liar's Fantasy," *Washington Post*, November 18, 1984.

21. Although Petrov was allegedly his "control," his existence had previously slipped

would appear that the security services were trying to make it easier for Agca to select the right people ("Remember, the one with a military uniform, and the *first two* in the album"!). Finally, the photo album shown to Agca had been used earlier in a trial involving Senzani, the Red Brigades prisoner who was in the next cell to Agca and in frequent communication with him. Senzani would have been well situated to brief Agca on the Bulgarian details that he needed to know in the identification parade.

• Antonov was allegedly introduced to Agca as "Bayramic." Bayramic is the name of a small town in Turkey located near Agca's home in Malatya. (This was disclosed by Antonov's defense counsel in his concluding remarks on March 6, 1986.) This would be another extraordinary coincidence if we were to take Agca's word that this was a code name fixed by the Bulgarians; on the other hand, it is entirely comprehensible if we assume that the name was another concoction by Agca.

• According to Agca, "Bayramic" was the only name by which he knew Antonov. But he allegedly communicated with Antonov by calling him at the Bulgarian Embassy, through the general switchboard. Martella never addressed the question of how Antonov could be reached through the switchboard operator, who presumably did not know Antonov's highly secret code name, by Agca, who knew Antonov only by the code name.

• Initially Agca identified Antonov as having a beard. While Antonov had a beard at the time of his arrest, his counsel was able to prove that he did *not* have a beard at a time when Agca claims they met. Agca identified Antonov on the basis of a later photograph, making the kind of mistake in timing that occurs with coaching, when the beard appearing later is carelessly assumed to have been worn earlier. How did Agca even *recognize* the bearded Antonov whom he had never seen in the bearded state? On the supposition that he might still have recognized him, would he not be likely to note his former nonbearded state? Agca subsequently suggested that Antonov probably wore a false beard. And the beard apparently changed color at each meeting, as in a bad spy thriller.[22]

• In his detailed description of Antonov's apartment, Agca mentioned a folding door that divided the apartment. But while such a door

Agca's memory.

22. For the actual sequence of Agca's changing claims about Antonov's beard, see the text below on pp. 116-17.

existed in the other apartments in the building, the folding door had been removed in Antonov's apartment and replaced by a curtain prior to Agca's alleged visit. Again, as in the case of Antonov's beard, we have the kind of mistake easily made by imperfect coaching, where the arrangements in Antonov's apartment are inferred from those in other apartments in the same building.[23]

• After Agca retracted his claim that he had been on reconnaissance missions planning to murder Walesa, he was asked to explain how he knew so much about Walesa's hotel if he had never been there? According to Michael Dobbs, "Agca claimed that he learned the details from magistrates who had interrogated him in connection with a parallel investigation into an alleged Bulgarian spy ring in Italy."[24] This admission once again displays a broken-down judicial process. But there are two further problems. First, at the time that Agca was interrogated by these magistrates, they themselves had not received the information which they supposedly passed on inadvertently to Agca. Second, the interrogations of Luigi Scricciolo, which he named as the source of his information, do not contain any descriptions of the building in question.[25] Agca also named a Bulgarian diplomat, Ivan Dontchev, as a partner in the Walesa murder plot, and he identified Dontchev from a photo album. Subsequently Agca admitted that he had never seen Dontchev in his life. How did he identify Dontchev's picture without coaching?[26]

Martella, Priore, and Italy's Investigation of the Plot

Just as the U.S. press has never seen fit to examine the Italian political environment, so also it has never analyzed closely Magistrate Ilario Martella and his handling of the Bulgarian Connection. Martella was often given laudatory and entirely uncritical accolades emphasizing his

23. Also living in the same apartment building in 1981 was Reverend Felix A. Morlion, a veteran reactionary and CIA asset. Perhaps the folding door idea was obtained from Morlion. See "The Role of Felix Morlion," *CovertAction Information Bulletin*, Number 25, Winter 1986, p. 30; *Il Mondo*, April 8, 1985; and *L'Espresso*, May 19, 1985.

24. Michael Dobbs, "Agca's Changing Testimony," *Washington Post*, October 17, 1984.

25. *Martella Report*, pp. 375-82 (490-500), 423-27 (557-63).

26. Coaching would include a disclosure by a magistrate during interrogation which the witness seizes upon and is allowed to use as confirmation of his special knowledge of the matter disclosed to him! See note 14 above on Agca's identification of Vassilev's mole.

determination, conscientiousness, and integrity; but his background and performance were never considered in any depth or with the slightest critical perspective. This allowed the press to proceed on the assumption that we were witnessing in Italy a thorough and unbiased judicial investigation, and it permitted the steady stream of fresh allegations and leaks to be given full propaganda value.

With an unbiased media, by contrast, we believe that the fraudulent character of the pre-trial proceeding would have been quickly made evident.[27] The preceding chapter described a political environment that seriously threatened the integrity of judicial processes, and in fact the antiterrorism law under which the case was brought suspends many of the traditional rules that distinguish democratic from nondemocratic societies. The passionate public statements by political leaders in Italy and the United States that clearly prejudged the case, the enormous media barrage that did the same, and the huge stake of Italian and U.S. conservatives in the outcome made this a political and politicized case from the very beginning. Would this not affect the judicial system, the choice of investigators and judges in Italy, and their ability and willingness to look for the truth? The question did not arise in the West.

The P-2 conspiracy penetrated the Italian judiciary. The 1984 Parliamentary Report, for example, states that Dr. Carmelo Spagnulo, chief prosecutor of the Rome Court of Appeals, attended a key meeting held in Gelli's home in 1973. In the Report's general enumeration of P-2 penetration into public administration, which counted 422 P-2-linked officials, 16 active and 3 retired magistrates were included. Whatever the affiliations of particular judges such as Martella, this is symptomatic of an unhealthy judicial environment.

By the late 1970s the Italian judiciary was saturated with the Sterling-Jonathan Institute perspective on terrorism. This framework was immediately applied to the plot against the Pope. Thus Martella's colleague Rosario Priore, Judge of the Court of Appeal and serving as Investigating Judge at the Rome Tribunal, produced a report entitled "The cases Moro, Dozier and the attack on the Pope," which is vintage Sterling.[28] After describing Agca's account of his stay in Sofia and presenting a number of alleged facts about the Bulgarians named by Agca,[29]

27. We are speaking of the initiation and investigative phase of the case, not the trial, whose conduct was fair, although subject to political constraints.

28. This document was circulated in the United States by the Italian Embassy.

29. Two of them were in Bulgaria at the same time as Agca, and two "were in service in Rome at the same time the structure discussed above was in operation—acquiring infor-

Priore says that this "network" shows "the interweaving of a number of international interests and the existence of centers that manipulate terrorism, which are located in other countries and in their intelligence services. . . ."[30] Priore quotes without qualification Agca's description of his own role: "I am an international terrorist, ready to help the terrorists of any nation."[31] Priore asserts that the manipulators of international terrorism "aim at destabilizing the western democracies,"[32] although he does not point to any evidence that would support this claim. This is of course a major theme of Claire Sterling's *The Terror Network*, which she could not sell to western intelligence agencies, but which found a happy home in the Italian judicial system.[33] Priore infers a "network" from an alleged Bulgarian Connection alone, and "international centers" of terrorism (plural) from the same evidence. He shows not the slightest skepticism concerning Agca's testimony, despite its continually shifting character and other deficiencies. He refers to Agca's statement—"I am an international terrorist" etc.—as "highly significant," not as a statement that would be significant if true. The extremely rote quality of Agca's remarks on international terrorism, which conform so precisely to—even caricature—the Sterling model of a modern terrorist, does not elicit doubts from this Italian judge, and coaching is not entertained as a possibility. The hypothesis that the Bulgarians and Soviets might have been set up by some other "centers of terrorism" (if any exist for Priore) is never addressed.

Judge Ilario Martella apparently shares Priore's frame of reference. He was put in charge of the case in November 1981. Like Priore, Martella started out with a prior assumption that the charges which he was supposed to be investigating were essentially true. The most remarkable

mation on the Italian trade unions. . . . " Rosario Priore, "The cases Moro, Dozier and the attack on the Pope," p. 24.

30. *Ibid.*
31. *Ibid.*, p. 25.
32. *Ibid.*, p. 26.
33. The judge in charge of the second trial in Rome, Severino Santiapichi, who also presided over Agca's initial trial for the attempted assassination of the Pope, stated at the conclusion of the earlier trial that Agca was merely the surface representation of a "deep conspiracy . . . orchestrated by secret forces, carefully planned and directed down to the smallest detail." This reference to "secret forces" has a Sterling-like ring, and as we discuss elsewhere in this book, the planning of the assassination attempt was remarkably mismanaged. In the second trial, just concluded, Santiapichi showed that he was not committed to the *a priori* "deep conspiracy" view, and the course of the trial as conducted by Santiapichi effectively undermined the "first conspiracy" scenarios of western disinformationists and their "secret forces."

illustration of this was his reaction to Agca's numerous lies and retractions. In a normal judicial process, lies and retractions that destroy *part* of the claims of a witness weaken the credibility of those parts that cannot be positively disproved. Disbelief is directly related to the number of lies and retractions. This was not true in the Martella investigation. Martella postulated that, having decided to tell the truth, Agca was always struggling to make that core truth more credible. He lied, according to Martella, in order to "give more credibility to his statement."[34] That the statement to which Agca desired to give credibility was not also a lie was, of course, merely Martella's gratuitous assumption, for which he gave no rationale. This assumption flies in the face of normal reasoning—which does not rationalize *selected* lies by *a priori* assumptions about the liar's intent. Martella's investigation was therefore hopelessly biased at the outset.

When Agca retracted evidence, for Martella this was to Agca's credit, as he was cleansing himself of excesses in his search for the truth. ("We cannot ignore the particular importance in the search for truth of the 'retraction' made by the same Agca during the course of judicial inquiry."[35]) An alternative explanation, which Martella never addressed, is that Agca shifted his testimony in order to make a new dramatic entry on to the stage. This would, of course, require that he say that which the audience (*i.e.*, Martella and his associates) wanted most to hear. Another possibility which Martella never mentioned is that Agca retracted claims because his lies had run into so many contradictions that they were no longer sustainable. Thus, Agca ultimately withdrew his claim that Aivazov was the man photographed from behind fleeing the Square on May 13, claiming instead that it was his friend Oral Celik. The reason for this recantation, according to Agca, was that he had determined "to tell the truth to the end even at the risk of harming a friend who like Celik is dearer to me than a brother but in the knowledge that I am telling the absolute truth."[36] Martella quoted this with admiration, although it was an assertion of a man who had lied incessantly up to that very moment.[37] Martella made no reference to the fact that Agca's retraction followed shortly after a press conference in Sofia, at which the opportunity to see Aivazov had made it clearly evident to the assembled

34. *Martella Report*, p. 377(492-93).
35. *Ibid.*, p. 769(986).
36. *Ibid.*, p. 127(172).
37. The trial has cast doubts on the truth of Agca's identification of Celik in the Square. It appears that Martella was gulled twice about the identification of the one photograph.

press that he bore no resemblance to the man in the Lowell Newton photograph, and thus it could not have been he in the Square. When the counsel for the defense suggested that this, rather than a sudden burst of sincerity, might have had something to do with Agca's recantation, Martella refused to accept such a cynical view!

Because for Martella Agca was a truth-seeker, he could adjust his evidence by a system of successive approximations. In fact, the great judicial innovation brought to the Bulgarian Connection case by Martella was allowing the witness supporting the *a priori* Free World truth about the assassination attempt to adjust his testimony by a trial-and-error process *with no penalty for error*. As Michael Dobbs pointed out, "The overall effect of these changes was to bring his evidence into line with events occurring outside the top-security prison where he was being held as well as with revelations about the case in the mass media."[38] Although he made errors on key points and radically contradicted himself time and again, this never fatally damaged Agca's credibility for Martella.

Agca's identification of Antonov and his claim to have done business with him were strategic points in the case. Consider, then, how Agca identified Antonov:[39]

(1) It took him six months after agreeing to cooperate with the Italian authorities even to mention Antonov's existence.

(2) In his first reference to Antonov, made at the end of October 1982, Agca was brief. He said only that on May 12, 1981, his Bulgarian "control officer" pointed out Antonov to him as the man who would drive him on the next day to the assassination rendezvous. Agca said that Antonov had a blondish beard.

(3) On November 8, 1982, Antonov was recognized by Agca in the photo album. He now had a *black* beard. Agca now remembered that he had seen Antonov on two or three previous occasions (whereas 10 days earlier he stated that he had seen Antonov only on May 12 and that he had had a blond beard).

(4) On November 19, 11 days after being shown the photo, Agca's recollections bloomed and finer details were forthcoming. He now remembered that Antonov had a broad forehead and a big nose, and that

38. Dobbs, *op. cit.*, n.24.

39. The facts in this account are taken from the chronology given by Michael Dobbs in his "A Communist Plot to Kill the Pope—Or a Liar's Fantasy," *Washington Post*, November 18, 1984. This article summarizes Martella's interrogation of Agca on pages 84-87 (103-7) of his *Report*.

he had been introduced to Agca not by his control officer but at the Hotel Archimede back in December 1980. At that time they discussed plans to assassinate Lech Walesa!

(5) On November 27, 1982, Agca now claimed to have first met Antonov in the apartment of his control officer at 36 Via Galiani.

(6) By late December, Agca had moved on to a version of greater complexity and intimacy. He now claimed that he had met Antonov and his wife in their own apartment several days before the assassination attempt—a version Agca retracted on June 28, 1983.

Agca also adjusted his story several times concerning the events of the day of the assassination attempt. It turned out that so many people had seen Antonov at the Balkan Air office on May 13, 1981 at 5 P.M.— the time when Agca claimed that Antonov was with him—that Agca's evidence was not sustainable. Well, Agca could then recall that he had in fact met Antonov somewhat earlier. This was perfectly understandable to Martella.

Agca's method was to adjust his claims until they fit times for which the Bulgarians had no ironclad alibis. His ability to get away with this depended on the fact that Martella disbelieved Bulgarians as strongly as he believed Agca (and anybody who supported his claims). For Martella, Bulgarians were not seekers after the truth. Their failures to remember all of the details of the events during a day two years earlier quickly aroused his suspicions. Numerous Bulgarian and Italian witnesses brought forward by the defense were dismissed for lack of precision and for contradictions in their recollections. But when Agca was caught unable to state on what floor Aivazov's apartment was located (he allegedly visited it a number of times), Martella says "it would have been much more surprising had Agca been not mistaken."[40]

The Martella process was completed by his further dichotomous treatment of possible coaching. Martella was extremely alert to the possibility that the Bulgarians might connive among themselves to create an alibi, and he was quick to dismiss new claims that corrected earlier inconsistencies. These he saw to be clearly based on collusion. But regarding the possibility that Agca was primed from the beginning, or step by step, one can observe a completely different Martella—more under-

40. Traikov, op. cit., n. 19, p. 38. When Agca tried to locate Aivazov's apartment, he got badly confused. He also misspelled the street name, using two 'ls' in Galiani, a mistake made in the telephone directory, but not on the street sign on the block. None of these errors impressed Martella.

standing of Agca's problems in searching for the truth, and remarkably naive and vague about the possibilities of connivance and collusion.

Here again was a double standard that protected a case which so well served western political interests. What makes Martella's naiveté about the possibility that Agca was coached especially ludicrous was that he maintained no control over the imprisoned Agca's visitors or activities, whether by lack of power or because he delegated it to the intelligence services and prison authorities. Martella was vague about this lack of control and its implications, but denied his own responsibility. Martella himself visited Agca only after a long delay, and shortly after the visit by the intelligence services. This suggests the possibility of a "two track" system, by which the intelligence services and prison authorities arranged for Agca to be primed, and Martella then accepted the new insights and sought to confirm them independently. This division of labor would allow SISMI and others to do the dirty work of getting Agca to see the light and feeding him the requisite information, while Martella would be left as an innocent if perhaps naive judge playing dumb about the SISMI preparations as he doggedly searched for the truth.

In the summary of his final Report Martella spoke of the plot as "a real act of war." This language was close to that demagogically used by Defense Minister Lagorio on the floor of the Italian Parliament, but it is an especially flamboyant and politically loaded phrase in a case resting strictly on Agca's claims and still untested in a jury trial. After noting that Agca had been provided with a perfectly forged passport and that he had received financial support and protection during his travels up to May 13, Martella concluded that "Ali Agca was only a pawn in a vast plot. . . . " The facts cited by Martella, however, were perfectly compatible with a "tiny plot" involving the Malatya branch of the Gray Wolves. The "vast" plot is political rhetoric not grounded in evidence.

Martella's political bias was also reflected in his affinity for U.S. disinformationists. Just prior to arresting Antonov, Martella visited the United States, where he was given a special viewing of the NBC-TV program "The Man Who Shot The Pope," and consulted with various government officials and experts on the case. One of his informants was Arnaud de Borchgrave, a Red Scare novelist and major disinformation source. From de Borchgrave Martella got the information that the head of the French secret services had learned about an "Eastern" plot against the Pope in advance, and had actually warned the Vatican.[41]

41. The ultimate source of this information is unclear. The head of the French intelli-

This point eventually showed up in Agca's testimony. Agca claimed that the Bulgarians urged speed in executing the plot, as the French and Rumanian secret services were aware of it and the papal authorities might take countermeasures. Martella cited these claims in his Report's summary, apparently taking them seriously. He never seems to have noted the contradiction between the claim that the alleged conspirators feared prior knowledge of the plot by the authorities, and the incredibly loose behavior of the Bulgarians in entertaining Agca and openly parading around with him for several days preceding the assassination attempt. We feel confident that this de Borchgravian information offered by Agca was fed to him by one of his interrogators, to be regurgitated for the delectation of the investigating magistrate.

Claire Sterling also appears to have had a close relationship with Martella. She states in *The Time of the Assassins* that she "dropped in on Martella" to check up on his agenda,[42] and apparently did so more than once,[43] although she notes elsewhere that he "was free to discuss the case only with competent judicial authorities."[44] It would appear to be no coincidence that the first journalist to obtain the Albano Report was Claire Sterling. The Sterling "imprint" is evident in both the Albano and Martella Reports in their Cold War premises and in their framing of the Bulgarian Connection case.

Under Martella's management the case was also notable for leaks and delays. Martella always reluctantly produced just enough copy to keep the pot boiling. After Agca was persuaded to implicate the Bulgarians in November 1982, Martella busily visited Antonov's apartment and otherwise displayed to the press that energy in pursuing Agca's claims that was one of his most distinctive attributes. On July 8, 1983, Agca was brought out of jail to be interrogated concerning the kidnapping of Emmanuela Orlandi, the Vatican official's daughter. The press was in-

gence agency that passed the story along to the Vatican, Comte Alexandre de Marenche, was a good friend of Francesco Pazienza, who was at that time a member of SISMI and collaborator with Ledeen. Pazienza claimed that he and de Marenche warned the Vatican of this threat six months ahead of the assassination attempt. (Jonathan Kwitny, "Tales of Intrigue: Why an Italian Spy Got Closely Involved In the Billygate Affair," *Wall Street Journal*, August 8, 1985, p. 12.) This was not the first time that de Marenche had warned the Pope about an alleged assassination attempt. De Marenche was himself an important disinformationist and recycler of the disinformation of other intelligence agencies.

42. Claire Sterling, *The Time of the Assassins* (New York: Holt, Rinehart and Winston, 1983), p. 64.
43. *Ibid.*, pp. 109, 194.
44. *Ibid.*, p. 144.

formed of the occasion; and Agca was allowed to speak before Italian TV cameras, where he presented a full litany of Sterling clichés, as a spokesman for law and order: "I was trained in Bulgaria and Syria . . . the Bulgarian services. . . . Yes, by the KGB." Martella disclaimed responsibility for allowing this organized press conference for Agca, but if this is true it indicates a serious lack of control over judicial processes. In December 1984 Agca was again allowed to be interviewed by an Italian journalist, although he was presumably scheduled for trial for conspiracy to murder. The leak of the Albano Report to Claire Sterling fits the same pattern.

Martella showed no interest in any possible locus of the plot other than Bulgaria, a point also stressed and criticized by Turkish analyst Ugur Mumcu.[45] Agca spent a great deal of time in Switzerland and West Germany, which are major Gray Wolves centers, and the Gray Wolves provided Agca with money and guns throughout his travels in Europe. It is important, too, that the details showing extensive Gray Wolves involvement are independent of Agca's testimony. Although Celebi, Agca's paymaster, lived in Frankfurt, Martella failed to go there and seek evidence of a possible Gray Wolves conspiracy.

Martella was also extremely unenterprising in seeking evidence that *contradicted* Agca's claims, and when he was confronted with it he tended to look the other way. In Bulgaria, Martella visited the Vitosha Hotel, where Agca claimed to have stayed and met his accomplices in Room 911. The Vitosha keeps extensive records—the guest register, passport data, and details on the occupants of each room. During the period of Agca's alleged stay, neither his name nor passport aliases appear on the hotel records. According to Bulgarian authorities, Martella didn't even bother to make a court-usable copy of these records, nor did he show any interest in checking out and verifying the complete record of all of the room occupants during the relevant period.[46]

Another important illustration concerns Agca's claim to have met Mrs. Antonov on several different occasions and to have visited Antonov, his wife, and daughter in their apartment. Even though these claims were extremely implausible, Martella believed them and failed to show any initiative in proving Agca wrong. The defense had to dig up the evidence that Mrs. Antonov had driven with friends to Yugoslavia. The defense—not the dogged investigator—got copies of hotel registers

45. Ugur Mumcu, *Papa, Mafya, Agca* (Istanbul: Tekin Yayinevi, 1984), p. 27.
46. Christian Roulette, *La Filiere: Jean-Paul II, Antonov, Agca* (Paris: Editions du Sorbier, 1984), pp. 245-52.

and affidavits of identification at hotels and border crossings. At the time Agca allegedly met Mrs. Antonov at the Picadilly restaurant, she was in Sofia. The defense was obliged to seek out and produce compelling data showing this. Martella never even bothered to check out Mrs. Antonov's movements through the Rome airport. The Bulgarians claim that when Martella finally interrogated Mrs. Antonov, his questioning was lengthy and hostile. Subsequently, Agca admitted that he had never met Mrs. Antonov.

Martella was clearly a "team player"—the team being the Italian political-intelligence elite and their allies in Washington, D.C. His function was to push the Bulgarian Connection as far as it could be pushed, to deflect criticisms as best he could, to keep the ball in the air as long as public relations points could be extracted from it. He performed this function well.

The Trial and The Coaching Hypothesis

The trial provided important support for the coaching hypothesis in two ways. For one thing, by exposing Agca to open view and by its failure to obtain confirmation anywhere for his claims of Bulgarian involvement, the trial stripped away the last vestiges of believability of the Sterling-Henze model. In doing this, the trial proceedings inevitably suggested questions about the route through which Agca came to latch on to the Bulgarians, although this line of analysis was not pursued relentlessly. The court apparently felt that testing Agca's claims was the first order of business. If they were not confirmed, the prosecution's case was lost. The issue of how Agca came to expound false claims, while indirectly relevant, was not regarded as worthy of a major inquiry. That area also happens to be especially sensitive politically.

The trial also contributed to validating the coaching hypothesis more directly by information that cropped up during the proceedings. Sometimes this information was thrust upon the court by independent developments in Italy. Pandico's interview in *L'Espresso* describing a coaching scenario in detail could hardly be ignored. During the interrogations of the Gray Wolves Ozbey and Catli, the court was taken aback by Catli's contention, and Ozbey's reluctant admission, that the West German police had offered a bribe to Celik to come to West Germany to testify in support of Agca's claims. This evidence added plausibility to the coaching hypothesis by showing that the willingness of intelligence services to manipulate evidence in support of the Bulgarian Connection was not confined to Italy. As for Italy itself, during the course of the trial another court, in Milan, issued its dramatic judgment against Pazienza, Belmonte, and Musumeci for crimes, including the forging of evidence. This also helped to focus attention on the question of the integrity of the Italian secret services, an issue that Albano, Martella, and Sterling had carefully avoided.

In sum, the trial greatly strengthened the case—already formidable— that Agca was coached while in prison, and that the Bulgarian Connection rested on a "second conspiracy."

6. The Disinformationists: Sterling, Henze, and Ledeen

As we have stressed, the Bulgarian Connection was exceedingly functional and met urgent political and ideological needs of the West. The Reagan administration's plan to build 17,000 new nuclear warheads and to deploy space-based battle stations is much more salable to the public and Congress when news headlines read: "Soviets Plot to Kill Pope." In Italy also the Bulgarian Connection served well the Craxi socialists, Christian Democrats, and the neofascist P-2 in their efforts to embarrass and isolate the Communist Party and to facilitate participation in the U.S.-sponsored New Cold War.

Given the great serviceability of a Bulgarian-Soviet Connection to powerful western interests, it was to be expected that the mass media of the West would quickly accept and then help extract publicity mileage from claims of Soviet involvement. U.S. conservatives, of course, contend that the media are hotbeds of dissent, the source of unceasing struggle against established government and corporate interests. We will show in this and the following chapter that the conservative model has no relationship to reality in the Bulgarian Connection case, where mass media coverage of the Connection was almost completely dominated by the conservative Sterling-Henze-Ledeen axis. It is ironic that this trio and their allies regularly assail the media, while at the same time maintaining their own full, almost exclusive, access and essentially complete freedom from criticism. But the conservative attacks are purposeful, designed to intimidate the media into keeping out dissident voices altogether[1] and moving the system toward a desired 100 percent con-

1. Given their position as established, brand name authorities, whose appearance will

formity. As Murray B. Levin points out in his *Political Hysteria in America* "A near unanimity of pro-conspiratorial communications may be a necessary precondition for the successful creation of a myth."[2]

Another important factor that causes the conservatives to attack the media is that they are themselves in the disinformation business. They all, of course, make periodic, usually brief, genuflections to Western Freedom, but their enthusiasm for the *practice* of political freedom is less evident.[3] This may be why they skirt so easily around the political crimes of rightwing states like Turkey and South Africa. Many conservatives contend that we are fighting a holy war against an enemy that has no scruple. We are at a disadvantage because of our tradition of honesty, etc. Fortunately, we have people like Henry Kissinger, Zbigniew Brzezinski, Robert Moss, Ray Cline, and a few thousand others who are prepared to overlook our tradition of honesty in the face of the challenge to our National Security. In short, they will lie without scruple and create and/or disseminate fabrications, but they will call it "news management."[4] Fred Landis argues persuasively that the recent spurt in rightwing attention to alleged Soviet disinformation and Soviet moles was closely related to the new surge of disinformation by the very individuals levying the charges:[5]

Because this group planned to use the technique of disinformation within the

not be protested by Accuracy in Media or the State Department, Sterling and Henze have been able to exclude contesting views from the media. An official of one TV network informed us that both Sterling and Henze refuse to appear on network programs with critics, insisting on a de facto exercise of veto power over participants. Only once in the years 1982-85 was a dissident voice on the Bulgarian Connection heard on national TV. On that occasion, when Claire Sterling was confronted by Alexander Cockburn, we are informed by network personnel that Sterling had vetoed participation by the present writers and Michael Dobbs of the *Washington Post*. When she appeared at the station and found that Cockburn was also to be on the program, she was outraged, and only at the last moment was persuaded not to walk out of the studio. See note 65 below on Henze's even more comprehensive prior restraints on media programming.

2. (New York: Basic Books, 1971), p. 118.
3. The same is true of their leader. See, *e.g.*, Walter Karp, "Liberty Under Siege: The Reagan Administration's Taste for Autocracy," *Harper's*, November 1985.
4. According to Arnaud de Borchgrave, Free World spokespersons never produce "disinformation," they only engage in "management of the news." See Fred Clarkson and Louis Wolf, "Arnaud de Borchgrave Boards Moon's Ship," *CovertAction Information Bulletin*, No. 24 (Summer 1985), p. 35.
5. "Spies and the Reagan Victory: 'The October 22 Movement,' " *CovertAction Information Bulletin*, Number 12 (April 1981), p. 36.

U.S. and because they realized that it would be used on such a scale as to raise questions among thoughtful observers, they raised the issue in advance themselves.

The best defense is a good offense. And if the U.S. disinformationists are able to command extensive and respectful attention in the mass media, they can kill two birds with one stone: disseminate their own disinformation, and protect themselves from serious criticism by threatening the media with accusations of being Soviet stooges in reporting any dissenting fact or opinion.

Claire Sterling, Paul Henze, and Michael Ledeen were the principal exponents of the Bulgarian Connection in the United States in the years 1982-85. It is our belief that they were important participants in the *creation* of the Connection, as well as its leading disseminators. The accounts which follow will show that they are disinformationists in the literal sense of the term.[6] We will describe more fully in Chapter 7 their dominance over the media's portrayal of the Bulgarian Connection.

Claire Sterling: Terrorism Pseudoscholar

For many years a journalist in Europe for the *Reporter* and other magazines, with the publication of *The Terror Network* in 1981, Claire Sterling became the leading publicist of the alleged Soviet-backed campaign of international terrorism. This work, which was immediately adopted as a fundamental text by the incoming Reagan administration, established Sterling's credentials in the eyes of the western media. *The Terror Network*, along with her more recent study of the papal assassination plot, *The Time of the Assassins*, and her frequent articles in the *New York Times* and *Wall Street Journal*, can be analyzed as primary materials in the study of the pseudoscience of terrorism.

This pseudoscience is illustrated by the infamous Lusk Report, a product of a post-World War I investigation by the New York state legislature which found a Red under every bed. Murray B. Levin describes

6. Disinformationists are those who originate and/or dispense disinformation. "Disinformation is an intelligence word which describes the covert attempt to manipulate the informational environment of a selected target group by such actions as planted stories, selective leaks, rumors, forged documents—all orchestrated toward a particular theme. . . . " *Ibid.*, p. 35.

the methodology of this Red Scare classic as follows:[7]

The data is presented without any effort—serious or otherwise—to evaluate its validity or relevance. Generalizations and conclusions, unsupported by data, are sprinkled throughout. . . . The pseudoscholar proceeds to laboriously accumulate vast numbers of "details" and documents. . . . Some of the details and documents refer to facts. Some of the details are fiction. Nothing remains unexplained. . . . The authors of the various parts of the report cite each other's analysis as authoritative.[8] Documents are taken at face value, regardless of their source or the context within which they originally were presented. . . . Simultaneity is taken as proof of cause and effect. . . . Possibilities are invested into certainties. Following the presentation of endless details, the conclusion is "inevitable." . . . [V]ast historical forces are assumed to be set in motion by the mere will of a few monstrously evil but brilliant men. They pull puppet strings and duped and compliant millions act out their will.

The qualities of the "pseudoscholar" are on full display in Sterling's writings on terrorism in general, and on the Bulgarian Connection in particular. We detail some of these qualities in the balance of this section.

Manicheanism: Us versus them, good versus evil. Terrorism pseudoscholars are committed ideologues who divide the world into people, movements, and states that are good and those that are evil. The former, which usually coincides with the analyst's fellow citizenry, country, leadership, and clients, are generous and kind, but also bumbling and insufficiently alert to the need to be harsh with the forces of darkness. The forces of evil are cruel, insidiously clever, and constantly plotting the downfall of the forces of decency.

In the case of the plot to assassinate the Pope, Sterling is convinced of Bulgarian-KGB guilt because this is just the kind of thing that the forces of darkness do. The truth flows so easily from fundamental preconceptions of good and evil that evidence is really required only for public relations service. With or without evidence, *one must choose.* For example, Sterling says that in "choosing sides" one must take one or the other "on trust: the Italian judiciary or Bulgaria's Communist establishment."[9] At the point when Sterling wrote these lines in 1983, the "Ital-

7. *Op. cit.*, n. 2, pp. 122-26.
8. See the discussion of the "echo chamber effect" in Chapter 7 under "The Intellectuals: Somnolence and Complicity."
9. *The Time of the Assassins* (New York: Holt, Rinehart and Winston, 1983), p. 163.

ian judiciary" had not "chosen." Antonov was being held for an investigation, but the investigating magistrate had not yet given an opinion, and of course a trial had not been held. For a terrorism pseudoscholar, however, the choice *precedes* careful investigation and a legitimate judicial finding. For the Sterlings of the 1920s, Sacco and Vanzetti were guilty before the trial because they were on the wrong side and one had to "choose."

Apologetics and coverup for rightwing terror. Sterling is a committed rightist. In *The Terror Network* she provides systematic apologetics for rightwing dictatorships, whose intelligence services are an important direct and indirect source for her claims about terrorism. She does not use the word "terrorism" to describe the torture and murder of political dissidents by the Chilean, Argentinean, and South African police, and she applies no indignant and sarcastic words to their actions. Even when their operations fit the category of "international terrorism" very literally, such as in their cross-border assassinations[10] and preventive invasions,[11] they fail to arouse her ire.

Her apologetics for military dictatorships take two forms. First, she repeatedly suggests that military takeovers were a consequence of leftwing terrorist provocations.[12] This is a complete fabrication for the important cases of Chile and Brazil, and is a misleading half truth for others. Her second mode of apologetics is to suppress the facts about what her favored military dictatorships *do*. Even if they were "provoked" into taking control of the state, how much killing, torture, and dismantling of democratic institutions followed? Sterling carefully averts her eyes,[13] as details on state terror would weaken the force of her attempt to make rebel movements the exclusive "terrorists."

10. Under "Operation Condor" in the 1970s the security forces of Argentina, Brazil, Chile, Paraguay, and Uruguay apprehended and murdered hundreds of dissidents by a collective monitoring and assassination system across borders. See Edward S. Herman, *The Real Terror Network: Terrorism in Fact and Propaganda* (Boston: South End Press, 1982), pp. 69-73. Sterling has never discussed this terrorist enterprise.

11. See Richard Leonard, *South Africa At War* (Westport, Conn.: Lawrence Hill, 1973); Sean Gervasi, "Secret Collaboration: U.S. and South Africa Foment Terrorist Wars," *CovertAction Information Bulletin*, No. 22 (Fall 1984), pp. 36-40.

12. In *The Terror Network* (New York: Holt, Rinehart and Winston, 1981), Sterling states that "the wall of police states" in Latin America in the mid-1970s was "largely of the terrorists' own making" (p. 110).

13. She says in *The Terror Network* that rightwing terrorism has big plans and is "well worth a book on its own" (p. 111), but she has not embarked on this book as yet.

Sterling's identification with the state terrorists is illustrated by her contrasting personal reactions to rebels and western officials in the killing business. She reports in *The Terror Network* that at one time she found herself on a plane with a rebel terrorist who had been trained in Havana, and "I was too frozen with fear to open my mouth."[14] On the other hand, Sterling frequently cites conversations with representatives of the secret police of the Free World, who kill as ruthlessly and at least as frequently as her rebel, but she never mentions the slightest trepidation or lack of sympathy. In fact, she tells us that:[15]

One of my more memorable conversations in France was with a personage of vast charm and qualified experience who assured me that he would brand me a compulsive liar if I quoted him. If, now and then, I should notice a small news item about a body washed up on a beach, he said, it might well be that of some trained and unregenerate professional terrorist, sent on "a long, long voyage— very long, madame," in the interests of preserving public order.

This was a "gentleman" of the Free World speaking to her, not a "terrorist."

Sterling's *The Terror Network* is a running attack on liberation movements in the Third World. She doesn't discuss how the West sustains the conditions giving rise to them nor how it arms the military services and death squads designed to keep the Third World majorities in their place. Instead, she stresses the frequency with which these liberation movements allegedly fall into the hands of leftists who are tools of Moscow or one of its surrogates. Sterling demonstrates in *The Terror Network* how it is possible for a rightwing journalist, by carefully ignoring the massive violence and oppression of the terrorist *states*, and by confining her attention to rebel violence and alleged rebel links (via arms supply and training) to radical states, to make the terrorist states and their allies look like victims, and the true victims look like baddies, wittingly or unwittingly part of a plot to "destabilize Western Democracy"!

It is interesting to see how Sterling deals with South Africa. She is careful not to smear the South African liberation movements directly and openly as terrorist, or to characterize the apartheid regime as fighting terrorism. But she does this indirectly. At no point does she discuss South African state terrorism against its black majority or its invasions

14. *Ibid.*, p. 248.
15. *Ibid.*, p. 68.

and subversive acts against its neighbors. Instead she focuses exclusively on alleged South African rebel ties to an external Red Network. Thus the implicit smear process contains the following sequence: Some rebels get some arms and training from the Soviet Union and its surrogates; the Soviets aim to destabilize the "democracies"; all the recipients of Soviet largesse are agents of a Communist Combat army;[16] therefore, all of these liberation movements are tainted as elements of the master conspiracy.

In *The Terror Network* Sterling brings in South Africa very cautiously, in a chapter on Henri Curiel, a Paris-based activist and supporter of Third World liberation movements, whom she tries to make out to be a KGB agent. (On her loss of a slander suit in Paris based on this accusation, see below.) In the course of that chapter she writes that all the Palestinian terrorists could count on Curiel's support, and "so could the front-line guerrilla forces of southern Africa, regularly supplied by Solidarité [one of Curiel's organizations] with funds and clandestine equipment."[17] Elsewhere in the same chapter she discusses the case of the South African poet Breyton Breytenbach, who set up a printing plant for the South African underground "and was soon arrested under the antiterrorist laws."[18] (We may note in passing that Sterling doesn't use quote marks, comment, or provide a word of sarcasm on this usage—as she would perhaps if the Polish government arrested an underground Solidarity worker under "antiterrorism laws.") She goes on to say that just as an international campaign of appeal for Breytenbach was getting under way, he pleaded guilty. She doesn't say what he pleaded guilty to, but implies that this was meaningful, proving something like real guilt. She states that he later suggested to his brother that he had been "manipulated" in Paris; in Sterling's words, "Gradually the conviction grew on Breytenbach that Solidarité fronted for a deep underground apparatus providing technical services to international terrorist groups."[19] Sterling gives no source for this information, very possibly provided her by the South African police. We may note also her seeming naiveté on the "growing conviction" which apparently came upon Breytenbach in a South African prison. Although it is well publicized that "terrorists" are regularly tortured in South African prisons, Sterling takes Breytenbach's alleged reconsiderations at face value.

16. *Ibid.*, p. 16. See the subsection on The Conspiratorial Imperative, below.
17. *Ibid.*, p. 54.
18. *Ibid.*, p. 51.
19. *Ibid.*, p. 54.

At the time Sterling wrote on Breytenbach's admission of guilt there was already in print an account of Breytenbach's trial in an Introduction by André Brink to a translation of Breytenbach's *A Season in Paradise*,[20] which reads as follows:

> After more than two months in detention he was brought to court on eleven charges of what, in South Africa, passes for "terrorism." Many of the charges were patently ridiculous, and the fact that all the persons charged with Breytenbach were subsequently allowed to go scot-free seemed to corroborate this impression. However, Breytenbach's interrogators had succeeded, during his months of solitary confinement and constant interrogation, in convincing him that he might well qualify for the death sentence should he try to contest the charges in court. Consequently an arrangement was made whereby some of the more far-fetched charges were dropped, in return for a plea of guilty to all the others. The plea was accepted, with the result that a minimum of witnesses were called.

Brink goes on to point out that in spite of this plea, Breytenbach got a nine-year sentence, that all appeal was refused, and that the documents in the case miraculously disappeared. Breytenbach himself, in a 1983 autobiography, also contradicts Sterling in both letter and in spirit. His work is a crushing indictment of the South African system, which "is against the grain of everything that is beautiful and hopeful and dignified in human history. . . ."[21] Curiel, on the other hand, is one of Breytenbach's heroes, "an inspiring man: a limpid ideologue, and a man who remained committed to the better instincts in mankind."[22] Speaking of George Suffert, the journalist who, based on intelligence leaks and forgeries, first attacked Curiel in print as a KGB agent, and on whom Sterling relies heavily, Breytenbach calls him a "cowardly French journalist . . . the mouthpiece of the South African masters."[23] And on his trial and confession, Breytenbach says that given "the atmosphere of terror created by the powerful political police" his lawyers felt obliged to tread very lightly. Of his short statement read to the court in these circumstances, he says: "Read it—you will also hear the insidi-

20. (New York: Persea Books, 1980), pp. 10-11.
21. *The True Confessions of an Albino Terrorist* (New York: Farrar Straus Giroux, 1983), p. 73.
22. *Ibid.*, p. 89.
23. *Ibid.*, p. 51. Suffert had on the top of his list of "terrorist" organizations the African National Congress, which suggests that the South African secret police may have had a hand in assisting Suffert's "researches" (and indirectly, Claire Sterling's work).

ous voice of the controller in it."[24]

The main point, however, is that in her not very subtle way Claire Sterling succeeds in tarnishing South Africa's liberation movements by tying them to the KGB—with no solid facts, no numbers, no evidence that these ties, if they existed at all, were not marginal, and by relying heavily on South African police interrogations for evidence. Focusing on local South African conditions would suggest that the African National Congress is fighting a ferociously terroristic and antidemocratic regime in a thoroughly just cause. Sterling never allows such considerations to surface—South Africa is part of the Free World, and she displays throughout her work a solidarity with it, its leaders, its secret police, and other similar terror regimes.

All disagreements with her views are enemy propaganda and often traceable to the Kremlin. Just as the world of states is divided into blocs, so is the world of ideas. In criticizing Michael Dobbs of the *Washington Post*, for example, Sterling asserts that Dobbs's statements lend "considerable credence to the Bulgarian argument."[25] This is taken as sufficient to invalidate Dobbs's argument. It also implies as a matter of course that the Bulgarian contentions are incorrect. Sterling never for a moment allows that she could be wrong.

In a speech on disinformation given in Paris on December 5, 1984,[26] Sterling attacked the effort of Italian newspapers to link what we call "second conspiracy"—the framing of the Bulgarians—to Ledeen, Pazienza, and the U.S. and Italian secret services. She does this, not by offering evidence, but by claiming to have traced the source of these allegations to a Communist paper in Italy and a Communist disinformation campaign. She does not give any *evidence* that these were the sources, or that the alleged disinformation campaign had any success, but she uses these assertions—essentially smears by association—to discredit an alternative line of thought.[27]

24. *Ibid.*, p. 63.
25. Claire Sterling, "The Attack on the Pope: There's More to the Story," *Washington Post*, August 7, 1984.
26. This speech was given at a conference on disinformation sponsored by Internationale de la Resistance, a coalition of rightwing resistance/"liberation" organizations and related support networks from Europe and the United States. John Barron of *Reader's Digest* and Arnaud de Borchgrave, an Adjunct Fellow of the Georgetown Center for Strategic and International Studies, were also in attendance. We are citing an offprint put out by the sponsoring organization.
27. Henze works the same way. In *The Plot to Kill the Pope* he spends a great deal of

Uncritical use of disinformation sources. One of the main weapons of
terrorism pseudoscience is the use of convenient facts from intelligence
agencies and defectors (the latter often themselves creatures of the intelligence agencies). Sometimes this is done knowingly—"planned gullibility"—but it is often a reflection of the loss of critical capacity in the
search for proof of that which the pseudoscientist knows by instinct.

It is well established that all intelligence agencies will forge and plant
documents and lie where useful and practicable, so that from at least *one*
of them it is possible to obtain any desired "fact." Intelligence agencies
also operate in an environment in which political "crazies" can survive
and even flourish. For example, James Angleton, long-time CIA chief
of counterintelligence, was firmly convinced that the apparent Chinese-
Soviet hostility after 1959 was a conspiratorial deception to lull the
West into a false sense of security.[28] What theory of Red Conspiracy
would not be sincerely believed by some intelligence source and thus be
confirmable for a Claire Sterling?

In his book *Deadly Deceits*, former CIA officer Ralph McGehee
states that the CIA has "lied continually," and that "Disinformation is
a large part of its covert action responsibility, and the American people
are the primary target of its lies."[29] Philip Agee's *Inside the Company*
provides dozens of examples of CIA sponsorship of violence, forging of
documents, and planting of fabricated stories with conduit journalists,

space on Soviet-Bulgarian responses to accusations of their involvement in the assassination attempt. Most of this is a venomous caricature, providing a straw man enabling
Henze to attack weak arguments. More important, it also allows him to identify criticism
of the Connection with the Enemy. In an article "From Azeff to Agca," in *Survey, a
Journal of East and West Studies*, Autumn-Winter 1983, for example, he dismisses the
present writers as Soviet apologists, based on their article critical of the Bulgarian Connection. No evidence was given that they relied on Soviet sources or arguments, or that
they have any ties to the Soviets. It is enough for Henze that their article contested the
Connection.

In the same article Henze refers to the Turkish journalist Ugur Mumcu as "well known
as a purveyor of Soviet disinformation in Turkey." Mumcu, in fact, has been highly critical of alleged Bulgarian involvement in the Turkish drug traffic, and he has rejected Andronov's (Soviet) thesis that the CIA is behind the assassination attempt on the Pope. For
the former CIA station chief in Turkey to be calling *anybody* else, let alone Mumcu, a disinformationist is audacious, as we will discuss in the next section.

28. See Thomas Powers, *The Man Who Kept the Secrets* (New York: Knopf, 1979), pp.
63, 289, 350.

29. Ralph McGehee, *Deadly Deceits: My 25 Years in the CIA* (New York: Sheridan
Square Publications, 1982), p. 192.

often for the purpose of demonstrating *Cuban* dirty tricks.[30] E.
Howard Hunt, a long-time CIA agent working with the Nixon "plumbers,"
even forged a document, with CIA knowledge and logistical support, in
a 1971 effort to embarrass Senator Edward Kennedy by publicly implicating John F. Kennedy in the assassination of Ngo Dinh Diem of
South Vietnam.[31] If CIA operatives will lie to discredit a U.S.
president for political purposes, of what would they be capable regarding foreign
enemies?

Although disinformation is one of her favorite words, to our knowledge Claire Sterling has never admitted that there is such a thing as
western disinformation. In her Paris speech on disinformation, she asserts with disdain that a Soviet author on the Bulgarian Connection,
Iona Andronov, "is a colonel of the KGB attached for the duration of
the Papal plot to the *Literaturnaya Gazeta.* . . ."[32] The implication is
that, as a KGB officer, Andronov could hardly be taken seriously as a
purveyor of information. Whatever the truth of her contention about Andronov's KGB affiliation, it is noteworthy that Paul Henze is not contaminated in her eyes by *his* extensive intelligence career. In the Mani-
chean world of Sterling and her associates, the intelligence agencies on
our side do not lie, forge documents, or engage in disinformation strategies; only those on the enemy side do these things. Whether this is deliberate suppression of known fact or the self-deception of the true be-
liever, it makes Sterling a superb instrument of propaganda.

Claire Sterling has long used, and served as a conduit for, the Free
World's intelligence agencies. In *The Terror Network*, she has 37 citations directly to intelligence sources, 31 of them anonymous, with still
larger numbers of references to individuals and works that themselves
depend heavily on intelligence sources (Brian Crozier, Robert Moss,

30. Philip Agee, *Inside the Company: CIA Diary* (New York: Stonehill, 1975), pp.
145-46, 279-81, 283-87, 292-95, 453-57, 468-69, 471-72. And see Warner Poelchau,
ed., *White Paper Whitewash: Philip Agee on the CIA and El Salvador* (New York: Deep
Cover Publications, 1981), pp. 28-41.

31. E. Howard Hunt, *Undercover* (New York: Putnam, 1974), pp. 178-81. And see
Powers, *op. cit.*, n. 28, pp. 254-55; Poelchau, ed., *op. cit.*, n. 30, p. 38.

32. *Op. cit.*, n. 26. Andronov vigorously denies the charge, with considerable logic.
Sterling was apparently unaware that he had been, quite openly, the *Literaturnaya Gazeta*
correspondent in the United States from 1972 to 1978, or that his work has appeared regu-
larly in that newspaper for more than 15 years. Moreover, in 1985 he returned to New
York to resume his foreign correspondent's work in this country, with the consent of the
United States government. If anyone other than Claire Sterling thought he was a nefarious
KGB colonel, is it likely he would have received such permission?

John Barron).[33] Conor Cruise O'Brien observes in his review of *The Terror Network* that Sterling "consistently assumes that anything she is told by her western intelligence sources must be true. Her copious but naive footnotes often refer to unnamed intelligence sources, whose veracity she simply takes for granted."[34]

In her use of Italian intelligence sources, Sterling quotes frequently from reports of SISMI, an intelligence agency run for a number of years by General Santovito, a member of P-2 and a sponsor of Francesco Pazienza. P-2, as we have seen, was an illegal rightwing conspiracy that heavily infiltrated the Italian intelligence, police, and army and whose members were involved earlier in major disinformation efforts, including the forging and planting of documents.[35] Sterling always quotes a SISMI statement as authoritative fact, never as one from a potential disinformation source. Nowhere in *The Terror Network*, nor in *The Time of the Assassins*, does she so much as mention P-2 or the "strategy of tension" pursued for many years by Italy's right wing, including elements of the security services. This non-discussion is essential to preserving the appearance of authenticity and integrity of handouts from SISMI.

As we noted earlier, in *The Terror Network* Sterling also passed on the claims of unidentified "intelligence sources" that Henri Curiel was a KGB agent. Sterling's comrade-in-disinformation, Arnaud de Borchgrave, asserted that it was an "open secret" in the intelligence world that Curiel was a KGB agent.[36] As Curiel had already been murdered by unknown assailants, his family and several associates sued Sterling for slander in the French courts. French secret police documents provided

33. Philip Paull, *International Terrorism: The Propaganda War*, M.A. Thesis in International Relations, San Francisco State University, June 1982, p. 73.

34. "The Roots of Terrorism," *New Republic*, July 25, 1981. When her sources say something convenient to her argument, Sterling's gullibility shows no limits. O'Brien gives an excellent illustration in his review in discussing Sterling's treatment of the Irish Provos. An even more spectacular example was her swallowing without blinking the "Tucuman Plan," supposedly prepared "under KGB supervision" in Argentina's Tucuman province in May 1975, and calling for the mobilization of 1,500 Latin American "terrorists" to be sent to Europe for an orchestrated destabilization effort. For a detailed discussion of this and other illustrations of her use of intelligence disinformation, see Diana Johnstone, "Disinformation: The 'fright story' of Claire Sterling's tales of terrorism," *In These Times*, May 20-26, 1981.

35. See Chapter 4, pp. 81-99

36. See the letter to George Suffert by de Borchgrave, reproduced in Frank Brodhead and Edward S. Herman, "The KGB Plot to Assassinate the Pope: A Case Study in Free World Disinformation," *CovertAction Information Bulletin*, No. 19 (Spring-Summer 1983), p. 15.

in connection with this judicial proceeding showed no evidence what-soever of Curiel having a KGB connection. Thus, in this rare event where the cover of "confidential sources" was lifted by legal process, the western intelligence service closest to Curiel's activities revealed de Borchgrave and Sterling to be playing a disinformation role, perhaps serving as a conduit for the same intelligence service that organized Curiel's murder. Sterling lost one of the slander suits and was assessed a fine; another she slipped out of on legal technicalities and by the court's acceptance of her claim that she had not accused Curiel of being a KGB agent, but was merely presenting a "hypothesis."[37] The Curiel trials, which bear so clearly on Sterling's credibility, were reported upon only in the back pages of the *Washington Post*, and were unmentioned in the *New York Times*, *Time*, or *Newsweek*, or on the TV networks.[38]

Defectors are also a prime source of information for Sterling. The use and abuse of defector evidence is discussed in more detail in Appendix C, but we note here that Sterling's *The Terror Network* rests heavily on the testimony of General Jan Sejna, a Czech defector of 1968, who, ac-cording to Sterling, had defected "a jump ahead of the invading Soviet army" during the Czech Spring.[39] This is a fabrication—Sejna was an old Stalinist who defected in the *middle* of the Czech Spring,[40] long be-fore the invasion, and in the midst of a corruption scandal in which Sejna was a principal.[41] Sejna was so forthcoming in his debriefings that the CIA finally decided to test his veracity by forging a document with elaborate but phony details on Soviet sponsorship of terrorism. Sejna immediately claimed the document to be authentic—it was one that had just slipped his mind![42] Ten years later, Michael Ledeen got Sejna to re-

37. See Jonathan Randal, "French Socialists Seek to Solve Slaying of Alleged Master Spy," *Washington Post*, August 19, 1981, and "Court in Paris Fines Author of Terrorism Book," *Washington Post*, March 30, 1982. Sterling made no effort in the Paris trial to prove the *truth* of her case by innuendo—she and her publisher used her reliance on the methodology of terrorism pseudoscience to disclaim having said anything definite.

38. In connection with the Curiel cases, Sterling was given unusual assistance by the CIA in aid of her defense against accusations of slander. See note 63 below.

39. *Op. cit.*, n. 12, p. 290.

40. According to Leslie Gelb, "The defector, Major Gen. Jan Sejna, was said to have been closely associated with Antonin Novotny, the Stalinist party leader of Czecho-slovakia. The General fled to the United States in early 1968 after Mr. Novotny had been replaced by Alexander Dubcek, the leader of the short-lived liberalization period." "Soviet-Terror Ties Called Outdated," *New York Times*, October 18, 1981.

41. See Diana Johnstone, "The 'fright story' of Claire Sterling's tales of terrorism," *In These Times*, May 20-26, 1981.

42. Lars-Erik Nelson, "The deep terror plot: a thickening of silence," *New York Daily*

peat this scenario, and *this evidence constitutes the heart of Sterling's proof of a Soviet terror network!*[43] This should have discredited Sterling completely and permanently, but she is under mass media protection for valuable services rendered and it appears that no fabrication or lunacy (see below under The Conspiratorial Imperative) can render her less than an authentic expert.

The manipulation of evidence. Sterling's misuse of evidence assumes many forms. One is to twist words to alter meanings. In *The Terror Network*, for example, Sterling purports to quote directly from a CIA report:[44]

"Warsaw Pact members' assistance to terrorists originates in Pankow (East Germany) and Prague," said the CIA in "International and Transnational Terrorism," April 1976, p. 21 of the CIA's Annual Report.

What the CIA report actually says is: "In any event, the only hard evidence of Warsaw Pact member assistance to individuals associated with the Baader-Meinhof Gang points to Pankow and Prague." Sterling's bogus quote distorts the meaning of the real quote. The CIA report speaks of "the only hard evidence" of assistance to individuals "associated with" a specific terrorist group (as opposed to the more generic and broader-based usage of the word "terrorists"). The original does not say that Warsaw Pact assistance "originates" in Pankow and Prague as Sterling writes, but "points to" Pankow and Prague, a looser connection. If this is what happens to verifiable quotes in Sterling's work, what happens to those quotes which are not verifiable?

Sterling's erroneous citations are numerous. In *The Time of the Assassins*, for example, she says that Bulgaria was responsible for "four-fifths of the arms reaching the Middle East."[45] Her source for this whopper, the *New York Times* of February 9, 1983, actually states that Israeli intelligence authorities attributed to Bulgarian sources four-fifths of the weapons the Israelis had captured from the PLO. As another il-

News, June 24, 1984, p. C14. In 1981, when then Secretary of State Alexander Haig asked the CIA to "produce the kind of evidence that Ms. Sterling had cited in her book . . . the CIA shamefacedly confessed that it was being asked to confirm its own phony document—and Haig had to let the issue drop."

43. See *The Terror Network*, pp. 14, 34, 221, 290-92.

44. *Ibid.*, p. 341.

45. *The Time of the Assassins*, p. 211.

lustration, she states that a SISMI report describes the gun dealer Horst Grillmaier as having "traveled often to Syria, East Germany, and other countries of Eastern Europe."[46] Looking up her reference, the SISMI report in question mentions Grillmaier in passing and does not say a word about his alleged travels to Syria and East Germany.

Another form of manipulation of evidence is her selective use of some facts, her suppression of others, and her simple refusal to discuss conflicting facts. As we discuss below, Sterling attempts to tie the leftwing Minister of the Interior in the Ecevit government, Hasan Fehmi Gunes, to Agca's escape from a Turkish prison in 1979. To show that he was a "leftist" she refers to him as a "Marxist" and mentions that his brother was a radical. The Turkish journalist Ugur Mumcu, who knew Gunes well, says that Gunes never considered himself a Marxist and that the term was not properly applied to him. Mumcu also points out that Gunes had another brother, who was a conservative, whose existence somehow escaped Sterling's notice.[47]

Another illustration of Sterling selectivity and suppression is her handling of Agca's letter in which he expressed his devotion to Türkes, the leader of the fascist Nationalist Action Party of Turkey. She and Henze do not like this letter, as it shows a rightwing political commitment that they consistently try to downplay as they strive to make Agca into a mercenary terrorist without politics. Sterling therefore dismisses the letter as a "laughably clumsy forgery."[48] A problem, however, is that this letter was introduced as evidence in a trial in Ankara by the Turkish military government, usually adequate proof for Sterling of authenticity. This provides considerable insight into Sterling's methods. On the one hand, if we have a "laughably clumsy forgery," what do we conclude about the quality of the Turkish judicial system that admits such a document into evidence? On the other hand, perhaps we should look more closely at the Turkish evidence, which Sterling does not find it convenient to do in this instance. Ugur Mumcu devotes five pages of his book *Agca Dossier* to a detailed account of the Türkes letter. He reports that the Turkish military government went to great pains to analyze its authenticity, putting it through many tests at the police laboratory and hiring an outside consultant from the Department of Graphic Arts at Istanbul University to study the document. The conclusion on all sides was

46. *Ibid.*, p. 34.
47. Ugur Mumcu, *Papa, Mafya, Agca* (Istanbul: Tekin Yayinevi, 1984), p. 205.
48. *The Time of the Assassins*, p. 70.

that the letter was authentic.[49]

Equally interesting, Sterling mentions that after his arrest for shooting Ipekci, even after a week or so in the hands of the police, Agca appeared in court without the slightest evidence of police maltreatment, which Sterling remarks was "customary under whatever political regime in Turkey."[50] When the military took over in 1980, torture was stepped up and many individuals died under torture. Neither Sterling nor Henze discuss this, nor do they allow it to qualify their faith in evidence from this source. So Sterling mentions police brutality when it serves her convenience (here to suggest that maybe Agca was being protected from on high), but usually ignoring it in reference to a favored police state.

In her *Reader's Digest* article, Sterling traced Agca's gun to the previously mentioned Horst Grillmaier, an Austrian gun merchant who, according to Sterling, had fled behind the Iron Curtain after May 13, 1981, to avoid questioning in the West. It turned out later that Grillmaier was a former Nazi who specialized in supplying rightwing gun-buyers; that he had not disappeared behind the Iron Curtain at all; and that the gun had gone through a number of intermediaries before finally being passed to Agca by a Gray Wolves friend. In the last pre-trial version of Agca's story, the Bulgarians supposedly gave him a package, including his gun, on May 13, 1981. Why would Agca have given up his gun to the Bulgarians, to have them return it to him on May 13? Why would the Bulgarians have had to go through all the transactions with Grillmaier and others to provide Agca with a gun, given their extensive facilities in Rome?

Sterling handles the disintegration of the original Grillmaier line in typical Sterling fashion, by simply shifting to new conspiratorial ground. Thus instead of showing a Bulgarian Connection by Grillmaier's eastern links, she turns things on their head—the sinister Bulgarians had Agca purchase a gun through a known fascist to strengthen the suggestion that Agca was a rightwinger who could not possibly be connected with the Communist powers! The Grillmaier readjustments show well that no matter what happens to facts, the Sterling methodology will yield the prescribed conclusions.

Possibly the most enterprising Sterling innovation in her efforts to rationalize Agca's lies and retractions is her elaboration of a *signaling theory*. According to this theory, if Agca releases evidence on the Bul-

49. Ugur Mumcu, *Agca Dosyasi* (Ankara: Tekin Yayinevi, 1984), pp. 106-10.
50. *The Time of the Assassins*, p. 48.

garian Connection slowly, makes mistakes, or retracts evidence, he is trying to convey a message to his sponsors. He is warning them to do something, or that he will say more. The empirical foundation for this notion was Agca's behavior in the last days of his trial in Turkey for the shooting of Ipekci, in October 1979, when he issued in court an explicit warning, that he had things to tell that some people would regret. Several days later the Gray Wolves heeded his message and he was escorted out of prison. According to Sterling, Agca adopted the same strategy after his imprisonment for shooting the Pope. The most important instance of Agca's alleged signaling in Rome came in June 1983, when a Vatican official's daughter, Emmanuela Orlandi, was abducted. A few days later, on June 28, Agca withdrew key elements of his previous testimony. To this day Sterling claims that by his renunciation Agca was signaling to his Bulgarian sponsors that he wanted to be either exchanged or rescued from prison.[51]

There are many difficulties with the signaling theory as an explanation of Agca's behavior in Rome. For one thing, he delayed his signaling for a very long time. Why? Then when he started to talk, in May 1982, he did so without any known prior signal; *i.e.*, without warning his sponsors of his intentions (as in the Ipekci case). Furthermore, in Rome neither the Gray Wolves nor the Bulgarians would be in a position to spring Agca in a prison break, and the idea that Agca would expect the Bulgarians to bargain for his release is far-fetched. His crime was one for which the Italians would not be likely to engage in political bargaining for a release. Even more important, to bargain the Bulgarians would have to acknowledge openly their own involvement in the plot. On Sterling logic, the Bulgarian-KGB strategy was to establish enough distance from the hired killer to be able to make a case for noninvolvement. Even Agca would realize that any signals to the Bulgarians and Soviets would be fruitless.

There are other problems with Sterling's signaling theory. Why did Agca produce inconsistent signals? While he retracted some of his

51. See the discussion of the Emmanuela Orlandi case in Chapter 2, pp. 33-35. Agca eventually adopted the signaling theory himself. After a particularly bizarre series of accusations and withdrawals while testifying in court, Agca refused to talk for several days. He then told the court that a kidnapping was part of a pre-arranged plan, and that "the Gray Wolves and the Bulgarians kidnapped Emmanuela Orlandi so that I would retract the accusations against them, confuse the trial, and then I was to discredit the western press." ("In New Account Agca Tells of a Fourth Turk at Shooting of John Paul," *New York Times* [AP], July 2, 1985.)

major claims just after the Orlandi kidnapping, he also made wild allegations of KGB and Bulgarian involvement in the assassination attempt at an impromptu press conference on July 8, 1983, just 10 days after his retraction. If he was trying to mend his fences with his would-be liberators on June 28, why would he publicly assail them shortly thereafter? Furthermore, how would his sponsors-rescuers know that he had made his retractions, and, in effect, receive his signals?[52] They were not reported in the press at the time, and were made public only when the Albano Report was leaked a year later.

Thus, the signaling hypothesis is neither plausible nor capable of explaining the actual pattern of confessions, errors, and retractions. The coaching hypothesis fits comfortably. It explains Agca's slow start by the circumstance that initially he had nothing to confess about the Bulgarians. Later on, the pump was primed: Agca was first persuaded and/or coerced to talk, and he was then given the basic data needed to get the Connection rolling. His enlarging "knowledge" came from the press, secret prison briefings, and other connections with the outside, as well as his own fertile imagination and quest for publicity. His retractions were the result of the disclosure of incompatible facts and contradictions that required the overworked slate to be tidied up. As we noted earlier, he mentioned Celenk only after reading a book by Mumcu on the Turkish-Bulgarian smuggling connection in which Celenk's name appeared. He withdrew his claim that his fleeing accomplice at St. Peter's Square on May 13 was the Bulgarian Aivazov only days after western reporters attending a press conference in Sofia were able to witness for themselves (and report) that Aivazov's physical characteristics were totally at odds with those of the individual in the photo. Agca's major retraction of June 1983, acknowledging that he had never met Mrs. Antonov or visited the Antonovs' apartment, followed press accounts of the defense counsel's having obtained substantial evidence that Mrs. Antonov had not been in Rome at the time of Agca's alleged rendezvous.

A key element in Sterling's argument that the Pope plot was controlled by the Soviet Union has always been her account of the events surrounding Agca's escape from a Turkish prison in November 1979. Both in her original *Reader's Digest* article and in her later book she tries hard to tie that escape to a social democratic Minister of the Inte-

---

52. We pointed out in Chapter 2 that the retraction preceded the kidnapper's demand that Agca be released.

rior, Hasan Fehmi Gunes, who she implies was complicit in Agca's prison break. Sterling says that "he [Agca] could not have done it without high level help." This is not true. It would seem quite possible to organize an escape if a prisoner has as allies a large number of the prison's guards and officers. And, in fact, the Gray Wolves and NAP were extremely well represented at Agca's prison. According to official accounts, about a dozen members of the Gray Wolves, three of them soldiers, dressed Agca in a military uniform and conducted him through eight security checkpoints to a waiting car. There is no doubt that this was a Gray Wolves operation, and in February 1982 three Gray Wolves conspirators were sentenced to prison by a Turkish martial law court for having helped Agca to escape.

After noting that Gunes was a radical, Sterling points out that at his trial Agca "waited in what appeared to be the expectation of getting sprung," and in mid-October he told the court that he had been offered a deal by Gunes: If he admitted membership in the NAP he would get off. Two weeks later, says Sterling, Agca told the court that "I did not kill Ipekci, but I know who did." He added "that he would reveal the true assassin's name at the court's next sitting. It was an explicit warning to his patrons to get him out," says Sterling, "and that is what they did."

It is clear that Sterling is trying to implicate Gunes—"a radical well to the left of Ecevit"—in Agca's prison break. Her assertion that high level help was necessary, as we have seen, is not convincing. Furthermore, she gives not a shred of evidence that Gunes had any Soviet ties or that he had anything to do with the escape. Finally, she either doesn't know or suppresses the important fact that Agca gave his courtroom speech at the very time when a new conservative government was being formed, after Ecevit's more liberal government had lost its parliamentary majority in mid-October. Thus, Agca's escape was engineered two weeks *after* Gunes had been replaced and a new conservative government—which had been a long-time ally of the Gray Wolves and NAP—had taken office.

The press is being overwhelmed by KGB propaganda. A favorite theme of Sterling and her colleagues is that the press regularly plays into the hands of the enemy. Sterling uses the Bulgarian Connection as an illustration of the successes of KGB disinformation. In her Paris Conference speech, Sterling claimed that disbelief in the Connection was a result of a Soviet-inspired propaganda barrage. She noted that the Soviets sent the 40-page book on the Plot by "KGB Colonel" Iona Andronov to "every important or unimportant journalist, columnist, newspaper commentator, television commentator, editor, of every western newspaper that I know of, in Europe and in the United States." This operation had great effect according to Sterling; disbelief in the Connection has become "the accepted position, the socially indispensable position. . . . Prodigious effort and one of the world's most expert craftsmanship [sic] had gone into generating such doubts."[53] At no point does she present evidence that Andronov's work was read, or that it influenced anybody in the West. Its theme, that the CIA was behind Agca's assassination attempt, has never been espoused or taken seriously in any mainstream publication in the United States or Western Europe. Andronov's book has been mentioned in the western media solely in derogatory references by Claire Sterling and Paul Henze.

Sterling asserts in *The Time of the Assassins* that if only she had argued for a CIA connection, her message would have been welcome. She portrays herself as a latter-day Joan of Arc, fighting a lonely battle against the forces of the establishment.[54] If only she had taken the easy road and blamed things on the CIA, "my fortune would have been made"—but the indomitable Sterling was blaming it on the KGB, and this message was very hard for the American elite to swallow. Despite the lunatic quality of this assertion, no establishment book review or article has ever noted the contradiction between Sterling's claims that she has been rejected by the U.S. political and media elite because of their détente-induced bias, and her obvious commercial and journalistic successes.

Sterling's vision of the media stands the truth on its head. Western propaganda sources are vastly more powerful and believable in the West than Soviet sources, as exemplified by former CIA propaganda officer Henze's role and authority and alleged KGB officer Andronov's effective nonexistence. Sterling and Henze *are* propaganda sources, or operate in close collusion with them, and they have full access to the mass media. Furthermore, there is a will-to-believe in the villainy of the

53. *The Time of the Assassins*, p. 141.

54. Of course, she did have the benefit of generous funding from the Reader's Digest Association, and the built-in audience of many millions that it commands. Sterling herself notes in *The Time of the Assassins* that "It isn't every day that a reporter gets an offer like the one I had from *Reader's Digest*: take as long as you like . . . " (p. 4). She gives specific numbers for the cost of the ABC 20/20 program of May 13, 1983, which raised doubts about the Bulgarian Connection. In contrast, she never provides dollar figures for her own expenses or those of the NBC programs with which she was affiliated and which peddled her line.

enemy in *every* country. In the case of the Bulgarian Connection this has helped to overcome doubts that might arise from the absence of evidence and the implausible and shifting scenarios dispensed by Agca. It is in such a world that a Claire Sterling can thrive.

The conspiratorial imperative. Another essential feature of terrorism pseudoscience is the elaboration of leftwing conspiracies. In *The Terror Network* the great conspiracy is of course the Soviet Union's attempt to destabilize the western democracies by aiding assorted dissidents and rebels. Sterling makes the blanket statement that all of these aided parties "come to see themselves as elite battalions in a worldwide Army of Communist Combat."[55] Terrorists aid one another and act as if unified. Killed terrorists "are unfailingly replaced," and defeats lead to changes in "pressure points," suggestive of a central planning body.

She also says that there is "nothing random in this concentrated assault," noting that the Red Brigades, "who like to think that they speak for many or most of their kind . . . have even published a terror timetable."[56] Sterling doesn't tell us how she knows what the Red Brigades like to think, but the truly Sterlingesque trick here is her use of this phony Red Brigade spokesmanship and timetable to establish nonrandomness, to suggest that the Red Brigades really *do* speak for all recipients of Soviet aid and that they all have a timetable!

What is the proof that the Soviets aim to destabilize western democracies? Sterling has nothing in the way of evidence except a few stale assertions of defectors. Her claim is an ideological premise of terrorism pseudoscience. Would destabilization of the West benefit the Soviet Union? For Sterling the answer is obvious and she doesn't discuss it. And her proofs of Soviet sponsorship of destabilizing terror, by selective illustration, all disintegrate upon close inspection.

She tries hard, for example, to tie the KGB to the Italian Red Brigades, and to their assassination of former Italian Prime Minister Aldo Moro. But Moro was murdered precisely because of his role in en-

---

55. *The Terror Network*, p. 16. Sterling later contradicts herself, noting that "Not all those who took the Cubans and Russians up on their aid offer were for sale, or even for rent. Many have proven to be a headache to their former benefactors." This suggests that some unknown but possibly very large fraction of those aided did not see themselves as a part of the "Army of Communist Combat," and that the Soviets didn't "control" the terror network. Sterling even concedes at various points that there is no central direction, only "links," and arms sales (pp. 10, 16). But these contradictions don't interfere with reiteration of her incompatible generalization.

56. *Ibid.*, p. 7.

gineering the "Historic Compromise," that sought to bring the Communist Party into a greater role in governing Italy. The Red Brigades fought violently against the Italian Communist Party, and the Communist Party was the strongest proponent of a policy of harsh repression against the Red Brigades. The murder of Aldo Moro was a major setback for the Communist Party and for détente. Was it in the interest of the Soviet Union to weaken the Italian Communist Party and détente? Is it not curious that killing Aldo Moro was a key element in a *rightwing* coup plan (Plan Solo) of 1964?[57] If the Red Brigades are an instrument of Soviet policy, is the Italian Communist Party not only independent of the Soviet Union but its actual enemy? Sterling never addresses any of these questions.

Sterling and Henze claim, without presenting any evidence, that the Soviet Union was pouring resources into Turkey to "destabilize" that country in the 1970s. Again, given the power of Turkey's military establishment, wasn't this foolish, likely to produce a military coup dominated by anti-Soviet forces? Furthermore, the terrorist acts themselves were in the majority *rightwing* attacks and murders, largely against leftist forces or areas. How would sponsoring rightwing terror help the Soviet Union? Sterling never tells us. She notes in *The Terror Network* that the military takeover of 1980 was "hardly in a manner living up to Soviet expectations."[58] It never occurs to Sterling that her understanding of Soviet expectations might be wrong and that the Soviet destabilization hypothesis, so conspicuously irrational and contrary to Soviet interests, might also be in error.

Sterling argues that the Soviet motive for shooting the Pope was to stop the Solidarity movement. Apart from its other deficiencies of logic and evidence,[59] this argument fails because shooting the Pope could not reasonably have been expected to stop the Solidarity movement. Furthermore, the risks involved in such an action would be very great, including the high probability that the shooting would be attributed to the Soviet Bloc. In their rational self-interest Soviet officials would have anticipated this and avoided any such risky and exceptionally stupid ventures.[60]

57. See Chapter 4, p. 79.
58. *The Terror Network*, p. 245.
59. See Chapter 2, pp. 14-15.
60. In Sterling's version of her interview with former Turkish Interior Minister Gunes, he made the point that, given the predictable results of an assassination attempt—that is, ready accusations and blame accruing to the Soviets—it would be a plausible *rightwing*

The most remarkable conspiracy doctrine in Sterling's works is her contention that the truth of the Bulgarian Connection has had to penetrate a longstanding "western intelligence shield" protecting the Soviet Union, which for many years has been concealing from public view the truth about Soviet terrorism.[61] The reason for the establishment coverup is that the truth was too shocking and would disturb international equilibrium and détente.

These contentions are crackpot nonsense. In order to facilitate its rearmament program and to help place new missiles in Europe, from 1981 onward the Reagan administration desperately sought means of portraying the Soviet Union as the Evil Empire. The Bulgarian Connection was exceptionally helpful in achieving that objective. If the absurd notion that Reagan seeks to protect détente failed to dent Sterling's credibility in the United States, it is a testimonial to the establishment's tolerance of congenial and serviceable propaganda.

What are we to make of the expressions of doubts about the Bulgarian Connection by the CIA and other government officials, and their refusal to embark on a massive propaganda campaign? One reason for their caution is that many officials probably knew that the Connection was a creation of Sterling, Henze, and the Italian secret services, and was thus unsustainable in the long run. The wise strategy, therefore, was to allow and encourage Sterling and her propaganda cohorts to milk the Plot for all it was worth, while the Reagan administration remained publicly uncommitted and ambivalent. This would permit a great deal of publicity, some even generated by debates between the Sterling forces and the ambivalent CIA, while giving the government an emergency exit.

A second reason for U.S. government caution is that it makes the CIA a "moderate" critic in the debates on the truth or falsity of the Connection. With Sterling, Henze, Senator Alfonse D'Amato, and Zbigniew Brzezinski accusing the CIA of dragging its feet, the CIA becomes an anti-establishment truth seeker (which it is not) rather than an instrument of the administration (which it is). Thus the debate on the case can be reasonably restricted to Sterling and company on the right and the CIA on the left.[62]

move, "to provoke a Polish revolt, and pull Poland out of the Warsaw Pact." *The Time of the Assassins*, p. 79. Sterling fails to discuss the point, as usual refusing to consider alternative hypotheses or the weaknesses of her own.

61. Although this point is strewn throughout her *The Time of the Assassins*, it is featured prominently in an exclusive interview with Sterling entitled "Why is the West Covering Up for Agca," *Human Events*, April 21, 1984.

62. See the discussion in Chapter 7 of Robert Toth's article in the *Los Angeles Times* on

A third reason for U.S. government reticence in commenting on the Connection was that the case was still being adjudicated in the Italian courts. For the U.S. government to organize an open press campaign arguing KGB guilt would be a blatant interference with the Italian legal process and would therefore be badly conceived even as a public relations strategy.

A final reason for official U.S. restraint is that the public relations job was being handled very well by the private sector, led by Claire Sterling and her friends. As we will describe in the next chapter, they dominated the media and established the Bulgarian Connection as true for the general public. Further government inputs have been unneeded. We believe that Sterling and her friends are well regarded by the administration and served a key role in propagandizing the case exactly as the administration desired. Sterling's assertions of administration and CIA cowardice are understood to be the crankish outbursts of a very serviceable instrument, who has an important part to play in a common enterprise.[63]

Paul Henze: "Specialist in U.S. Propaganda"

Paul Henze began his long CIA career under Defense Department cover as a "foreign affairs adviser" in 1950. Two years later, he began a six-year hitch as a policy adviser to Radio Free Europe (RFE) in Munich, West Germany.[64] By 1969, Henze was CIA chief of station in Ethiopia,

CIA opinion on the case and the Sterling reaction. This was in fact the lineup of contestants organized on a MacNeil/Lehrer program in January 1983.

63. In spite of her attacks on the CIA for cowardice and footdragging, the CIA entered into an agreement with Sterling to help her out of her legal difficulties in the Curiel case. By a signed agreement of March 24, 1983, the CIA provided Sterling with an Affidavit verifying that the published document "International Terrorism in 1978" from which Sterling had quoted was in fact an official CIA document, and that, going beyond the assertions of the 1978 report, the CIA was prepared to swear that Curiel "headed an apparatus that provided technical support to groups that engaged in terrorist acts." The CIA also agreed to provide Sterling with any documents subsequently released to anybody else on Curiel under the Freedom of Information Act. As Sterling's counsel noted in a letter to Sterling dated March 24, 1978, "That means that you do not have to wait on the Freedom of Information Act line. The Office of General Counsel [of the CIA] will tag your file and respond expeditiously." It is not everybody that gets this kind of expedited and special service from the CIA.

64. In the early 1970s, a time of increased interest in the activities of U.S. intelligence agencies, it was learned that the Munich-based RFE of the 1950s was controlled by the CIA, which managed RFE's Cold War propaganda.

and he served as station chief in Turkey from 1974 through 1977. When Zbigniew Brzezinski assembled his National Security Council team for President Jimmy Carter, Henze was hired as the CIA's representative to the NSC office in the White House. Throughout Henze's determined media campaign to link the Soviet Union to the shooting of the Pope, including his articles in the *Wall Street Journal* and the *Christian Science Monitor*, and in his regular appearances on the MacNeil/Lehrer News Hour, Henze has consistently refused to allow himself to be identified as a former career officer of the CIA.[65] A case in point is the jacket cover of his book, *The Plot to Kill the Pope*, where Henze is described as follows:

Paul Henze spent thirty years in various government and government-related organizations, including Radio Free Europe and U.S. Embassies in Ethiopia and Turkey. During 1977-1980 he was a key member of Zbigniew Brzezinski's National Security Council Staff. Since his retirement from government, Henze has been a free-lance writer, lecturer, and business consultant.

Thus, Henze's readers are not informed that his position in the "U.S. Embassies in Ethiopia and Turkey" was as CIA station chief, and that as "a key member of Zbigniew Brzezinski's National Security Council Staff" he was the CIA liaison to the White House. In addition, even though much of his book is written in the first person narrative style ("The sun had just set, bringing to an end a cool, bright autumn day when I stepped off the bus near the central square of Malatya. . . . I had come to probe Mehmet Ali Agca's background"), there isn't a single word from Henze about his CIA career in Turkey or anywhere else.

Henze and the Board for International Broadcasting (BIB). In May 1980 four members of the Senate Foreign Relations Committee—Frank Church of Idaho, Jacob Javits of New York, Claiborne Pell of Rhode Island, and Charles Percy of Illinois—wrote a letter of protest to President Jimmy Carter concerning certain proposed appointments to the Board

65. We were informed by one TV network producer that as a condition for his participation in a program Henze requires that his long association with the CIA not be mentioned. Another network official told us that Henze, like Sterling (see note 1, above), will not participate in a program where a seriously dissenting view would be expressed. Beyond this, he insists on control over the script, which helps explain why he is never asked embarrassing or penetrating questions (see the analysis of the MacNeil/Lehrer News Hour treatment of the Bulgarian Connection in Chapter 7). The stations, networks, and printed media that go along with these demands are committing serious acts of suppression and deception on the public.

for International Broadcasting (BIB). The BIB was created by Congress in 1973 to oversee the operations of the two U.S. government-operated radio stations based in Munich, West Germany: Radio Free Europe (RFE) and Radio Liberty (RL). The BIB had been organized following disclosures that the CIA was behind the two radio stations. The senators complained that "former intelligence officials are trying to redirect the board away from its oversight role to one more compatible with the two stations' old role as a tool for propaganda."

The former CIA official within the Carter administration "trying to redirect" the BIB was Paul Henze, described by the *New York Times* as "the National Security Council specialist on United States propaganda." Henze had been the policy adviser at RFE when it was controlled by the CIA. The BIB controversy centered around two Henze nominees to fill vacancies on the board. This was an effort, according to the senators, "to make the board more responsible to the National Security Council," *i.e.*, to Henze. One of Henze's nominees, Leo Cherne, reportedly received CIA money in the 1960s. The senators commented in their letter:[66]

We believe that the work of a decade in assuring the professional integrity of RFE/RL would be undone if any of the present members were to be replaced by persons who could even be remotely identified as presently or formerly associated with the CIA or intelligence activities in any capacity.

It is profoundly ironical that Henze's attempt to influence the oversight authority of the BIB was strongly opposed by the senators on the ground that broadcast integrity demanded a severed relationship between news journalism and intelligence officials. In sharp contrast, there has been no audible protest, or even minimal disclosure, as this intelligence figure became a leading mass media source of information on the Bulgarian Connection.

Henze and the Media. Henze was the first prominent American to accuse the Soviets in print of conspiring to shoot Pope John Paul II. His November 1981 article in *Atlantic Community*, in which he made this charge, provided no evidence to show that the Soviets had anything to do with the shooting. For Henze, however, the question of evidence was

66. Quoted by A. O. Sulzberger, Jr., "U.S. Overseas Radio Stirs Dispute Again," *New York Times*, May 15, 1980.

an unpatriotic consideration in discussing hypothetical Soviet crimes:[67]

> The extent to which the Soviet Union has encouraged, underwritten, and insti-
> gated political destabilization is a complex and widely debated question. I be-
> lieve we are past the point where it serves the interests of any party except the
> Soviets to adopt the minimalist, legalistic approach which argues that if there is
> no "documentary evidence" or some other form of incontrovertible proof that
> the Government of the U.S.S.R. is behind something, we must assume that it is
> not.

Although this article played an insignificant role in U.S. media coverage of the investigation into the shooting, it is important because it
openly denies the need for documentation in a case where Henze was
shortly to become a leading source of evidence for the Free World's
media. As Philip Taubman and Leslie Gelb noted in the *New York Times*
shortly after the arrest of Antonov: [68]

> Several former government officials, including Henry A. Kissinger, Secretary
> of State in the Nixon and Ford administrations, and Zbigniew Brzezinski, na-
> tional security advisor to President Carter, have said that they believe that Bul-
> garia and the Soviet Union were involved in the assassination attempt.
>
> Support for this theory has come from Paul Henze, a former CIA station chief
> in Turkey and an aide to Mr. Brzezinski. Mr. Henze, now a consultant to the
> Rand Corporation, was hired by the *Reader's Digest* after the shooting of the
> Pope to investigate Mr. Agca's background.
>
> Mr. Henze's findings, which included information about links between Mr.
> Agca and Bulgaria as well as the Soviet Union's use of Bulgaria as a surrogate
> to spread unrest in Turkey, were incorporated in a *Reader's Digest* article on the
> shooting of the Pope that was written by Claire Sterling and published last Sep-
> tember.
>
> Mr. Henze said he later sold his reports to *NBC-News* and *Newsweek*, which
> have explored possible Bulgarian and Soviet involvement. Mr. Henze made his
> research material available to the *New York Times* for a fee.

In brief, Henze's researches were incorporated into virtually all of the
major mass media pieces which introduced the Bulgarian Connection to
a U.S. mass audience and established the Plot's hegemonic position in
the U.S. media: Claire Sterling's article in the *Reader's Digest* of Sep-

---

67. Paul Henze, "The Long Effort to Destabilize Turkey," *Atlantic Community*,
Winter 1981-1982, p. 468.
68. "U.S. Officials See A Bulgarian 'Link'," *New York Times*, January 27, 1983.

tember 1982; Marvin Kalb's special White Paper broadcasts in September 1982 and January 1983; and the *Newsweek* cover story of January 3, 1983.

Thus, Paul Henze, long-time CIA officer and specialist on propaganda, who had openly denied the need for hard evidence in supporting accusations against the Soviets, was probably the most important individual source of information for the U.S. media in its coverage of the alleged Soviet-Bloc conspiracy. Furthermore, having helped *generate* the Connection, Henze was then used by the media to confirm the truth of the Plot. He was a prime mover in establishing the "echo chamber effect," whereby the originators of disinformation on the Bulgarian Connection were then called upon by the mass media to verify its accuracy.

Henze and Turkey. Henze's unsuitability as a media expert on the Bulgarian Connection is strikingly revealed in his writings on Turkey. We discuss them briefly here because they display not only his uncritical attachment to the Turkish military regime and his apologetics for state terrorism—if advantageous to U.S. interests—but also his lack of self-discipline as a purported journalist or analyst.[69] Henze's basic methodological precepts are: Anything helping my cause I will accept and rationalize; anything hostile to it is not only wrong but is probably Soviet disinformation. This methodology was transferred intact to his analysis of the Bulgarian Connection.

On the quality of the Turkish martial law regime, Henze is rapturous. Assessing the military takeover of September 12, 1980, he writes: "The country heaved a collective sigh of relief. There was no resistance. Instead there was jubilation. With quarreling politicians silenced and massive arrests of terrorists, the country quickly returned to order."[70] Note the rhetorical "collective sigh," the implication that a lack of resistance was a mark of general approval, and the enthusiasm for stilling quarrels among unruly politicians (a normal characteristic of nonauthoritarian states). In a letter to the *New York Times* a year and a half after the coup, Henze said that "evidence of political oppression is hard to find in Turkey," and he claimed that "to a man I have found Turks enthusiastic" about economic developments. He maintained that the new process of

---

69. The Turkish journalist Ugur Mumcu, after recounting a series of episodes in which Henze told plain lies, suggests that Henze is not only a bad journalist, but could hardly even serve as a quality intelligence agent! Ugur Mumcu, *Papa, Mafya, Agca* (Istanbul: Tekin Yayinevi, 1984), p. 230.

70. Paul Henze, *The Plot To Kill the Pope* (New York: Charles Scribner's Sons, 1985), p. 40.

"devising a more viable democratic system, which is now under way, has the support of the overwhelming majority of the people."[71] In the 1985 revision of *The Plot To Kill the Pope*, Henze makes no qualification to his comprehensive apologetic for the martial law regime. Henze's fondness for martial law Turkey may help us understand his statement that "In reality fascism is no force in Italy. Communism is."[72] We showed in Chapter 4 that fascism is an enormous force in Italy, extensively organized within the security forces and state apparatus, and involved in numerous subversive attempts at coups and terrorist activities over the past several decades. We may interpret Henze's statement that fascism is no force to be partly simple misrepresentation of fact. But it is also a reflection of his belief that fascism is no *threat*. Something is not a threat if you like it and if your country regularly builds it up as an asset to contain other groups. The military in Turkey was not a threat, it was an agent of stability. We would wager that Henze did not view the military as a threat in Greece before (or after) 1967.

Nowhere in his letter or book does Henze mention torture in reference to Turkey. He says exactly what a public relations spokesman for the military regime would say, and when he runs into insurmountable difficulties he resorts to silence or smears.[73] A report by Amnesty International released in July 1985 states that the torture of political detainees in Turkey continues to be "widespread and systematic." The report provides detailed testimony on the use of electric shocks, beating of the soles of the feet, burning with cigarettes, hangings for long periods of time, assaults with truncheons, and violence directed to the sexual organs.[74] According to Helsinki Watch:[75]

71. Letter published on February 22, 1982.
72. *The Plot to Kill the Pope*, p. 65.
73. In his February 22, 1982 letter to the *New York Times*, attacking five prominent U.S. critics of the Turkish military regime, Henze wrote: "The judgments about the current situation in Turkey which the five professors in the social sciences express in their letter are almost identical to those which *Pravda* prints." This is typical Henze (see his references to the present authors and Mumcu in note 27, above). It results in part from the extreme Manicheanism that Henze shares with Sterling, Ledeen, and their colleagues. It is also a part of their program of deliberately tarring all opposition as part of an immense Soviet disinformation campaign. It is, of course, very convenient to be able to dismiss any hostile point as a product of insidious enemy propaganda.
74. Amnesty International, *Turkey: Testimony on Torture* (London: AI, 1985).
75. Helsinki Watch, *Ten Years Later: Violations of the Helsinki Accords* (New York: Helsinki Watch, 1985), pp. 140-41.

Under torture, which is used routinely during interrogation to gather information about terrorist movements, individuals are often forced to confess any crime and to name as many individuals as possible. In this way, thousands of people—particularly young people—have been gathered into police stations and military jails. Many were convicted on the basis of "confessions" obtained through torture or upon the testimony of other tortured victims.

Ali Briand, a correspondent for *Milliyet*, claims that between 1980 and 1984 178,565 people were detained, 65,505 were arrested, 41,727 were condemned for political motives, 326 were sentenced to death, and 25 were executed.[76] Henze mentions in his book that the martial law government had arrested "43,140 terrorists and terrorist collaborators," and he notes that "during much of 1982, the national television service, TRT-TV, broadcast almost nightly roundups of confessions and proceedings at trials of terrorists in all parts of the country."[77] Henze takes all of this at face value—the people taken are all "terrorists," and their confessions are all bona fide.

Regarding Henze's claim of the overwhelming support for the more "viable democracy" being installed by the military government, it is notable that when the opportunity arrived for the Turkish people to pass judgment on the military government in the 1983 parliamentary elections, the party supported by the military finished last. Referring to the 1983 Turkish election, Helsinki Watch reported: "The Turkish people overwhelmingly rejected the military-backed party and gave their support to the Motherland Party, which in the absence of any real opposition, was the only alternative to the junta." Before permitting elections to occur in the first place, the military regime had forbidden all previously established political parties and politicians from participating in the election: 12 of the 15 political parties that sought to participate were banned. This arrangement assured that the winning party or coalition would be acceptable to the generals and would be prepared to abide by the rules that they had already built into Turkey's now "viable democratic" system.

The generals also rigged the election by institutionalizing their power through a new constitution, which legalized the extension of martial law in many provinces and guaranteed the continued presidency of General Kenan Evren until at least 1989. The military was to be the real behind-the-scenes government that defined the rules of the political game. Part

76. *Ibid.*, p. 138.
77. Henze, *op. cit.*, n. 70, pp. 62-63.

of these rules were the 631 laws it had enacted following the 1980 takeover, which could not be changed or criticized by the new Turkish parliament. On January 28, 1984, the *Washington Post* reported the consequences of the new constitution and press laws:

> Bound by these limits, the Ozal government is seen by many observers here as no more than a token step in the direction of democratic civilian rule, with little chance of exercising more than a moral influence on Evren and the determined officers who joined him in the military coup of 1980.

As noted, Henze cites without qualms or qualifications the evidence of Turkish prisoners who "confess." Similarly, if the Turkish military government claims that its arrests and censorship of writers and journalists are based on the latter's support of "terrorism," Henze raises no questions. He also takes the government's announced discoveries of weapons caches at face value, using them to implicate the accused organizations in terror and subversion: "Most of them [the weapons] were discovered in hideouts in former 'liberated areas' in premises of organizations such as TOBDER [a teachers' union], DISK [a major trade union organization], and groups associated with the National [*sic*] Action Party."[78] Helsinki Watch points out that these claims of discoveries of weapons caches, which are used as the basis for fresh waves of arrests, are never verified by independent investigation. Henze never addresses the question of the validity of the government pronouncements or their possible use as disinformation and propaganda. Given the fact that Henze is a long-time professional propagandist, this uncritical use of contaminated materials must be a conscious act, and one serving a propaganda function.

Just as everything the Turkish military government says is taken as true, the other side of the coin is Henze's reliance on assertion without evidence to castigate the Enemy. A central feature of Henze's writings is his claim that in the 1970s Turkey was the victim of a comprehensive Soviet plan for destabilization through terrorism. He asserts that "The Soviet modus operandi included multi-faceted infiltration and build-up of rightist groups to serve as a foil for the left and accelerate the destabilization process."[79] He cites no independent evidence to support

78. *Ibid.*, p. 61. Ugur Mumcu states that Henze's comments on TOBDER and DISK as terrorist organizations "are based on straightforward lies." Mumcu, *op. cit.*, n. 69, p. 230.

79. Henze, *op. cit.*, n. 70, pp. 63-64.

these claims, nor does he explain how the alleged Soviet plan would serve Soviet interests. Proof that the Soviets provided arms is that "there is no other logical source,"[80] whatever the trademark of weapons manufacture. There *are* other "logical" sources, but Henze does not discuss them. By what logic would the Soviet Union support right-wingers as a "foil" for destabilization, when strengthening the Right would shift the balance of power toward an adverse result—a crackdown by the rightwing and pro-NATO military—which did in fact occur? Henze never bothers to explain. The fact is that the real beneficiary of the decade of terrorism was not the Soviet Union, but rather the United States, as Henze himself acknowledges—"Turkey's relations with her NATO allies were probably, on balance, strengthened rather than weakened by terrorism"—without awareness of his internal contradictions.[81]

Given the results of the decade of terrorism, the question arises whether it might have been the beneficiary—the United States—who sponsored terrorism. Henze never mentions U.S. intervention and destabilization efforts in Turkey. As we discussed in Chapter 3, however, U.S. intervention in that country was massive and its links to terror groups clearer than any Soviet connections. Henze is perhaps constrained in discussing these U.S. activities, not only from his political commitments, but also because he was an *actor* in the events of the terror years. In the spring of 1985, former Turkish Prime Minister Bulent Ecevit was quoted in the Italian weekly *Panorama* as saying that he was certain that Henze, as the CIA station chief in Turkey in the 1970s, was a behind-the-scenes organizer of rightwing violence and massacres in those years.[82] The United States had been upset with Ecevit, who pursued a policy of détente with the Soviet Union and closed the U.S. military bases in 1975 after the U.S. arms embargo following the Turkish invasion of Cyprus. The U.S. "loss" of Iran in 1978-79 greatly increased the strategic importance of Turkey and its facilities. Turkey's reliability as a military partner and host to key U.S. surveillance posts was only reestablished following the outbreak of terrorism that led in turn to the military coup of 1980. This pattern of alleged Soviet-sponsored terrorism, with the United States consistently reaping valuable gains in consequence of these foolish Soviet acts, recurs in the Bulgarian Connection. Henze, of course, never addresses this paradox.

80. *Ibid.*, p. 62.
81. *Ibid.*, pp. 51-52.
82. *Panorama*, May 26, 1985, p. 107.

Henze on the Bulgarian Connection. Henze has devoted considerable energy to proving that Agca is neither unbalanced nor a fascist, as this is important for making him a credible witness. Given Agca's courtroom performance and repeated claims to be Jesus Christ, it is useful to have Henze's assurance that "He [Agca] was too rational, too proud to be able to make himself appear deranged."[83] In his proof of Agca's lack of political commitment, Henze cites a neutral statement by Agca's brother Adnan, but suppresses Adnan's highly political explanation reported in *Newsweek*, that Agca wanted to kill the Pope "because of his conviction that the Christians have imperialist designs against the Muslim world and are doing injustices to the Islamic countries."[84] Although Agca spent the better part of his life with Gray Wolves, this has no evidentiary value for Henze. Agca's friends like Gray Wolves militant Oral Celik are only "allegedly" rightists, who were "claimed to have been" close friends of Agca's.[85] Henze's standards of proof here are greatly different from those required to demonstrate Agca's alleged Bulgarian links.

Henze attributes all of the voluminous evidence tying Agca to the Turkish Right to Soviet disinformation. For example, after the Ipekci murder Agca was arrested at the Marmora café, a Gray Wolves hangout. Henze says: "It was almost as if the arrest had been staged to substantiate the impression that Ipekci had been killed by the extreme right, at the connivance of Alparslan Türkes."[86] This is a wonderful illustration of terrorism pseudoscience, which allows its user to make a point by purely verbal manipulation. Note the "almost as if," which is gibberish, but which allows Henze to suggest that the arrest at the café was arranged by the Reds to give the impression that the Right was involved in the Ipekci shooting. There is, of course, no evidence for this, and it is absurd in that Agca was well-known in Turkey as a rightist without having to be arrested at the Marmora. (Henze uses this bit of pseudoscience to influence an American audience, not one in Turkey.) The technique used here is to attribute a "cover" in any situation in which we want a role reversal. As another illustration, Henze says that Agca's connections with Celebi in Frankfurt, West Germany, "which on the surface appeared rightwing," were in fact a rightwing cover for Red control.[87] No evidence is provided that the surface was not the reality. Further-

83. Henze, *op. cit.*, n. 70, p. 7. See also p. 41.
84. *Newsweek*, May 25, 1981.
85. Henze, *op. cit.*, n. 70, p. 147.
86. *Ibid.*, p. 148.
87. *Ibid.*, p. 160.

more, within a week after the shooting of the Pope in Rome, Celebi called a press conference to announce that while Agca's attack might create the appearance of Gray Wolves involvement, in fact the Bulgarians and KGB were behind the assassination attempt. Henze does not mention Celebi's press conference, but his and Sterling's methodology can cope with it (or anything else).[88]

Henze's method is also illuminated by his analysis of the 1979 threat by Agca to kill the Pope in Turkey. He tells us that Agca's letter threatening the Pope was very probably written under Bulgarian instructions and was "his first open move toward implementing a plan that could have been developing for nearly a year."[89] Henze offers no evidence for this scenario; it is entirely hypothetical. The fine-tuning by the KGB was remarkable: They supposedly anticipated the Solidarity crisis by hiring Agca well in advance and got him to make threats as a cover several years before the actual assassination attempt. Still more remarkable, the KGB organized the rightwing press to denounce the Pope's visit, to give the further impression that the Turkish Right was hostile to the Pope and the things he stands for.[90] Why, with all this fine-tuning, the KGB then sent Agca for a long, visible stay in Sofia, and used a legion of Bulgarian employees to help Agca in Rome, is a puzzle. Henze's position is that the KGB got careless after its numerous "successes" in Italy, but he never explains the contrast between the careful planning in Turkey and the foolishness elsewhere.

Although the key to demonstrating a Bulgarian Connection is presumably to be found in Agca's supposed links with the three Bulgarians charged with conspiracy to shoot the Pope, only four and a half pages of Henze's 217-page book are devoted to developing an actual Agca-Bulgarian link—two pages for the "Bulgarian Connection in Rome" and two and a half pages for "Bulgarian Big Brothers." Henze's first attempt to link Agca directly with the Bulgarians proceeds as follows:[91]

Agca made his way back to Rome. There he was no longer on his own but in

88. They would cope with it as follows: Celebi was using a double deception in which, while on the surface this rightist denied involvement and blamed the KGB, in reality he did this because he knew he would be disbelieved. By blaming the KGB he helped exonerate it!

89. Henze, *op. cit.*, n. 70, pp. 204-05.

90. Henze denies that the rightwing press was hostile to the Pope's visit. Ugur Mumcu, however, gives numerous citations from the rightwing Turkish press of the time to demonstrate that Henze was telling another whopper. Mumcu, *op. cit.*, n. 69, pp. 213-20.

91. Henze, *op. cit.*, n. 70, p. 171.

direct contact with Bulgarian intelligence officials. According to his statements to the Italian authorities in the summer of 1982, Agca met with these Bulgarians at the Hotel Archimede in early January 1981 to discuss the assassination of Lech Walesa. The talk was of blowing up his car it seems.

As there has never been anything in the way of evidence or eyewitnesses linking Agca to Bulgarians, Henze relies entirely on Agca's own story. Agca eventually withdrew his claims that a plan to assassinate Walesa had materialized, or that a meeting at the Hotel Archimede ever took place, and he recanted on other major contentions that had been used to confirm his links to Bulgarians. The 1985 edition of Henze's book never mentions these retractions.

Following the meeting in which the Agca-Bulgarian team supposedly planned to assassinate Walesa, "The Bulgarians must have continued frequent contacts with him."[92] No evidence is presented to sustain this assertion. Henze goes on to further fancies:[93]

The Bulgarians there [in Rome] were neither the architects nor the prime contractors for Agca's activities. They were journeymen with the task of seeing that plans drawn up and approved elsewhere were executed efficiently. Control rested in Sofia or Moscow. The architects remained in Moscow. They were pressing the men in Rome to get on with the job. Something had to be done about this Polish pope.

He writes that the "architects remained in Moscow" with the same assurance that "the Bulgarians must have continued frequent contact with Agca," although there is no evidence for either and the underlying premise rests only on Agca's word. As with Sterling, a secret of Henze's persuasiveness for the media is the breezy confidence with which he presents his alleged facts and conclusions and glides over his omissions and contradictions.

Boris Henzoff: KGB Propaganda Specialist. One of the most remarkable features of the history of the Bulgarian Connection has been the ability of Henze to assume a dominant position as news analyst and reporter, given his badly compromised credentials. Henze's bias, and the media's culpability in not recognizing and acknowledging this bias, may be made clearer by constructing an experiment.

92. *Ibid.*, p. 172.
93. *Ibid.*

Let us imagine that there was a Soviet KGB officer with the following characteristics:

He had been the KGB station chief in the country from which the would-be assassin came, one where the Soviet-backed regime routinely tortured its own citizens;

He had at one time been the policy adviser for a European radio station that the Soviets now admit was a KGB operation to spread the Soviet version of the news throughout Western Europe;

He had recently nominated known intelligence experts and suspected KGB agents to oversee this same radio station; and

His most recent assignment within the Soviet apparatus was the post of propaganda specialist in the Politburo.

Let us now imagine that this same KGB officer undertakes a propaganda task, allegedly "on his own," at the precise moment that the Soviet Union is about to deploy an increased number of nuclear missiles on European soil. The new missiles are opposed by many Europeans, including substantial numbers of citizens in countries allied with the Soviet Union. The "former" KGB officer's endeavor—as the Kremlin is dramatizing the U.S. threat to the Soviet Union and manipulating information about the military balance in Europe—is to orchestrate a behind-the-scenes media campaign to persuade international opinion that the highest leaders of the United States government have conspired to shoot the Pope.

While the KGB officer's campaign finds a ready acceptance in the Soviet press and in communist party publications throughout the world, it must be admitted that his story raises doubts in other quarters. But even though he can provide no real evidence—no "smoking gun" or eyewitness testimony—that demonstrates that the papal assassination attempt was a U.S. plot, he argues that a "minimalist, legalistic approach" to the U.S. conspiracy "would only serve the interests of the Americans." This reminder about patriotic duty apparently convinces *Pravda* and *Izvestia*, which print the front-page news that the United States has conspired to shoot the Pope.

As the story gains in credibility with each retelling, new confessions by the would-be assassin issue from his Bulgarian prison. These are confirmed by the Bulgarian investigators. The KGB officer is called upon by the "quality" Soviet media to comment on these startling revelations. In fact, the KGB officer becomes a prime source for the communist media throughout the world. The communist media pay no attention to protests from the West about the credibility of their source, for they quickly trace these protests and alleged contrary evidence to the CIA. And why should they take the western allegations of fraud seriously? For the KGB man is a former intelligence officer of their own country; and, as for each country in the world, it is an article of faith that only intelligence officers of somebody else's state tell lies.

Michael Ledeen

Like Sterling and Henze, Michael Ledeen has had a long career of service to the U.S. foreign policy establishment, and durable links to the establishment's conservative network. In his 1980 efforts on behalf of Reagan, Ledeen co-authored a series of articles with Arnaud de Borchgrave, and Ledeen's recent book *Grave New World* [94] was enthusiastically reviewed in de Borchgrave's (and the Reverend Moon's) *Washington Times*. In his acknowledgments in *Grave New World*, Ledeen expresses in groveling language his indebtedness to a large number of the key members of the rightwing network, from Henry Kissinger to Vernon Walters ("one of the great personages of our time, whose tireless service and remarkable personal qualities have done so much for our country").

An important institutional base of Ledeen has been the Georgetown Center for Strategic and International Studies (CSIS), a research center "affiliated with" Georgetown University. (Although no courses are taught there, this affiliation furnishes an academic cover for a rightwing propaganda agency/thinktank.) Funded by conservative foundations and corporate interests, CSIS provides a revolving door between government-CIA personnel and journalist-academics. Former CIA Deputy Director for Intelligence Ray Cline has been a leading official of the Center, and the senior researchers tend to be former intelligence officials of the CIA and State Department. The CSIS has specialized in reports on various forms of the Red Threat. Fred Landis makes a good case that it also provides an outlet for CIA and other intelligence reports and a cover for CIA black propaganda. [95] Perhaps most important, the CSIS provides a means for organizing the preparation and dissemination of

94. Michael Leeden, *Grave New World* (New York: Oxford University Press, 1985).

95. Fred Landis, "Georgetown's Ivory Tower for Old Spooks," *Inquiry*, September 30, 1979, pp. 7-9; Landis, "The Best Selling Lies of 1980," *Inquiry*, September 29, 1980, pp. 17-23.

the appropriate conservative "lines" on various subjects, and for providing "experts" like Michael Ledeen, Robert Kupperman, and Walter Laqueur to appear on the TV networks to expound these views. The intellectual status of the organization is enhanced by the affiliation of scholar-notables like Kissinger, Brzezinski, and Adjunct Fellow Arnaud de Borchgrave.

Ledeen's role within the rightwing intellectual establishment has been based on his credentials as an expert on Italy, and especially on political extremism and "Soviet-sponsored terrorism" in Italy. As Italy has provided a dramatic example of these phenomena for conservatives, Ledeen has become a leading spokesperson for the thesis of Soviet manipulation and disinformation.[96]

In Italy in the mid-1970s Ledeen served as a journalist for the rightwing paper *Il Giornale Nuovo*, a 1974 breakaway from *Corriere Della Sera*, and probably funded by the CIA.[97] During the Italian election campaign of 1976, the Italian Communist Party was expected to make great gains, which aroused acute alarm in the U.S. foreign policy establishment. In these dire circumstances Ledeen played an important role in trumpeting both at home and in Italy itself the fearsomeness of the Red Threat. In collaborative articles with Claire Sterling, Ledeen alleged that Soviet money was flowing into Italian politics. (Characteristically, and once again revealing a feature of Sterling and Ledeen as disinformationists, this was a period of enormous secret inflows of *U.S.* money into the Italian electoral process.[98])

While Ledeen has close links to the U.S. hard-line Right, perhaps his most notable distinction lies in his affiliations with the extreme Right in Italy. As we saw in Chapter 4, he was associated with Francesco Pazienza, a friend of Licio Gelli and the Mafia and a member of the Italian secret service organization SISMI, and Ledeen himself was on the SISMI payroll and participated in its dirty tricks. According to Italian press reports, furthermore, Pazienza and Ledeen foisted some stale U.S. intelligence reports about the Communist Plot on SISMI for large consulting fees. Ledeen's manipulative operations in Italy were of sufficient scale and quality to cause a new head of SISMI to denounce Ledeen on the floor of the Italian Parliament in 1984 as an "intriguer" and

---

96. With the cooperation of the mass media, in which they are a powerful force, the conservatives have succeeded in pushing under the rug the massive rightwing destabilization and terrorism in Italy in the period 1969-80. They pretend that Italian terrorism is predominantly a product of the Left. (See Chapter 4.)

97. See Landis, "The Best Selling Lies of 1980," *op. cit.*, n. 95.

98. See Chapter 4, p. 73.

unwelcome in Italy.[99]

It even appears that Ledeen had a significant relationship with Licio Gelli, the head of P-2 now wanted in Italy for a variety of crimes. On March 29, 1982, the Italian weekly *Panorama* reported that a phone call from Gelli in Uruguay to Florentine lawyer Federico Federici, which was intercepted by the police, had instructed Federici to pass the manuscript of Gelli's new book on to Michael Ledeen. When Gelli's files were seized by the Uruguayan police, Michael Ledeen went down to Uruguay on behalf of the U.S. State Department to try to acquire some of the files.[100] One can only wonder what Michael Ledeen was looking for in those files!

Ledeen's disinformation role. Michael Ledeen's function as an intellectual-propagandist of the hard-line Right is to find plausible reasons to oppose détente and to justify a renewed arms race, the free use of force, and support for the enlarging network of rightist regimes and counter-revolutionary Freedom Fighters. His objective is to move the frontier of accepted premises as far to the right as is at present feasible. In the summer of 1985, for example, Ledeen aggressively pushed the desirability of bombing the Lebanese Shiites in retaliation for the TWA-hostage incident, as part of a harder-line policy of force in dealing with the taking of hostages;[101] and during the same period he urged the higher morality of invading Nicaragua in the interest of Freedom.[102]

The themes addressed over the years by Ledeen in pursuit of this basic agenda are very similar to those pressed by Sterling, Henze, de Borchgrave, Brzezinski, Robert Moss, and Henry Kissinger. The Communists are gaining power, pursuing their fixed agenda of conquest, infiltrating everywhere, and posing ever more serious threats to Liberty. The Free World's defenses are down and sagging. The First Amendment is an encumbrance that allows the liberal-dominated media to play into the enemy's hands. We need to organize and behave more ruthlessly to contend with the forces of Evil. This means providing more consistent support to our allies (*e.g.*, the late Somoza, the late Shah, Pinochet, Botha, and Marcos) and being more willing to move militarily

99. Maurizio De Luca, "Fuori l'intrigante," *L'Espresso*, August 5, 1984.

100. Diana Johnstone, "The Ledeen connections," *In These Times*, September 8-14, 1982.

101. "Be Ready to Fight," *New York Times*, June 23, 1985 (Op-Ed column).

102. "When Security Preempts the Rule of Law," *New York Times*, April 16, 1984 (Op-Ed column).

against the forces of the enemy (Angola, Nicaragua, the Shiite Moslems).

Ledeen's role in developing and propagating the Bulgarian Connection was thus only one of many threads of conservative thought he has been pursuing. What unites these threads is Ledeen's determination to show the Soviet hand everywhere. This can be seen by examining his recent volume of essays, *Grave New World*. Our examination will illuminate the place of the Bulgarian Connection within a family of rightwing themes, and it will reveal more clearly the pseudoscientific quality of the entire body of thought of Ledeen and his fellow disinformationists centered in the CSIS.

Soviet military superiority. Ledeen consistently acts as if certain partly or fully institutionalized propaganda lies are true, and proceeds from there. For example, a premise of the rightwing establishment is that the Soviet Union achieved military superiority in the late 1970s. Ledeen presents this as an assured truth, without bothering to provide argument or citations: "This [earlier Soviet] inferiority has now been overcome, and insofar as one side now has an overall edge in military power, it is the Warsaw Pact that leads the NATO countries."[103] This statement can be refuted by reference to numerous U.S. Defense Department estimates and posture statements. NATO defense expenditures have always exceeded those of the Warsaw Pact countries, its naval fire power is twice that of the Warsaw Pact countries, it has comparable levels of military manpower, and it has numerical and technical superiority in nuclear weapons. In a significant exchange on May 11, 1982, Senator Carl Levin asked the Chairman of the Joint Chiefs if he would trade Soviet military capabilities for our own. General Vesey would not trade. On April 29, 1982, Senator Charles Percy asked Defense Secretary Caspar Weinberger whether he would trade nuclear arsenals with the Soviets. Weinberger said that "I would not for a moment exchange anything, because we have an immense edge in technology."[104] Part of the genius of the system is that military officials can acknowledge our military superiority and plans for destabilization of the Soviet Bloc based on increases in military advantage,[105] while maintaining for the general pub-

103. Ledeen, *op. cit.*, n. 94, p. 5.
104. These quotes and a full range of statistics are available in Center for Defense Information, "U.S.-Soviet Military Facts," *The Defense Monitor*, Vol. XIII, No. 6, 1984.
105. See Chapter 4, n. 7 and associated text.

lic the vision of Soviet superiority and menace. This requires the services of intellectuals like Michael Ledeen.

The Soviet terror network. Another established premise of the disinformationists is that there is a Soviet-supported terror network. This idea therefore enters Ledeen's writings as a truth not requiring evidence. "The terror network was (among other things) a way of intensifying the pressure on the West to make space for the extreme Left."[106] As we noted earlier, the overall effect of the activities of the "terrorists" in Italy, Turkey, and West Germany has served *western* interests, not those of the Soviet Union. The Soviets have never been keen on the "extreme Left." And their stress on détente and building economic relationships with the West runs counter to building a Terror Network. Ledeen never discusses these points.

The Korean airliner 007 as a case study in Soviet terrorism. An example of Soviet terrorism in action, according to Ledeen, was the shooting down of Korean airliner KAL 007 in September 1983. This incident was quickly capitalized on by the Reagan administration, which alleged that the Soviets had knowingly shot down a civilian airliner without warning. The extreme Right contended that this was a Soviet bullying act, or even one designed explicitly to eliminate rightwing Congressman Larry McDonald, a passenger. Ledeen accepts and builds on the propaganda line and the Soviet coercion theme, using it to try to portray the then Soviet Premier Andropov as a villainous bully. According to Ledeen, the shooting down of the airliner was a "show of force . . . brutally threatening those who did not behave as he [Andropov] wanted."[107] The incident was actually a disaster for the Soviet Union, which shot down the plane not knowing that it was a civilian aircraft,[108] and then stumbled badly in confusion before a well-organized Reagan administration propaganda onslaught. That it was a *planned* effort to bully the West is the effusion of a propagandist.

The Grenada Threat. The Grenadian revolution of 1979, according to Le-

106. Ledeen, *op. cit.*, n. 94, p. 196.
107. *Ibid.*, pp. 192-95.
108. This point was even belatedly conceded by the CIA, but this did not diminish the effectiveness of the propaganda campaign. See David Shribman, "U.S. Experts Say Soviet Didn't See Jet Was Civilian," *New York Times*, October 7, 1983.

deen, established an important Soviet outpost, and was part of "a major direct [Soviet] commitment in the Caribbean."[109] Of course, this was all by proxy, but the Soviet commitment to the Grenadians was "quite explicit when Marshall [sic] Ogarkov told the ranking officer of the Grenadian army, Major Einstein Louison, that the revolution in Grenada was irreversible, thus extending the Brezhnev doctrine to the Caribbean region."[110] But why should the Soviets operate carefully only through proxies if they were willing to make an "explicit" extension of the Brezhnev doctrine to the Caribbean? Ledeen provides no direct quotation from Ogarkov. It is obvious that if Ogarkov had made a Soviet promise that they would not *permit* a reversal of the revolution, Ledeen would have mentioned this. As it is, he is forced to transform what was probably a rhetorical flourish at a cocktail party into a Soviet commitment. Here propaganda trickery attains the comic.

The Reaganite history of El Salvador. Ledeen's rewriting of Salvadoran history is in the same mold as his treatment of the 007 incident. That is, he knows that the Reagan administration was successful in selling the 1982 and 1984 Salvadoran elections as marvels of the democratic process. He therefore feels able to take their integrity at face value and go on from there. His manipulation of evidence also illustrates the larger disinformation function of turning all popular movements against U.S.-supported dictatorships into minority attacks on reformist governments. According to Ledeen:[111]

A group of progressive generals had seized power in 1979 from an oligarchic group that had long ruled the country. This coup constituted a moderate revolution: Some thirty thousand of the old ruling class left El Salvador. . . . In 1980, the generals brought Napoleón Duarte in to head the government, and Duarte and his colleagues promised constitutional reform, democratic elections, and a continuation of the redistribution program. All of these promises were maintained [*sic*]—an achievement in itself. It was only after this progressive coup that a unified guerrilla movement came into being. . . .

We may note the following fabrications and misrepresentations in this account:
(1) The economic oligarchy had ruled the country in close collusion

109. Ledeen, *op. cit.*, n. 94, p. 195.
110. *Ibid.*, p. 196.
111. *Ibid.*, pp. 97-98.

with a military oligarchy. The 1979 coup was engineered by progressive junior officers, not generals. These progressive officers were quickly ousted in a countercoup that left power in the hands of the same military elements that had collaborated with the old economic oligarchy for decades. As noted by Raymond Bonner:[112]

The young, progressive officers who carefully plotted the coup lost control of it as swiftly as they had executed it. Their ideals and objectives were subverted by senior, more conservative officers who had the backing of Devine [U. S. Ambassador to El Salvador] and the U.S. Embassy in El Salvador and key Carter administration officials in Washington. These senior officers were not about to surrender their unfettered sovereignty to civilians. They recoiled at the prospect of having criminal charges lodged against any of their colleagues. They blocked the implementation of economic reforms. And they continued to use excessive force against dissent: More people were killed in the three weeks following the coup than in any three-week period during the Romero regime [the dictatorship which preceded the coup].

(2) Duarte was brought into the junta in March 1980 after the resignation of the progressive elements in the junta. His function was to serve as a figleaf for the escalating violence, in the course of which over 20,000 unarmed civilians were killed by the security forces in 1980-81 without audible protest from Duarte. He was elevated to President of the junta in December 1980, following the rape-murder of four U.S. religious women, an action by the security forces that required a public relations response. Duarte himself conceded just prior to the 1982 elections that he had lacked any real power and served as a figurehead.[113]

(3) Ledeen suppresses the fact that a state of siege was imposed in March 1980, from which ensued a level of state terror that far exceeded the violence of the preceding Romero dictatorship. This was the period in which the "death squads" became important factors in Salvadoran life.

(4) The promise of "constitutional reform" was nullified immediately after the progressive junior officers and civilians were ousted. Instead of a constitutional process a new reign of terror descended on El Salvador. Even William Doherty, head of the CIA-funded American In-

---

112. *Weakness and Deceit: U.S. Policy and El Salvador* (New York: Times Books, 1984), p.149.
113. See the interview with Duarte by Raymond Bonner, *New York Times*, March 1, 1982.

stitute for Free Labor Development, stated in 1982 that "there was no system of justice in El Salvador."[114]
(5) The Salvadoran guerrilla movement came into existence in the early 1970s. It gained strength as popular movements of peasants, workers, and professionals were brutally repressed, and as the electoral path to reform was closed. It then grew rapidly under the reign of terror that followed the countercoup in early 1980.

Ledeen on the media. One function of the disinformationists is to make the media more pliable in accepting without question *their* disinformation handouts. As we have noted, one way they do this is to trumpet loudly about *Soviet* disinformation, as part of the larger campaign of bullying the media into submission to their own. Ledeen's attack on the media fits the standard neoconservative format.

(1) The media are a separate "largely homogeneous political class with the usual overriding class interest: increasing their own power."[115] The neoconservatives pretend that the lower echelons of journalists-producers are all there are in the media. But the media are a very complex set that includes reporters, anchorpersons, producers, owners, publishers, and corporate parents. The large media are all sizable corporations or affiliates of very large companies, and the bulk of their revenue is derived from the advertising outlays of other large companies. The media are owned and controlled by powerful corporate interests and wealthy individuals. What is *their* "class" and class interest? Why would they be opposed to a foreign policy geared to the interests of their corporate confreres? Do these owners, managers, and publishers have no influence over their employees' activities? Would these owners stand by helplessly in the face of systematic attacks on the corporate system and the essentials of national foreign policy agreed upon by the corporate community? Ledeen, of course, never addresses these questions.[116]

(2) The media culture is liberal and represents a liberal conformity. "Theirs is a view of the world in which the United States is a major problem, not a major contributor to solutions."[117] Interestingly, Ledeen and his neoconservative allies never ask whether the liberals are an-

114. Committee on Foreign Affairs, House of Representatives, Hearings on *Presidential Certification on El Salvador*, 97th Congress, 2nd Session, 1982, vol. 2, p. 105.
115. Ledeen, *op. cit.*, n. 94, p. 108.
116. See generally, Michael Parenti, *Inventing Reality: The Politics of the Mass Media* (New York: St. Martin's Press, 1986), especially Chapters 2, 3, and 4.
117. Ledeen, *op. cit.*, n. 94, p. 107.

ticommunist and whether they consider the Soviet Union to be a source of problems or a major contributor to solutions. The answers to the latter questions are so blatantly obvious that the neoconservatives have to evade them entirely. The trouble with the liberals is that, while usually highly patriotic and very hostile to communism, many of them actually believe in the principles of political democracy and competitive enterprise. Thus, they will sometimes criticize radical deviations from these principles on the part of Free World governments. It is this margin of dissent that the neoconservatives can't stand; they want a full mobilization of propaganda resources, in the interest of National Security!

The statement by Ledeen quoted above is of course wildly inaccurate. The press in the United States occasionally portrays its own country as having erred, but it invariably ascribes these errors to miscalculation in the national desire to do good. For the Free World media, U.S. interventions or violations of international law are deviations from a general tendency to do good in the world. By contrast, the press almost uniformly regards the Soviet Union and its allies as sources of problems, not means of their solution.

(3) "Most journalists these days consider it beneath their dignity to simply report the words of government officials—and let it go at that."[118] This is a fine illustration of Ledeen's (and the general neoconservative) view that the media should properly serve as an uncritical conduit for government handouts. Some might argue that Big Government threatens to dominate the media and gradually to become Big Brother. The neoconservatives have little fear of this, as long as their pals are in charge of the government! Big government is bad only in its intrusions into the *economy*, and even there, only where it tries to curb business excesses and redistribute income downward. In short, Ledeen is a spokesman for a National Security State and unbridled corporate domination of the economy.

(4) "The United States and its allies are held up against standards that are not applied to the Soviet Union and its allies. Relatively minor human rights transgressions in a friendly country (especially if ruled by an authoritarian government of the Right) are given far more attention and more intense criticism than far graver sins of countries hostile to us."[119] This is one of those neoconservative and Ledeenean whoppers that astound by their sheer audacity. Abuses of peasants and trade un-

118. *Ibid.*, p. 111.
119. *Ibid.*, p. 131.

ionists in Guatemala and Turkey are given more attention in the U.S. media than abuses in Poland? The murders of human rights activists in El Salvador are given more publicity than the treatment of Sakharov, Orlov, and Shcharansky in the Soviet Union? The media have paid a lot of attention to human rights violations in Indonesia and mass murder by the Indonesian government in East Timor, while neglecting Pol Pot and the trials and tribulations of the Vietnamese boat people?

Ledeen demonstrates the media's "ideological double standard" by comparing "the relative authority given statements from western and non-western sources."[120] He illustrates by the fact that "a denial by Qaddafi leads 'CBS News' to speak of 'alleged' Libyan involvement in Chad (after all, it was only alleged by the American government, and thus it was somehow suspect). . . . "[121] As Ledeen gives neither date nor source for this quotation, it is not clear whether the use of the word "alleged" accompanied Qaddafi's denial, but the implication that Qaddafi is treated with deference in the U.S. media as an authority superior to U.S. government officials is grotesque nonsense. The fact that Qaddafi was given a few minutes of time on CBS News proves nothing about *how* he was used—which is usually as a straw man to knock down. The main point, however, is that Qaddafi is the long-established bogeyman of both administration and press. Any negative allegation about Qaddafi is publishable, and his credibility as a source is absolutely nil. Ledeen's suggestion to the contrary, based on the application of a single word, is silly even for a propagandist.

(5) "Perhaps the greatest success of Soviet disinformation is the constant cynicism about American motives that characterizes so much of contemporary journalism."[122] The assertion of media cynicism about American motives is nonsensical, and the reverse of the truth. The standard liberal format is to postulate beneficent motives which are regrettably not being implemented properly. No matter how many Latin American dictatorships are brought into being and loyally supported by American power, the mass media never fail to find its country pursuing democracy and other reasonable ends.

Ledeen also uses here the standard disinformationist technique for smearing the media spelled out in *The Spike*.[123] Note how he makes the

120. *Ibid.*, p. 132.
121. *Ibid.*, pp. 132-33.
122. *Ibid.*, p. 134.
123. Robert Moss and Arnaud de Borchgrave, *The Spike* (New York: Crown, 1980). The authors argue that a substantial sector of the "establishment" media is deeply pene-

cynicism a success of Soviet disinformation, suggesting a cause and effect relation. He provides not one jot of evidence that any domestic criticism of U.S. policies is based on Soviet sources. He just implies this by word manipulation. He actually goes on to explain that it must be Soviet influence that causes suspicion of motives because the United States is good,[124] and when forced into conflict "will strain to support democratic forces"—as it has done for so many years in Guatemala and Zaire, for example. Although Ledeen is supposed to be a political scientist, he offers no serious discussion of U.S. interest and policies, only propaganda clichés.[125]

(6) Ledeen is deeply bothered by the First Amendment, especially in its claims for "unlimited free speech" and its lack of requirement for "responsible use of that right."[126] He sees this claim as the slogan of the "new class" that dominates the media and as a weapon in a "class struggle." We have to do something about the First Amendment in order to ensure serious debate, because you can't have serious debate when one side (*i.e.*, the media) "is itself an interested party."[127] The notion of the media as a "class interest" in systematic opposition to the government is pure neoconservative ideology and indefensible, as discussed in points (1) and (2) above. It is interesting to note, however, Ledeen's complaisance in the face of centralizing government power. Liberals ask: Isn't the government very powerful and doesn't it pose the problem of manipulating consent and overwhelming the public in a centralizing system? If the media is more "responsible" in a Ledeenean sense (*i.e.*, serves as a conduit for State Department handouts), where will we find any debate at all? Ledeen is silent on these points.

Ledeen does end up on a constructive note, however. He would provide for easier libel suits, an ombudsman, and more competition (how, he does not say). His positive recommendations, in short, are dangerous (libel suits), vague (more competition), and trivial (an ombudsman).

trated by KGB moles and well-populated with KGB dupes.

124. In an Op-Ed column in the *New York Times*, Ledeen even refers to our respect for law as "innate." Ledeen, *op. cit.*, n. 102.

125. On the history of the U.S. struggle *against* democracy in Guatemala, see especially, Blanche Wiesen Cook, *The Declassified Eisenhower* (New York: Doubleday, 1981); Richard Immerman, *The CIA in Guatemala* (Austin, Texas: University of Texas Press, 1982); Stephen Schlesinger and Stephen Kinzer, *Bitter Fruit* (New York: Doubleday, 1981). On the U.S. role in Zaire, see Jonathan Kwitny, *Endless Enemies* (New York: Congdon & Weed, 1984), pp. 8-103.

126. Ledeen, *op. cit.*, n. 94, p. 109.

127. *Ibid.*, p. 111.

His function, however, is to discredit the media and set the stage for antimedia pressures that will reduce dissent and enhance the power and freedom from criticism of the *preferred* and *relevant* disinformation.

Ledeen on the Bulgarian Connection. Ledeen discusses the Bulgarian Connection in the framework of his critique of the media. He tries to show that the media were lax in not pushing the case more aggressively. He also uses the case to reinforce the contention that the Bulgarian Connection is true and the Evil Empire evil. This is a precious theme for the disinformationists, and all of its members and associates try as best they can to stress that the Connection is *proved*, and to make it into an institutionalized truth which no reasonable person could question.

In pressing the Connection, Ledeen relies heavily on Sterling-Henze arguments, to which he adds his own quota of alleged facts and supportive innuendoes. He commends Sterling for her "careful article" which was subjected for many months "to checking, cutting, and rewriting" (which if done for Andronov's work in Moscow, would presumably add to *its* validity for Ledeen).

Ledeen follows the Sterling-Henze line on motive—that is, the Soviets had a clear motive to shoot the Pope, and the Italians had no motive to put the blame for the shooting on the Bulgarians and KGB. On the latter subject, Ledeen asks: Would Italian judges of "impeccable reputation" (*i.e.*, Ledeen likes what they are doing) push the case "without compelling evidence? Would they jeopardize Italy's national interest (which includes, at a minimum, good commercial relations with the Soviet Empire) without something approaching solid proof?"[128] Like Sterling-Henze, Ledeen never mentions P-2, the "strategy of tension," Pazienza, SISMI, or the politics of the Cold War in Italy. He doesn't even ask whether the pursuit of the case might have any spinoff benefits to the Socialist and Christian Democratic Parties. The dishonesty and hypocrisy here are extraordinary: Just as Henze, the "expert" on Turkey, ignores the Turkish roots of the assassination plot, Ledeen, the "expert" on Italy, ignores the Italian context of Agca's confession.

"Bit by bit the logic of the case began to assert itself. . . ."[129] "*Time* revealed that the Pope himself believed that Agca was part of a KGB plot and went on to deal with the growing evidence."[130] The Papal Office denied this alleged belief, but even if it were true, of what eviden-

128. *Ibid.*, pp. 127-28.
129. *Ibid.*, p. 127.
130. *Ibid.*, p. 126.

tial value is the Pope's belief? These allegations about "beliefs" and "growing evidence" are rhetorical tricks that Ledeen resorts to time and again.

His own touch is "that Agca's network of Bulgarians and Turks . . . provided Agca with money, with the gun he fired at the Pope, and with other forms of organizational assistance. . . ."[31] What is proven is that Agca's network of *Turkish Gray Wolves* gave him money, his gun, and organizational assistance; what still rests entirely on Agca's belated, contradictory, and unverified claims is that these Turks were involved with Bulgarians in the plot to shoot the Pope.

Ledeen alleges that the American press stayed away from the Bulgarian Connection. Initially, he tells us, the media suppressed the "facts" of the Connection "because it would give added credibility to Haig's claim that the Russians were behind a good deal of terrorism in the world."[132] No supporting evidence is given for this assertion, which is clearly shown to be totally false by the news story summaries in Appendix A. He rules out the possibility that something convenient to a patriotic line may be disbelieved because it is incredible and untrue. There must be a hidden subversive motive. We will show in the next chapter that his basic factual claim is false—the mass media swallowed and wallowed uncritically in the Connection as soon as a remotely plausible James Bond scenario was provided by Sterling and company.

Ledeen's statement on why journalists were hostile to the KGB plot is followed by this:[133]

But in several stories in early 1983 it was casually revealed that most knowledgeable people in the West are thoroughly convinced of this Soviet connection, particularly in the case of Italy. When Henry Kamm quoted his unnamed Israeli intelligence source to undermine the Bulgarian connection, he went on to provide considerable proof of Communist bloc involvement in international terrorism. Sari Gilbert, the *Washington Post*'s stringer in Rome, revealed on March 20 that the Italians were quite convinced of a long-standing connection between Eastern Europe (primarily Czechoslovakia) and the Red Brigades, a point also made by *Time* and *Newsweek*. Thus, those of us who for years have been arguing for such a connection—and were subjected to the most remarkable scorn from our colleagues in the elite media—have been vindicated. But the acceptance of these views is done in such a way as to deprive it of any political impact.

131. *Ibid.*, pp. 119-20.
132. *Ibid.*, p. 127.
133. *Ibid.*, pp. 129-30.

These lines combine direct lies, unproven allegations, faulty inferences, stripped context, and innuendo. Note first the opening reference
to several stories that "casually revealed" that "most knowledgeable
people in the West were thoroughly convinced . . . ," etc. Ledeen
doesn't cite a single one of these alleged sources, nor does he discuss
their sampling procedures. Who are "knowledgeable people"? Note the
rhetorical ploy "casually revealed," which suggests authentic truth
("revealed") unreasonably given inadequate attention (only "casually"
advanced despite the staggering implications of the revelations). The
knowledgeable people are convinced of a Soviet Connection which in
the preceding sentence refers to a generic "terrorism." It is not even
clear that the knowledgeable people were asked anything specific about
the Bulgarian Connection (as opposed to a looser Soviet connection to
spies and assorted villainy).

Ledeen refers next to Henry Kamm's article in the *New York Times* in
which Kamm cited several intelligence officials who expressed doubts
about the Soviet involvement in the plot against the Pope. Both Sterling
and Ledeen jump on this to prove media negativism and attempts to
"undermine the Bulgarian Connection." This is patent nonsense that
misreads Kamm's article, takes it out of context, and misses the forest
for a single tree. Kamm's article was full of accusations and innuendoes
about Soviet and Bulgarian support for terrorism. More important, as
we describe in the next chapter, the Kamm article was exceptional in allowing *any* negative assessments of the Connection to surface at all. Ledeen thus suppresses the fact that surrounding the cited Kamm article
were dozens that passed on the Sterling-Henze view of the plot uncritically and helped build up the critical mass of a propaganda campaign.

Consider the next series of sentences, about Sari Gilbert and the Red
Brigades. Note the use of the words "revealed" and the "Italians were
quite convinced." If Sari Gilbert had "revealed" that Italians were convinced that Michael Ledeen was a CIA flak, Ledeen would say that "revealed" is a grossly inappropriate word because it implies that something is true. He would prefer "alleged." But in the case of a point that
he likes, where Sari Gilbert is saying something agreeable, she "revealed" it. And "the point [is] also made" by *Time* and *Newsweek*—
not the "allegation" or "claim" is made, the *point* is made. The point
is now doubly established, because if Sari Gilbert and *Time* and *Newsweek* agree, given the fact that they are subject to the bias of liberal class
interest and are very possibly manipulated by the KGB, their admissions
are contrary to interest—by neoconservative premise. That is why Sari

Gilbert's statement is a "revelation" and true—and vindicates Michael Ledeen. The point that is being made, or "revealed," is that the "Italians" allegedly *believe* something to be true. Presumably if "the Italians" believed in flying saucers, that would be all that Ledeen would require for the establishment of the truth of flying saucers.

In the passage quoted above, Ledeen concluded that "the acceptance of these views is done in such a way as to deprive it of any political impact." He suggests that this applies to the publicity on the plot to kill the Pope. As we indicated in discussing the Kamm article, Ledeen and Sterling pick and choose their evidence of critical attacks on the Bulgarian Connection and ignore the massive, supportive publicity. In the next chapter we will provide evidence that the mass media of the United States have presented the Bulgarian Connection in a systematically biased fashion, featuring the disinformationists, and in such a way as to *maximize* its political impact. In reading Michael Ledeen, the rule should be: Take anything he says, stand it on its head, and you have a better than average chance of approximating the truth.

7. The Dissemination of the Bulgarian Connection Plot

A propaganda system is one which uses—and sometimes manufac-
tures—a politically serviceable fact or claim, gives it aggressive
and one-sided coverage, and excludes from discussion all critical facts
and analyses. An imperfect propaganda system will allow a small quantum of leakage, but not enough to prevent the effective mobilization of
bias and the establishment of the convenient story as a patriotic truth in
the minds of the general public. In its handling of the Bulgarian Connection story the U.S. mass media behaved as an imperfect propaganda system.

Media Processes in a Propaganda Campaign

Propaganda takes its effect, first, by repetition—by day-in-day-out
coverage which drives home the fact that something is important. It is
significant that the U.S. media do not provide day-in-day-out coverage
of the victims of death squads in Latin America, or assaults by South
Africa on its neighbors, or Indonesia's invasion and continuing pacifica-
tion of East Timor. These are actions and victims of "friendly" nations,
who provide an excellent investment climate and align themselves as
clients and military allies with the dominant powers of the Free World.
With them we therefore enter into "constructive engagement," and es-
chew boycotts and threats no matter how violent and unconscionable
their behavior.[1] On the other hand, victims of enemy powers—Cuban

1. The "human rights" policy of the Carter years did constitute a deviation from this
pattern, but it was a deviation. A residue of the Vietnam War era, it was pressed by Congress, and was frequently vigorously resisted and used heavily for rhetorical purposes by
the administration itself. Loaded with exceptions and weak in implementation against
client states, it was subject to intense and ultimately effective opposition by the business
community and military-industrial complex. See Noam Chomsky and Edward S. Herman,

and Vietnamese refugees, Lech Walesa and Soviet dissidents—are subjects of day-in-day-out coverage. A tabulation in *The Real Terror Network* shows that between January 1, 1976 and March 30, 1982, the *New York Times* had more than twice as many articles on Anatoly Shcharansky as it ran on an aggregate of 14 notable Free World victims of state terror. Shcharansky generated five different spurts of intensive coverage during that period.[2]

The process of mobilizing bias depends heavily on the initiatives and power of the mass media, with perhaps a dozen entities capable of getting the ball rolling and sustaining interest. If several of these, like *Reader's Digest*, NBC, and the *New York Times* decide to push a story, it quickly becomes *newsworthy*. Many people hear of it, and thus other members of the media fraternity feel obliged to get on the bandwagon because *this is the news*. When one of the authors (Herman) wanted to write on both Cambodia *and* East Timor in 1980, not Cambodia alone, the editor of a liberal magazine objected on the ground that "nobody had heard of" East Timor. The *Reader's Digest* had had no article on the subject; William Safire, Hugh Sidey, and William Buckley had not discussed the matter; and the coverage of East Timor by the *New York Times* had been inversely related to Indonesian state violence (starting from a modest level and a pro-Indonesia bias to begin with).[3] With this silence at the top of the media power structure, and thus "nobody having heard of East Timor," only eccentricity could cause the lesser media to bring up a subject so obviously unnewsworthy.

For news that is more acceptable to major power groups, if circumstances are ripe a propaganda campaign can be mobilized. Especially during periods when the business community is in an aggressive mood, eager to discredit unionism, regulation, and the welfare state, and has succeeded in bringing a conservative government into power and frightening liberals into quiescence, Red Scares and even repressive violence can occur. The press will then provide daily coverage of the latest revelations of Red linkages, confessions, and newly found documents, and will carry speculation by notables on the intent of the conspirators. The aggressive and assured portrayal of the conspiracy as clearly proven by the media elite produces an equally uncritical "popu-

The Washington Connection and Third World Fascism (Boston: South End Press, 1979), pp. 33-37.

2. Edward S. Herman, *The Real Terror Network: Terrorism in Fact and Propaganda* (Boston: South End Press, 1982), pp. 196-99.

3. See Chomsky and Herman, *op. cit.*, n. 1, pp. 145-51.

lar belief" that helps stifle any opposition views in the rest of the media. Such views are quickly seen as very "far out" and even subversively deviant.

The mobilization of bias is helped along by the large number of right-wing columnists who come into prominence in conservative eras. It is the *function* of people like William Safire, George Will, and Ben Wattenberg to take advantage of any opportunity that presents itself to shift the political spectrum farther to the right, and they leap into the fray without any encumbrance by intellectual scruple. They are quickly joined by conservative academics and thinktank operatives (Walter Laqueur, Michael Novak, Ernest Lefever), who bring their "expertise" to the proof of Red Evil and to the important task of keeping the issue alive. In such an environment, with critical judgment by the mass media suspended, rightwing propagandists given free rein, and dissident opinion effectively excluded, lies can be institutionalized. As Murray Levin concluded in his study of the Red Scare of 1919-20, millions of people were led to believe in the existence of a Red Conspiracy "when no such threat existed."[4]

The Bulgarian Connection as a Media Propaganda Campaign

The mass media buildup of the Bulgarian-KGB Connection is a model illustration of the principles and processes just outlined. Once again, it is an alleged *enemy* act of villainy that is shown to be capable of generating day-in-day-out coverage. The process started with Claire Sterling's *Reader's Digest* article and the NBC-TV program of September 21, 1982. But the real media buildup followed Agca's "confession," which led to the arrest of Antonov in late November. The *New York Times*, for example, had only two articles on the Bulgarian Connection in September 1982, none in October, and two in November; then it had 20 in December, 15 in January 1983, and a modest fall-off to 8 in February. All the other major media enterprises—*Time*, *Newsweek*, the *Washington Post*, the *Wall Street Journal*, and the TV networks—had a comparable escalation of coverage in December 1982 and January 1983. The second layer of media followed in close order with a spate of articles; and commentators, humorists, and cartoonists attended to the

4. Murray B. Levin, *Political Hysteria in America* (New York: Basic Books, 1981), p. 3.

Bulgarian Connection frequently during the high intensity period.

Besides its intensity, another indicator of the propagandistic character of the campaign was that its news content was minimal. Of the 32 news articles in the *New York Times* on, or closely related to, the Plot which appeared between November 1, 1982 and January 31, 1983, 12 had no news content whatever, but were reports of somebody's opinion or speculation about the case—or even their refusal to speculate about it! The *Times* carried one news article whose sole content was that President Reagan had "no comment" on the case. More typical was the front-page article by Henry Kamm, "Bonn is Fearful Of Bulgaria Tie With Terrorists" (December 22, 1982), or Bernard Gwertzman's "U.S. Intrigued But Uncertain On a Bulgarian Tie" (December 26, 1982). In "news report" after news report unnamed officials are "intrigued," their interest is "piqued," evidence is said to be "not wholly convincing," or "final proof is still lacking." Four of the news articles in the *Times* were on peripheral subjects such as smuggling in Bulgaria or Vatican-Soviet relations. Of the 16 more direct news items, *only one* covered a really solid news fact: the arrest of Antonov in Rome. The other 15 news items were trivia, such as Kamm's "Bulgarians Regret Tarnished Image" (January 27, 1983), or another Kamm piece entitled "Italian Judge Inspects Apartment of Suspect in Bulgarian Case" (January 12, 1983). All of these expressions of opinion, doubt, interest, supposition, or news of minor details served to produce a lot of smoke, and kept the issue of possible Soviet involvement before the public. The *New York Times* was so aggressive in smoke creation that its article on smuggling in Bulgaria was placed on the front page, with the heading "Plot on Pope Aside, Bulgaria's Notoriety Rests on Smuggling" (January 28, 1983)—a little editorial reminder of the Plot for the benefit of the reader, plus a further editorial judgment on "notoriety," all in a single headline!

Smoke was also generated by the large stable of rightwing journalists and scholars—Safire, Will, Buckley, Pipes, and of course the Big Three—who took advantage of the newsworthiness of the Plot, added to it, and kept the pot boiling. Another of their functions was to make it appear that not only was the proof clear, but that there was also a sinister coverup in high places of the true extent and enormity of Soviet guilt. In a charming little game, the CIA—reported to be "not sure," although believing that the Soviets "at a minimum" *knew* about the Plot—was made to appear the epitome of caution and judiciousness, not as a

longstanding participant in rightwing disinformation.[5] *Time* magazine
played this game with considerable flair, following Sterling in suggesting that foot-dragging in Washington was based on the fear that the true
story "might scuttle any arms-control talks" (February 7, 1983). This
delightful gambit, which patriotically assumed Reagan's deep devotion
to arms control in the face of obvious evidence to the contrary, thereby
converted a factor that might arouse suspicion as to the source of the
Plot into a basis of administration regrets and coy protection of the
Soviets.

   Time also did a masterful job of building up its favored sources of evidence—"normally cautious Italian politicians . . . exude confidence,"
"circumstantial evidence [which] . . . seems overwhelming" to U.S.
intelligence, the British alone remaining skeptical. On the other hand,
the Soviet reply was "emotional," with attacks on western journalists,
but not on Marvin Kalb, "which tends to add credibility to the facts as
well as to the tone [*sic*] of his reporting" (February 22, 1983). There
was the necessary playing down of the problem of the credibility of
Agca, his confession, his photo identification in the Italian police-
prison-political context; but *Time* threw in just enough in the way of intelligence doubts and admissions of lack of *final* proof so that their completely uncritical use of sources and packaged *sell* of the Connection
was not obvious.

   As we noted earlier, rightwing analysts like Sterling and Ledeen took
articles like those of Toth and Kamm, in which intelligence agencies
were quoted as expressing doubts about Soviet involvement, and tried to
use these articles as evidence of CIA "foot-dragging" and reluctance to
pursue the "truth." But not only did the cited articles invariably implicate the Soviets and Bulgarians one way or another,[6] they were also part
of a large cloud of smoke whose net effect was to sell the Connection.
The occasional qualified doubt or reservation actually contributed to the
net effect by giving the impression of fairness and reasonableness on the
part of the press. The modest qualifications that were allowed to surface
were swamped by the larger enthusiastic chorus of nondoubters.

   A further characteristic of mass media coverage of the Bulgarian-

   5. Robert Toth, "Bulgaria Knew of Plot on Pope, CIA Concludes," *Los Angeles
Times*, January 30, 1983.
   6. Toth's article incriminated the Bulgarians by suggesting that they knew about the
plot but did nothing to prevent its implementation. Kamm transmitted western intelligence
agency doubts about Soviet involvement in the plot to assassinate the Pope, but conveyed
strong claims about Soviet contributions to "terrorism."

KGB Connection that fits a propaganda model has been the virtually complete exclusion of dissenting opinion. The "debate" is confined to assertions and speculations by western terrorism experts, intelligence sources, and politicians, on the one hand, and Soviet and Bulgarian denials on the other. Communist denials, obviously to be expected, come from a source that the public will not find believable. Western critics of the story, who might have greater credibility, are not admitted to the debate.

In the news articles and opinion pieces in the *New York Times* between November 1, 1982 and January 31, 1983, for example, not one serious voice of opposition is to be found. (This characteristic also applied to the *Times*'s coverage up to the time of the trial in 1985.) The *Times*, like *Time*, conveyed the views of the CIA, Italian politicians, the establishment terrorism experts, other intelligence services, and of course Zbigniew Brzezinski. Brzezinski's belief in Soviet involvement was put forth in a "news" article devoted solely to this enlightening fact; and the *Times* then gave Brzezinski Op-Ed column space to restate his opinion. This is a good illustration of the main form of editorial writing in the mass media—confining questions and answers in purported "news" articles to those whose conclusions preclude the necessity of the editor expressing his or her personal judgment.

A final important propaganda characteristic of media coverage of the Bulgarian Connection, implicit in a number of the preceding points, was the media's suspension of critical analysis and investigatory zeal. For system-supportive claims of enemy evil, the mass media do not require much in the way of evidence or plausibility. They join a herd-like chorus with patriotic enthusiasm. As we have noted, the 1982 Sterling *Reader's Digest* article and the associated NBC-TV special contained no credible evidence of a Bulgarian Connection, and were crudely demagogic. Analogous claims of CIA involvement in the Plot, if recognized at all, would have been carefully examined and scornfully dismissed.[7] A propaganda system chooses its preferred myths and scenarios, disseminates them without critical scrutiny, and protects them from attack. Disinformation has free sway, eliciting no threatening flak; critics of that disinformation, who *would* elicit flak, are marginalized.[8]

7. We show in Appendix D that the Soviet journalist Iona Andronov made a case for a CIA connection to Agca and the assassination attempt that is certainly more persuasive than the case made by Sterling against the KGB. Andronov's work is unknown in the United States.

8. One media official told the authors that for any *criticisms* of the Connection, the pro-

Following the huge spurt of publicity between December 1982 and February 1983, press coverage of the Bulgarian Connection fell to a lower level. But it was periodically renewed with fresh disclosures and new leaks from Rome. For example, in a long article in the *New York Times* on March 23, 1983, Nicholas Gage passed on claims made by French counterintelligence that a Bulgarian defector had implicated both the Bulgarian state security agency and the Soviet KGB in the papal assassination plot. The defector was Iordan Mantarov, supposedly a former deputy commercial attaché at the Bulgarian Embassy in Paris, who repeated information he had allegedly received from one Dimiter Savov before defecting in July 1981. Mantarov identified Savov as a high ranking Bulgarian counterintelligence official. The Bulgarian government responded that Mantarov had actually been a maintenance mechanic at a Bulgarian-owned company in Paris called Agromachinaimpeks, which exports farm equipment. In a small article reporting the Bulgarian government's response on April 8, 1983, Craig R. Whitney, foreign editor of the *New York Times*, admitted that Mantarov was not listed on the Bulgarian Embassy roster, which as a commercial attaché he certainly would have been. (The Bulgarians also denied that any "Savov" worked for the state security agency, and noted that this was a common Bulgarian surname.)[9] Despite the quick collapse of this apparently new evidence, the Mantarov story has retained its usefulness to the disinformationists: On the opening day of Agca's trial, for example, Paul Henze reminded Judy Woodruff on the MacNeil/Lehrer News Hour that the testimony of the Bulgarian defector Mantarov had con-

gram would have had to make sure "of every comma." He noted that such care was not required for pro-Plot programming.

9. Gage's story, on which he supposedly spent two months while traveling to seven countries, appeared only days before his cover story in the *New York Times Sunday Magazine* describing his search, while working as a *Times* reporter, for the Greek Communist who reportedly murdered his mother during the civil war in the 1940s. In the article Gage described himself as armed and seeking vengeance, though he ultimately could not bring himself to act when he found the alleged murderer. The movie version of his book on the subject was reviewed critically in the *New York Times*. Jimmy Carr reports that Gage "thinks it may have stemmed from his unfashionable antileftist stance. 'I think there is a double standard in judging evil people if they're rightist or leftist,' he says." ("Gage says 'Eleni' 'payment' to mother," *Boston Globe*, November 10, 1985.) In assigning Gage to investigate the Bulgarian Connection, the *Times* undoubtedly considered him "objective" in reporting on a matter of potentially great East-West tension.

For a devastating account of Gage's background and misrepresentations of history in *Eleni*, see Nikos Raptis, " 'Eleni': The work of a 'Professional Liar,' " *CovertAction Information Bulletin*, Number 25 (Winter 1986).

firmed Agca's original testimony, which was suddenly threatened by Agca's announcement that he was Jesus Christ.

Considerable news coverage was also generated by Agca's informal news conference of July 7, 1983. Emmanuela Orlandi, the daughter of a Vatican official, had been kidnapped, and messages purportedly from the kidnappers had demanded Agca's release in exchange for the kidnap victim. Agca was brought from his prison cell to a courtroom to testify on these events. In the process, the media were assembled and Agca was allowed to engage in some verbal exchanges with reporters. Agca reiterated his new devotion to liberty and shouted that the Bulgarians and the KGB were both involved in the assassination attempt. Agca's claims were broadcast on all U.S. television networks that evening; the introductory lead-in was that Agca had at last brought the KGB directly into the case. The new and highly significant retractions that Agca had made two weeks earlier, by contrast, were not leaked to the press (or were not reported by the press). In fact, Agca's retractions were not even hinted at by the media for the entire year that followed.

The case took off with renewed vigor in June 1984 with a front-page article in the *New York Times* by Claire Sterling herself, giving an account of the Albano Report.[10] This sparked a new set of follow-up articles and interviews which stressed the enhanced likelihood of Bulgarian guilt, given the claims of the Italian prosecutor. Another surge of publicity took place in late October 1984, when Magistrate Martella issued his final Report, claiming the evidence sufficient to send the accused Bulgarian Antonov and others to trial. The beginning of the trial itself sparked a further stage of media interest, although the events of the trial, with Agca finally exposed to full public view, quickly began to erode the established presumption of Bulgarian guilt.

The Dominance of Sterling, Henze, and Ledeen in Media Coverage

As we noted in Chapter 2, for some months following the assassination attempt the main thrust of media attention was on Agca's Turkish fascist background. With the publication of Sterling's *Reader's Digest* article,

10. *New York Times*, June 10, 1984. See below, pp. 190-94. In an extraordinary departure from its standard practice, the *Times* gave Sterling a page-one by-line, and did not indicate that she was not a staff reporter (until the end of the article, on an inside page).

the airing of the NBC-TV programs of September 1982 and January 1983, and Agca's declarations in November 1982, the media shifted *en masse* to an uncritical acceptance of the Bulgarian Connection. Sterling and Henze were quickly established as the "experts" on the Plot, and their line was institutionalized and preserved more or less intact until the beginning of the trial in May 1985. The predominance of Sterling and Henze (and to a lesser extent Ledeen) in mass media coverage of the subject cannot be described with precision, because much of their influence was indirect, as others in the mass media read, heard, and absorbed their message. However, we have attempted to summarize their hegemonic position in the accompanying table, which describes their importance in nine major media outlets during two and a half years of a virtually uncontested line.

Table 7.1. Sterling-Henze-Ledeen Dominance of Mass Media Coverage of the Bulgarian Connection, September 1982-May 1985.

Media Outlet	Domestic Circulation or Broadcast Audience	Extent of Dominance	Evidence
Reader's Digest	18,012,397[a]	Complete	Sponsor of Sterling (see text); no deviation to be found
NBC-TV	7,500,000[b]	Virtually complete	Kalb close ally of S-H; latter consultants on 2 major programs; no serious deviation[d]
MacNeil/ Lehrer	3,000,000[c]	Virtually complete	76% of time given to S-H-L; no dissident allowed (see text)
Wall Street Journal	1,959,873[a]	Virtually complete	Sterling only outside commentator, with 3 separate items, favorable book review and editorial citations; no dissent[e]

a. Taken from Audit Bureau of Circulation figures for March–September 1984, *The 1985 IMS/Ayer Directory of Publications*, IMS Press, Fort Washington, Pa.

b. Number of households estimated by Nielsen to have watched the NBC-TV program of September 21, 1982 on "The Plot Against the Pope."

c. Average household audience in early 1985 as estimated by staff of the News Hour.

d. For an analysis of the September 21, 1982 program, see Frank Brodhead and Edward S. Herman, "The KGB Plot to Assassinate the Pope: A Case Study in Free World Disinformation," *CovertAction Information Bulletin*, Number 19, Spring–Summer 1983.

e. Reflecting the dichotomy between the quality news offerings and pre-Neanderthal

Table 7.1 Continued.

Media Outlet	Domestic Circulation or Broadcast Audience	Extent of Dominance	Evidence
Christian Science Monitor	141,247[a]	Virtually complete	Henze primary reporter-commentator, accounting for 12 of 14 articles, Jan. 1, 1983–July 15, 1985
CBS-TV News	11,200,000[f]	Virtually complete	3 in-depth interviews with Sterling; no dissent or critical analysis at any time (see text)
New York Times	934,530[a] (daily) 1,533,720[a] (Sunday)	Virtually complete	Bought Henze information; used Sterling as news reporter; adopted S-H line intact; no deviant facts or analyses allowed December 1982–May 1985 (see text)
Newsweek	3,037,277[a]	Virtually complete	Henze primary source of major article January 3, 1983; no deviation from S-H line
Time	4,630,687[a]	Substantial	No evidence of direct use, but as with *Newsweek*, no deviation from S-H line[g]

Editorial Page, while the latter offered pure Sterling through August 1985, the news column put out the excellent pair of articles by Jonathan Kwitny cited in the text, although these did not appear until August 1985.

f. An average value for households watching the daily evening news program in December 1984 and January 1985, taken from the Nielsen National TV Rating Reports.

g. Not only did *Time* follow the Sterling-Henze line, in an unusual footnote to one article it paid homage to Sterling as follows: "Late last year, Sterling brought out a book, *The Time of the Assassins*, that meticulously expounded the theory of a Bulgarian connection. It was greeted with some skepticism in many quarters, including the pages of the *New York Times*" ("Thickening Plot," June 25, 1984). As we discuss in the text, the slight skepticism shown in the *New York Times* was confined to two superficial and overgenerous book reviews.

The essence of the propaganda line that the Big Three successfully institutionalized had six main elements:

(1) Agca is a credible witness. The belatedness of his confession, his lies, his retractions, and the lack of independent confirmation of his

claims can all be explained and do not cast reasonable doubts on his primary allegations.

(2) The core evidence is Agca's stay in Sofia, Bulgaria, his claims of meetings with Bulgarian emissaries there, and his identification of Bulgarians in Rome with whom he allegedly conspired to carry out the assassination attempt.

(3) The Bulgarians would not initiate such an act on their own. They were obviously being directed by the KGB.

(4) The Bulgarians and Soviets may be presumed guilty on the basis of Agca's claims.

(5) The motive which led them to this despicable act was their desire to quell the uprising in Poland by eliminating an individual lending the Poles moral support.

(6) The wanton immorality and recklessness of the assassination attempt are the kinds of things we would expect of the Soviet leadership.

The line was institutionalized by giving the Big Three the floor and making no effort to probe beneath their renditions of the Plot. As we described earlier, once a system-supportive propaganda theme is accepted and pressed by the top media, it is sustained by popular belief as well as an institutional nexus. It becomes difficult and even risky to challenge the new line and easy to ignore dissent. In most instances the major media would not want to encourage dissent anyway. This was obviously true in the case of the *Reader's Digest*, where the line was conveyed by exclusive reliance on Sterling. Other major media also pressed the party line with positive and uncritical enthusiasm. In the two major NBC-TV programs of 1982-83, Sterling and Henze were consultants and their imprint is clear throughout. Marvin Kalb, the narrator of these programs, provided the bulk of NBC-TV's subsequent coverage of the case, which continued to argue energetically for the Connection. Even CBS-TV News and the MacNeil/Lehrer News Hour, supposedly the more "liberal" purveyors of TV news, served as straight conduits of the propaganda line. A closer look at CBS and MacNeil/Lehrer, to which we now turn, shows how the disinformationists and media use each other.

CBS-TV News. A review of CBS-TV News's coverage of the Bulgarian Connection between November 25, 1982, and September 30, 1984, shows that the program gave great play to Claire Sterling and attention to other supporters of the Bulgarian Connection hypothesis, but allowed not a single witness hostile to the line. Sterling was used in three long, in-depth interviews, during which she made all her standard points: The Bulgarians and Soviets are surely guilty, western intelligence agencies are dragging their feet, and the Pope himself believes in a Soviet-Bloc conspiracy. She was asked no critical (or intelligent) questions. CBS News also cited three different Bulgarian defectors to make the same points. Zbigniew Brzezinski was given an opportunity to assert his belief in the Bulgarian Connection and the need to take aggressive retaliatory action. Agca's various claims of Bulgarian and Soviet involvement were broadcast on several occasions, without critical comment. No contrary views were provided.

CBS News also used a number of unnamed sources to allege Bulgarian involvement in the kidnapping and interrogation of General Dozier and in other unnamed Bulgarian "operations" in Italy. CBS used selected Italian news accounts that supported claims of a Bulgarian Connection and avoided the large number of news accounts that raised doubts about the Plot. In short, CBS News did not depart even once from an uncritical dissemination of the Sterling-Henze line in the period from November 1982 through September 1984.

The MacNeil/Lehrer News Hour. The coverage of the Bulgarian Connection by the MacNeil/Lehrer News Hour was also extraordinary for its conformist bias and absence of any application of critical intelligence. This is in line with the general character of the program, which has chosen the easy road of accommodating the powerful: obtaining established and mainly conservative brand names as news respondents, and then never asking them challenging questions.

In the three programs on which the Bulgarian Connection was addressed, there were only five individuals interviewed:[11] Paul Henze, Michael Ledeen, Claire Sterling, Harry Gelman, and Barry Carter. The Big Three accounted for 76 percent of the discussion time on these programs.[12] Gelman was a former CIA officer and Carter a former member of the National Security Council. In short, there was no dissident or crit-

11. We exclude from this count interviewees in a video insert on the subject from the Canadian Broadcasting System, which was a segment of the News Hour program of May 27, 1985. The quotations below are from the official transcript.

12. The percentage would fall to 60 if we include the CBC documentary film, which itself used Sterling and did not depart in any way from the Sterling-Henze party line. The documentary, apparently based on an earlier Italian State Television production, used actors to dramatize Agca's version of his movements and those of the Bulgarians immediately prior to the assassination attempt.

ical voice in any of these programs. CIA officer Gelman cautiously raised a few possible objections to the standard line, which in the end he did not dispute. He failed entirely to offset the aggressive and assured propaganda outpourings of the Big Three.

The bias in news sourcing was reinforced by the failure to identify properly the Big Three. While Gelman was identified as a former CIA officer, in all three appearances on the News Hour Henze was described only as a consultant to Rand and a former member of Carter's National Security Council, not as a long-time CIA officer and former CIA chief of station in Turkey. (Mention of Henze's position on Carter's NSC may have been intended to suggest program balance, offsetting Ledeen's link to the Republicans.) Ledeen was identified only as associated with the Georgetown Center for Strategic and International Studies and the State Department. No mention was made of his link to Francesco Pazienza or Licio Gelli of P-2, facts which were already in the public domain in January 1983. Sterling was introduced by an awed Jim Lehrer as perhaps the "only" journalist expert on terrorism, and the first to report "authoritatively on the networks about terrorists."[13]

Putting before the public a trio of "experts" with enormous biases, the MacNeil-Lehrer team then proceeded to ask them a series of unintelligent and open-ended questions that almost always assumed in advance the truth of the Bulgarian Connection.[14] Of 55 questions asked on the three programs, only one had critical substance. (Robert MacNeil asked Henze about the 1979 Agca letter threatening to kill the Pope, sent out before Solidarity existed.) Otherwise the questions ran like this: (MacNeil) "Mr. Ledeen, is the Bulgarian Connection with Agca and this plot credible to you?" (Lehrer to Sterling) "And there is no doubt in your mind about it, is there?" and "No question in your mind that the Soviets knew what was going on?" A great many of the questions were vague inquiries about opinions on Soviet involvement, Soviet reactions, and what our responses should be if the case should be proved. Judy Woodruff even asked Henze whether the Soviets might have "any desire to try this again," as if the fact of their guilt was already established. Jim Lehrer asked Henze, "Well, one piece of speculation I read today was that he [Agca] went from Iran to the Soviet Union. Is there

13. In fact, reviews in the quality newspapers did not find her analysis of the terror network "authoritative," and scholarly reviews considered her work distressingly inadequate.

14. As we mentioned in Chapter 6, Henze insists on control over the script, which may help explain the almost complete absence of probing questions.

anything to that?'' Instead of a question based on fact or the internal logic of the case, Lehrer threw out a giveaway and biased piece of speculation that a professional propagandist would quickly take advantage of. Henze answered ''Well, it is entirely possible.''

In his introductory remarks to the program of January 5, 1983, Lehrer gave a summary of the ''facts'' of the case that was both biased and erroneous. For example, he said that in Turkey Agca was arrested for the assassination of ''a prominent newspaper editor.'' In fact, Ipekci was also a leading *progressive* editor, but including that would raise a question about Agca's affiliations. Lehrer said that after his escape from Turkey Agca traveled around, ''ending up eventually in Sofia, Bulgaria.'' This is a distortion of fact. Agca started out through Bulgaria and ended up in Italy, and spent most of his travel time in countries of Western Europe. Lehrer stated as an unqalified fact that Agca ''met three Bulgarians'' in Sofia, and ended up asking Henze whether there is ''anything you would add to my description of what the evidence is up 'til now?''

Besides open-ended questions without substance, the most notable feature of the interviewing style of the MacNeil-Lehrer team was their failure to ask questions that beg to be asked in the flow of the interview. For example, Henze said that ''It's inconceivable that the Bulgarians, which [*sic*] does, after all, follow Turkish affairs closely and which is right next door, didn't know who Agca was.'' No question was raised by MacNeil or Lehrer on either how a single Turk with a false passport would be readily identifiable, or why Agca was not known to the authorities in West Germany, Switzerland, and Italy by similar reasoning. Henze also suggested that Agca was instructed by the Kremlin to write his 1979 letter threatening the Pope: ''I can see no other reason why Agca would write a letter about the Pope. The Pope's visit to Turkey went off very successfully and there was no opposition to it.'' If MacNeil and Lehrer had done the least amount of homework they would have discovered that Gray Wolves ideology could explain the letter, and that Henze's statement that there was ''no opposition'' to the Pope's visit was a fabrication—the Nationalist Action Party-Gray Wolves press was violently hostile to the visit.[15] The idea that Agca was under KGB discipline to the point that they would instruct him to write a specific let-

15. In his book, *Papa, Mafya, Agca* (Istanbul: Tekin Yayinevi, 1984), Ugur Mumcu provided extensive evidence, including numerous quotations from the Turkish newspapers *Hergun* and *Tercuman* strongly hostile to the Pope's visit, to show that this claim of Henze's is a plain falsehood.

ter is not only lacking in a trace of evidence, it suggests further questions. Henze had just told his interviewers, rather indignantly, that the Bulgarians surely must have recognized Agca when he entered from Turkey shortly after writing the 1979 letter. But if he was already under tight KGB discipline, the problem of recognition is foolish: Why would the Bulgarians want to "recognize" a KGB agent? A question that would arise with a coherent analysis is: How could the KGB and Bulgarians be so foolish as to bring Agca to Sofia for an extended stay to get his instructions? But Henze's confusion and the questions staring one in the face are never confronted by the kindly MacNeil-Lehrer interrogators.

MacNeil-Lehrer never once asked about the massive violations of "plausible deniability" in the KGB-Bulgarian hiring of Agca, bringing him to Sofia, and then involving numerous Bulgarian officials in his Rome operation. They never raised a question about the enormous time lag in Agca's naming Bulgarians, nor the reports in the Italian press that Agca was given substantial inducement to talk, or the great convenience of the Plot from the standpoint of western political interests. Although the MacNeil-Lehrer show had run a program on the P-2 scandal, they never raised a question about the Italian political-judicial context or the conduct of the case. Sterling cited a report by the Italian secret service SISMI on the Soviet connection to Italian terrorism, but Lehrer never asked about SISMI's links to P-2 or the long history of Italian intelligence agency forgery and participation in rightwing destabilization plans.[16] When Sterling spoke about Agca's confessions being "corroborated in astonishing detail," Lehrer was too ignorant or politically biased to ask an intelligent question based on Agca's retractions and the ability to produce "astonishing detail" about things he admitted he had never seen in his life.

Sterling, Henze, and Ledeen all stressed with great energy how marvelous Magistrate Martella was and how beautifully the Italian judicial process was working. Barry Carter added that "The Italians appear to be doing a good investigative job." MacNeil-Lehrer once again asked no questions. (*E.g.*, "Mr. Carter, how do you know how good a job the Italians are doing given the secrecy of much of the process? How do you reconcile your statement with the frequent leaks that are supposedly contrary to Italian legal rules of secrecy?")

Paul Henze told Judy Woodruff on June 25, 1985, that except for the

16. See Chapter 4, pp. 86-99.

Soviet blaming of things on the CIA, "nobody has ever advanced any other explanation of the plot." This was a knowing fabrication, as a number of investigators in Europe and the United States, including the present authors, had given a two plot version of events: a Turkish plot to kill the Pope, and an Italian secret services/Mafia/rightwing plot to implicate the Bulgarians and Soviets by manipulating Agca. But Henze could contradict himself and tell outright lies without opposition on a program that allows the spokespersons for a propaganda line free and uncontested play.

The New York Times-Sterling-Ledeen Axis

In an editorial published on August 15, 1985, the *New York Times* finally announced that the Plot being acted out in Rome was reminiscent of "a farce by Pirandello." By a coincidence, the present writers had described the case in similar terms many months earlier, but we explicitly mentioned the *New York Times* as an active participant in the farce:[17]

The Bulgarian Connection thus provides a scenario worthy of a plot by Pirandello: Influential disinformation specialists linked to the Italian secret services and the Reagan administration create a useful scenario, sell it to the slow-moving Italians, who then implement it—with the final touch being that the *New York Times* [*et al.*] . . . then rely on Henze, Sterling, and Ledeen to elucidate the real story on what the nefarious KGB has been up to!

The *Times*'s editorial, however, took no credit for the farce. It is just that Agca now lacked credibility; there was no "independent confirmation" of his claims; he altered details at will; and there was a simpler hypothesis available—namely, "that the roots of the plot were in Turkey." The *Times* asserted, of course, that Agca's earlier account "was sufficiently convincing" to have justified proceeding to a trial. But this is disingenuous. The *Times* swallowed Agca's earlier assertions without question, although they were not independently confirmed, and although he had a reputation as a "chronic liar" (in the words of the *Times*'s own correspondent Marvine Howe). In its editorial of December 18, 1982, the *Times* asserted as a positive fact that "he [Agca]

17. Frank Brodhead and Edward S. Herman, "The KGB Plot to Assassinate the Pope: A Case Study in Free World Disinformation," *CovertAction Information Bulletin*, No. 19 (Spring-Summer 1983), p. 5.

checked into Sofia's best hotels,'' although this Agca claim was never "corroborated.'' In an editorial of June 21, 1984, the *Times* asserted that Agca's "detailed accounts of meetings with Bulgarian agents in Sofia and Rome . . . [have] been cross-checked and, with conspicuous exceptions, corroborated where possible.'' This evasive statement fails to mention that the corroborations were only negative; that is, the Bulgarians did not have alibis two years after the event adequate to satisfy Martella.[18] No evidence has ever been produced verifying the delivery of money for the assassination attempt or the rental of the getaway car, nor has a single person been found to testify that he or she had seen Agca with a Bulgarian. That is, by August 1985 nothing in the case had changed, except the *Times*'s assessment of its public salability.

We described earlier how the *New York Times*'s coverage of the Bulgarian Connection from December 1982 through March 1983 fits well a model of a propaganda operation. Apart from the initial flurry of investigation in the immediate aftermath of the shooting (see Appendix A), the only independent research commissioned by the *Times* was that of Nicholas Gage, whose deeply flawed effort was discussed above. We saw in the previous section that the *Times* did not mention Agca's major retractions of June 28, 1983, for over a year. It also refused to entertain a word of dissenting opinion or analysis in that period, although these were available and offered to it.[19] In effect, the editors of the paper adopted the Sterling-Henze line as either true, politically useful, salable, or some combination of these, and refused to look at the issue critically or even allow minimal debate in its pages.

The Albano Report. The low point in the *Times*'s coverage of the Bulgarian Connection was reached on June 10, 1984, when the paper featured a long front-page story by Claire Sterling on the still "secret" Albano Report. Sterling was a strong-minded partisan on this issue, and while she had a background as a reporter, her recent work with the *Reader's Digest* and in her book *The Terror Network* indicated that she had deteriorated from a mediocre Cold War reporter to a rightwing crank. Given her record, it was inevitable that Sterling would distort any news

18. This is the subject to which Martella devoted his maximum energies. See Chapter 5.

19. An excellent Op-Ed article by Diana Johnstone, European Editor of *In These Times*, which discussed the already impressive evidence that Agca had been threatened and induced to implicate the Bulgarians, was rejected by the paper in 1983. A minor exception to the generalization in the text was a single letter to the editor attacking the Connection written by Carl Oglesby.

as a result of her commitment and ideology, and this is what she did with the Albano Report.

The Albano Report is a highly political document, full of rhetorical flourishes and simple misstatements of fact ("Extraordinary is the attempt on his life [the Pope's] as the only such case in history").[20] Albano dismissed the notion that there could be a frameup of Bulgarians as outmoded Cold War propaganda, because Italy had no grudge against Bulgaria and no political purpose could be served by such actions.[21] On the other hand, as the Bulgarians had been accused by Agca, any Bulgarian statements (as opposed to those of the politically neutral Italian police) were statements of an interested party and must be regarded with suspicion.[22] Furthermore, although the idea of any Italian advantage or interest in attacking the East was old Cold War stuff, there was an "iron logic" (a phrase repeated more than once) in the case suggesting an eastern assault on the institutions of the West.

People who Albano found credible were: (1) Albano himself. Although a devout Catholic, a matter brought up by him in his Report, he was "without any political, religious or moral prejudice whatever."[23] (2) Agca. Although Albano acknowledged that Agca told many lies, he was cited as an authority for dozens of unconfirmed statements. (3) Arnaud de Borchgrave, whose statements the Report refers to as "absolutely unquestionable."[24] (4) Officials of the Italian intelligence services. Because they stated for the record that they had not spoken to Agca on any serious matters, this settled the question of coaching for the Prosecutor. (5) Claire Sterling. Albano's Report parrots the Sterling line

20. Report of May 8, 1984, of state prosecutor Antonio Albano (hereafter *Albano Report*), p. 2. A papal assassination had many precedents. According to one account:

"Few popes in the century following John VIII died peacefully in their beds. As we have seen, John VIII himself was murdered; Stephen VI (896-97) strangled in prison; Benedict VI (973-74) smothered; John XIV (983-84) done to death in the Castel Sant' Angelo." Geoffrey Barraclough, *The Medieval Papacy* (New York: Harcourt, Brace & World, 1968), p. 63. This quotation is far from exhausting the record of papal assassinations and assassination attempts.

21. *Albano Report*, p. 3. We pointed out earlier that the P-2 hearings on SISMI provide evidence from SISMI head Santovito himself that the organization had spent considerable effort trying to pin various crimes on the Communist Party and other political enemies. These documents were available to Albano (and to any American newspaper with enterprise and integrity).

22. *Albano Report*, p. 4.

23. *Ibid.*, p. 5.

24. *Ibid.*, p. 30.

in such detail that she must be regarded as the intellectual godmother if not an actual co-author. Thus the Report uses the signaling theory, for example, with Agca bargaining for release by cautious disclosures. It stresses à la Sterling that Agca has always been consistent on the core of his charges—namely, that the originally named Bulgarians are guilty. It asserts that the changes Agca made in his testimony were always "spontaneous," at his own initiative, and would not have occurred but for Agca's voluntary acts.[25] As we discussed in Chapter 5, this is highly misleading: The initiatives frequently followed real world events that made his prior claims untenable.

Albano added his own original touch to the motives for Agca's retractions. He was signaling, but he was also telling Antonov and the Bulgarians that he bore them no grudges: "Essentially this is the hand held up to Antonov, an undoubted indication that Agca holds no malice, no perverse acrimony, no venomous vindictiveness."[26] Another wonderful touch is the Report's explanation of how Agca could know facts about apartments that he subsequently admitted never having visited. The answer is that Agca's *retractions* were false; Agca really had been to all of those places! Albano is the iron logician. Having disproved the coaching hypothesis—*i.e.*, SISMI had no axe to grind, and *said* it was innocent—it follows by iron logic that Agca must have been to places he denied ever having seen. This is extremely convenient for the prosecution: Only assertions fitting the *a priori* iron logic of the case will be taken as true; others are disposed of as "the" lies! Thus the Albano Report states that "At these collective sessions [held by Agca with the Bulgarians in Rome] they also planned an attempt on the life of Lech Walesa who was visiting Italy in January 1981, and the possibility was contemplated to attack Walesa and the Pope simultaneously, as the two were scheduled to meet."[27] This Albano puts as fact, even though it is far-fetched, was never "independently corroborated" by anybody, and even though Agca later denied some of the meetings and his participation in the alleged Walesa plot.

Another illustration of the power of logic in Albano's Report is its use of Agca's lavish expenditures in Europe as evidence for eastern involvement in the assassination plot. At one point Albano noted that the Turkish drug Mafia had money, citing Agca's escape from prison in Turkey as a demonstration of "what the Mafia's money and efficiency can

25. *Ibid.*, pp. 15-16.
26. *Ibid.*, p. 71.
27. *Ibid.*, p. 21.

do.''[28] He gave no evidence that the prison escape was not a strictly Gray Wolves operation, nor that money was important for a prison break. Later on, however, he asked, "How can we account for the money Agca squandered so lavishly on hotel accommodations, restaurants,'' etc., unless we trace it to a political source and by iron logic to the Bulgarians? The answer he gave earlier and had forgotten was that the Turkish-Gray Wolves drug connection yielded a great deal of money.

Reading Sterling in the *New York Times* of June 10, 1984, one would have missed all sense of the bias, incompetence, and comedy that Albano's Report affords. Readers would also not have been informed about the one new major fact in the Report that up to that time had been kept out of the U.S. press—namely, that on June 28, 1983, Agca had retracted a significant portion of his evidence. Sterling's only hint at the retraction runs as follows:

Despite widespread press reports, Mr. Agca will probably not have to face the curious charge of "self-slander and slander" that arose from his brief retraction of some testimony that had already been corroborated. Judge Martella sent him a communication that he was under investigation for such charge last September in regard to certain confusing allegations of his in the Lech Walesa plot.

The serious misrepresentations in these sentences may be seen from the following:

(1) What Sterling calls "confusing allegations" was Agca's statement that he had lied about having participated in a plot to murder Walesa! Although he had described Walesa's hotel in detail, he admitted that he had never seen it, and that he had never met the Bulgarian diplomat whom he had identified from a photo as a co-conspirator. There is nothing "confusing" in these allegations.

(2) Sterling states that Agca only retracted testimony that "had already been corroborated." This is a fabrication. Agca withdrew the claims that he had met Mrs. Antonov and her daughter and visited Antonov's apartment. Agca's ability to recall precise details of the apartment had been previously advanced by the Sterling school as proof of his claims. His description of Mrs. Antonov was taken as "corroboration" of his claim to have met her. In no other sense were Agca's claims "corroborated," and the dishonesty of Sterling's assertions in the face of Agca's admitted lying about "corroborated evidence" is extraordi-

28. *Ibid.*, p. 9.

nary. Even the prosecutor admitted the serious effect of these retractions on Agca's credibility, but in her purported news article Sterling suppressed both Agca's retractions and Albano's statement on the meaning of those retractions.

Following the June 10, 1984 front-page article, the *New York Times* ran another front-page article by Sterling on October 27, 1984, in which she finally acknowledged Agca's retractions of June 28, 1983. Even here, however, the bulk of the article was devoted to presenting the details of the claims which Agca had withdrawn, and she tried to minimize the significance of the retractions by her usual formulas. Once again she asserted that Agca's original confessions provided a wealth of details that were "independently confirmed." But if Agca wasn't there—either at Walesa's hotel or Antonov's apartment—independent corroboration is not only meaningless, it also points to judicial fraud. Sterling then resorted to her signaling theory, claiming like Albano that Agca really *was* there, and that his retractions were false. According to Sterling, he was responding to the kidnapping of Emmanuela Orlandi on June 22, 1983. We have discussed her signaling theory in Chapter 6 and shown its complete implausibility, but also its great utility for *ex post facto* rationalization of anything one wishes to prove.

The Trial. Once the trial in Rome was under way, the *Times*'s on-the-scene reporter was John Tagliabue. Tagliabue had been the *Times*'s reporter in Germany when the assassination attempt occurred. At that time he contributed several useful articles on the Gray Wolves in West Germany, and on the West German government's unsuccessful efforts to determine whether and how long Agca stayed there and the nature of his activities. His performance during the trial, by contrast, illustrates the hegemony of the Sterling model in shaping the *Times*'s coverage of the Connection.

Tagliabue's troubles began on the first day of the trial, when Agca declared that he was Jesus Christ. This extraordinary claim was not featured in the headline of his article the next day ("Prosecutor Asks Broader Inquiry in Trial of Agca"), nor in the first paragraph of the text, although the day before (with Sterling's collaboration[29]) Tagliabue had stressed Agca's credibility as the key issue in the case. Immediately after noting Agca's self-identification as Jesus, Tagliabue hastened to

29. Articles by Sterling on the trial appeared in the *New York Times* of May 27, 1985 (the opening date of the trial) and on August 6, 1985.

stress Agca's "thoughtful and measured account of how he obtained the gun." It was still backup time, not bailout time. The trial next made the front page on June 12, when Agca claimed to have heard that a Soviet aide had paid money to have the Pope killed. On the other hand, when the Pandico revelations appeared, providing something close to a "smoking gun" for the coaching hypothesis, an article about that was rather inconspicuously placed on page 5.[30] In the course of the latter article, Tagliabue said that Ascoli Piceno prison, where Agca was housed, is "notoriously porous." This symbolized the beginning of a shift from backup to bailout time—the *New York Times* had never before thought Agca's prison conditions were relevant to the case, and they had certainly never alerted their readers to the fact that Agca's prison was "notoriously porous." But the *case* was becoming notably porous, and the rats were getting ready to abandon ship.

Up to the recess of the trial in August 1985, however, Tagliabue essentially held fast to the Sterling line, peddling Agca and his claims as objective news. A number of elements of the Sterling perspective can be traced in his reporting.

(1) The Bulgarians and the Soviets had an adequate motive for the assassination attempt based on Polish unrest and the Pope's opposition to leftism in the Third World. No counterargument was ever suggested by Tagliabue, and his news coverage tended to suppress incompatible facts or claims. On June 7, for example, Judge Santiapichi asked Agca about the note found on his person on May 13, 1981, which described the shooting as a political act, a protest against "the killings of thousands of innocent peoples by dictatorships and Soviet and American imperialism." Agca acknowledged that the note represented his views and that he had acted for "personal motives." Michael Dobbs, writing in the *Washington Post*,[31] pointed out that:

The note appeared to contradict his subsequent attempts to present himself as "a terrorist without ideology" who had agreed to shoot the Pope in return for the equivalent of $1.2 million by the Bulgarian secret service. The mercenary motive has been accepted as accurate by an Italian state prosecutor.

These themes were also central to Claire Sterling's analysis. John Tagliabue in the *New York Times* failed to mention this exchange during

30. *New York Times*, June 17, 1985.
31. "Agca Refuses to Testify on Accomplices," June 8, 1985.

the trial. Similarly, in testimony given by Yalcin Ozbey on June 19, the witness suggested that Agca's real motive in shooting the Pope was his hunger for fame. This claim also never reached the readers of the *Times*.

(2) The case was an embarrassment to the Italian government, which pursued it reluctantly. This classic Sterling line was pressed in the article Tagliabue wrote jointly with Sterling on May 27, 1985. Characteristically, no mention was made of any possible political benefits that might have accrued to Craxi and others in bringing the case.

(3) No mention was made by Tagliabue or Sterling of P-2, Pazienza, Ledeen, or Italian political conditions until *after* the Pandico bombshell.

(4) There was a steady reiteration of the Sterling cliché that Agca "has not budged from his basic contention that Bulgarians, and thus the Soviet Union, commissioned and financed the plot to murder the Pope."[32] And this cliché is not true. As noted above, Agca stated before the Court on June 7, 1985, that he had acted for "personal" motives with the intent of making a political protest, which contradicts the mercenary hypothesis. Even more dramatic, on March 3, 1986, Agca returned to the witness stand after a long absence, immediately after Marini's summing up and request for dismissal of the case against the Bulgarians, to reiterate the point he made in the letter threatening to shoot the Pope in 1979: that he had committed his act because of the crimes of western Christianity. "I thought I should strike at western civilization and Christianity in the person of the Pope because they have been repressive and oppressive of the people." In explaining his actions of May 13, 1981, he made no mention of the Bulgarians or KGB. Tagliabue and the *Times* blacked out this statement.

(5) Tagliabue swallowed the signaling theory and Agca's "double game." "By his own admission," wrote Tagliabue, Agca was playing a double game, which seemed "to play into the hands of the defense attorneys" who claimed that Agca was coached.[33] The use of "admission" we have already seen to be a manipulative device of the Sterling-Henze school. Tagliabue does not say that Agca "admitted" he was Jesus Christ. There are alternative explanations to the signaling theory; Agca could be a crazy opportunist, in which case he is revealing his true nature. The phrase "playing into the hands of" the Bulgarian defense reflects Tagliabue's and the *Times*'s identification with the case for the prosecution.

(6) Tagliabue regularly understated the number of contradictions in Agca's testimony. As Michael Dobbs wrote in the *Washington Post*: "Agca has changed elements of his story almost continuously in the last

32. *New York Times*, August 6, 1985.
33. *Ibid.*, June 22, 1985.

four years. The session of the conspiracy trial yesterday, however, appeared to set a record for the scale and rapidity of corrections offered by Agca to earlier descriptions of the logistics of the assassination attempt."[34] John Tagliabue, writing in the *New York Times*, was much more circumspect.

(7) Tagliabue raised no questions about how Martella assembled a case based on Agca's testimony, given the evidence accumulating in court that Agca lied and contradicted himself on an hourly basis and suffered from serious delusions.

(8) Following prosecutor Antonio Marini's recommendation on February 27, 1986, that the Bulgarian defendants be acquitted for lack of evidence, Tagliabue chose to feature heavily the prosecutor's attack on the judge for failing to admit additional witnesses, and the fact that Marini called upon the jury to make its own decision.[35]

The Times *and the Disinformationists.* We noted earlier that the *New York Times* not only used Sterling as a reporter and source of data and themes, it also suppressed information about her credentials. Her books were regularly reviewed: *The Time of the Assassins* was reviewed in both the daily and Sunday *New York Times*. Her reliance on Czech General Sejna, an established liar-informer, as a key source in *The Terror Network* has never been disclosed to *Times* readers; and the slander suits over her smearing of Henri Curiel were never mentioned in the *Times*.

Equally compromising has been the *New York Times*'s alliance with and protection of Michael Ledeen. Ledeen was given Op-Ed column

34. *Washington Post*, June 26, 1985.

35. "Rome Prosecutor Urges Acquittal of 3 Bulgarians," *New York Times*, February 28, 1986. Tagliabue pretended that there was a serious chance that the jury would override the prosecutor and find the Bulgarians guilty, which was foolish and naive. He also displayed the same kind of political naiveté that we noted above under (2); Marini's rhetoric was taken at face value, and Tagliabue never hinted at the possibility that the prosecutor might be protecting his colleagues in the Italian establishment, who had initiated and enthusiastically supported a case that was suffering such a dismal ending. Tagliabue offered no analysis of the causes of the failure, despite the long record of claims by the *New York Times* and its favored sources that Bulgarian guilt was all but proved. Apart from the Marini gambit, Tagliabue blamed the dénouement on Agca's undermining of the case, without explaining why none of Agca's claims of Bulgarian involvement had ever been confirmed by a single independent witness over the course of a four-year period of investigation and trial.

space twice in 1984-85,[36] allowing him to issue a call for the greater application of force in Lebanon and to stress the greater importance of National Security than individual liberty—themes that would delight the heart of Licio Gelli. Ledeen's book *Grave New World* was given a substantial and favorable notice in the Sunday *New York Times Book Review*.

Perhaps more serious has been the *New York Times*'s cover-up of Ledeen's role in Italy and his unsavory linkages to Italian intelligence and the Italian Right. The *Times* has never mentioned his connections with Santovito, Gelli, and Pazienza,[37] his controversial sale of documents to SISMI, or the fact that the head of Italian military intelligence stated before the Italian Parliament that Ledeen was an "intriguer" and unwelcome in Italy.[38] Actually, the *Times*'s suppressions on Ledeen have been part of a larger package of suppressions that excluded any information that would disturb the hegemony of the Sterling-Henze line. Thus, just as Sterling and Henze never mention P-2 in their writings, so the *Times* failed even to mention the Italian Parliamentary Report on P-2 of July 12, 1984, which raised many inconvenient questions about the quality of Italian society and the intelligence services. The Parliamentary Commission, which held extensive hearings on SISMI (published in five volumes), was also blacked out for readers of the *Times*. In July 1985 an Italian court pronounced sentence against Francesco Pazienza and other officials of SISMI for serious crimes. The accompanying 185-page report described spectacular abuses of secret service authority in Italy,[39] including the forging and planting of documents. Although these crimes were committed by individuals regularly linked in the Italian press to the Bulgarian Connection, this report and sentence were also suppressed by the *Times*. We believe that it is precisely this connection—and the fact that these sensational documents would raise questions about Ledeen and the Sterling-Henze portrayal of the Bulgarian Connection—that caused the *Times* to avoid providing its readers with such information.

For years the Italian press carried reports of SISMI and Mafia involvement in threatening and coaching Agca. The *New York Times* refrained from mentioning, let alone investigating, these matters. The first reference to Pazienza in the *Times* came only with his arrest on March 24, 1985, and the article appeared in the Business Section of the paper.

36. Michael Ledeen, "Be Ready To Fight," *New York Times*, June 23, 1985; and "When Security Preempts the Rule of Law," *New York Times*, April 16, 1984.

37. A minor exception is noted in the text below.

38. Maurizio De Luca, "Fuori l'intrigante," *L'Espresso*, August 5, 1984.

39. See Chapter 4, pp. 00-000.

The author, E. J. Dionne, never asked why Pazienza, wanted in Italy for over a year, had never been extradited. He failed to mention that Pazienza was wanted in Italy in connection with serious abuses by the intelligence services, including involvement in the Bologna railroad station bombing. When it came to Pazienza's involvement with Michael Ledeen, the reporter telephoned Ledeen, who told him that Pazienza had exaggerated his influence with the Reagan administration, and that he himself had had only a very brief, unspecified relation with Pazienza. Dionne raised no questions and tapped no alternative information sources. He had all the news fit to print.

From December 1982 through February 1986 the *New York Times* featured heavily and almost exclusively claims of prosecutors and proponents of the Plot. After a long trial in which the claims of the prosecutor were once again explored in great detail, the prosecution rested at the end of February, acknowledging its lack of an adequate case against the Bulgarians by asking for a dismissal for lack of evidence. It was finally the defense's turn to present its case. The Italian counsel for Antonov took the floor March 4, and finished his presentation on March 8. His powerful statement, which assailed the Martella investigation mercilessly, described in detail the evidential weakness of the case, and gave powerful support to the coaching hypothesis, was blacked out in the *New York Times* (and the rest of the mass media). This completes the circle of propaganda service, with the preferred line pushed as long as it could be issued as news without gross embarrassment, and then failing to give the defense even minimal coverage, even after it is apparent to all that the preferred line has been discredited. This process suggests the unlikelihood that any retrospectives will be provided that might explain the reasons for the failure—and the media's gullible and uncritical transmission—of a case long portrayed as cogent and true.

The Small Voices of Dissent

There were serious voices of dissent in the mass media, but they were few and without serious effect on the general run of media opinion and reporting. The only major TV program to challenge the Sterling-Henze line before the 1985 trial was an ABC-TV News "20/20" show on May 12, 1983. In that program ABC did some very remarkable and unique things: It investigated the obvious leads and implausibilities in the Sterling-Henze line with diligence, it went at it with an open and somewhat skeptical view of the truth of the case, and it tapped a wide array of sources. The results were devastating. It established from drug enforcement officials that Agca's travels fit well into the pattern of movement of the international drug trade. Citing Mumcu and others, it stressed Agca's psychopathic personality and overweening desire to be in the limelight. It effectively disposed of the alleged letter from the Pope to Brezhnev, citing Cardinal Krol (a Vatican-appointed spokesman) and other Vatican officials, who denied the existence of such a letter and claimed that verbal messages from the Pope at the time were conciliatory. It pointed out the many ways in which the implementation of the plot violated basic laws of spycraft (*e.g.*, planning meetings in Bulgarian residences). It pointed up strategic errors in Agca's evidence (mistakes in describing Antonov's apartment, and the alleged presence of Mrs. Antonov, who was in Sofia). It showed how Agca adjusted his testimony to take account of Bulgarian counterclaims (*e.g.*, pushing back the meeting time with Antonov on May 13, given Antonov's strong alibi for the originally "confessed" time). Examining the Bulgarian alibis, ABC found them partly convincing. It discussed the problem of the language barrier between Antonov and Agca. And it cited ABC's own intelligence and police contacts to cast doubts on the testimony of Mantarov and on the general validity of the case.

In brief, the ABC inquiry was an eye-opener, raising many questions and providing partial and skeptical answers. Nevertheless, the program's information fell still-born from the tube. Although it received powerful support from Agca's retractions one month later, the retractions were not leaked and publicized, and so did not strengthen the skeptical case. The Sterling-Henze line held firm in the mass media for another year.

The most important dissenting voice in the mass media was that of Michael Dobbs, the *Washington Post*'s Rome correspondent, who began to present an alternative and cautiously critical view following Sterling's June 10, 1984 misrepresentation of the Albano Report. In a series of articles beginning on June 18, 1984—eight days after the *Times* carried Sterling's rendition of Albano's Report—Dobbs began to provide U.S. readers a second opinion. While featuring Albano's conclusion that the Bulgarians were behind the plot, Dobbs also noted in his opening paragraph that the evidence was "largely circumstantial"; and in the fifth paragraph he said that "much of the circumstantial evidence . . . could undermine rather than confirm the conspiracy theory. . . ." The remainder of Dobbs's lengthy article questioned Agca's reliability, noted Agca's June 28, 1983 retraction of most of his previous declarations, and presented evidence that appeared to undermine fatally the Truck Ploy. A month later, on July 22, 1984, Dobbs returned to the attack, noting in an article headlined "Probers Divided Over Evidence in Pope Attack" that there were many loose ends in the case and that Agca lacked credibility.

This was too much for Claire Sterling. In an Op-Ed column in the *Washington Post* ("Taking Exception," August 7, 1984), Sterling accused Dobbs of "numerous omissions or misstatements." She alleged "a curious ignorance of how this investigation developed," and maintained that "while Dobbs dwells on [Agca's] retraction," he failed to take note that "practically everything Agca tried to take back had been substantiated already, and not a single point in the retraction changed the basic lines in Agca's story."

In a reply in the *Post* a few days later (August 10, 1984), Dobbs noted Sterling's "tendency to conclude that anybody who questions her thesis that the assassination attempt has already been shown to be a Soviet-bloc conspiracy is accepting Bulgarian arguments." But he dwelt primarily on Sterling's essential dishonesty in failing to include in her story that Albano's Report had raised the issue of Agca's "retractions" of June 28, 1983. In a separate document, made available to readers on request, he accused Sterling of omitting sections of the Report "that call into question Agca's credibility." This document lists a further dozen errors that Sterling made in her statement in the *Post* about Dobbs's reporting on the case, including clear misstatements of what Albano's Report actually says. Later, in a four-part series in the *Washington Post* in mid-October 1984, Dobbs relocated the root of the assassination attempt in the Turkish right wing, raised severe doubts about Agca's credibility and his allegations of working for the Bulgarians, and traced the evolving "confessions" to show that they were merely embellishments on a first-approximation tale that was corrected by information learned from the media and perhaps from the questions asked him by his interrogators.

During the last half of 1984 and in the early phase of the 1985 trial Michael Dobbs's writing on the Plot gave readers of the *Washington Post* (and some subscribers to the *Post*'s news service) a nearly unique channel of information, providing a well-reasoned alternative to the near tidal wave of pro-Plot outpourings from the publishers of Sterling, Henze, and their allies. Dobbs raised many questions, pointed up Agca's numerous lies and contradictions, and showed in a variety of ways the weaknesses of the Italian handling of the case. One of Dobbs's chief contributions was to trace a large proportion of Agca's claims to the Italian media, and to demonstrate the extensive access that Agca had to outside information which would help him develop his claims and declarations.

Despite these merits, Dobbs was unable to break free of the clichés that Martella was "wise" and "judicious," and that the coaching hypothesis was a "Bulgarian argument."[40] In his exchange with Sterling, Dobbs was on the defensive, claiming that his own role was reporting "both sides, in contrast to Sterling." In the end this lone mass media reporter, who had built up an impressive case against the Connection, was unable to state a firm conclusion. This is arguably reasonable; a reporter can give the facts and let readers make up their own minds. In the context, however, nobody in the mass media was drawing negative conclusions on the Plot. Sterling, Henze, and their allies suffered no such constraints. They were free to assert Bulgarian and Soviet guilt, and even to denounce doubters as victims of Soviet disinformation. The contrast tells us a great deal about the power of the political forces that originated and sustained the case.

The Intellectuals: Somnolence and Complicity

Between 1982 and 1985, when the Bulgarian Connection became incorporated into the public's consciousness, the academic community remained almost totally silent on the subject. Journals in the fields of political science, international relations, and Near Eastern studies record only a single article on the Bulgarian Connection. Academic intellectuals were content to allow this issue to be monopolized by the Big Three and their allies at the Georgetown CSIS. While the academicians

40. As late as June 19, 1985, Dobbs was still asserting that "Soviet Bloc propagandists and leftist Italian newspapers have claimed for some time that Agca was 'fed' in prison with details on the Bulgarians he later accused of being his accomplices, but have so far failed to provide convincing evidence to support their assertions." This reference to "Soviet Bloc propagandists" is the same kind of Sterlingesque designation that Dobbs objected to when applied to himself. Furthermore, it isn't even accurate. A fair number of analysts not reasonably designated as "Soviet Bloc propagandists and leftist Italian newspapers" have claimed that Agca was coached. What is "convincing evidence" is a matter for debate, but Dobbs has never explained how Agca could have given details about Antonov's apartment that were never previously published and that Agca admitted he had never seen.

were no doubt dealing with more important matters, they may also have been constrained by the fact that the links between academic political scientists, international relations specialists, conservative thinktanks, and the federal government are extensive and pervasive. The silence of the academy is evidence that these are to a great extent coopted disciplines, "handmaidens of inspired truth."[41] The Bulgarian Connection is an inspired truth.

We mentioned earlier that Michael Ledeen's book *Grave New World* was favorably reviewed in the Sunday *New York Times Book Review*. The reviewer, William E. Griffiths, a Professor of Political Science at MIT, remarked parenthetically that "his [Ledeen's] discussion of the probable Soviet involvement in the plot to kill the Pope is surely correct."[42] Griffiths gives no support for this statement. But Griffiths, who is a "roving editor" for the *Reader's Digest*, is also on the Editorial Board of *Orbis*, a semi-academic journal which carried the lone "scholarly" article on the plot. Perhaps this was the source from which Griffiths deduced the validity of the Connection.

The "scholarly" article was published in *Orbis* in the Winter 1985 issue. Entitled "The Attempted Assassination of the Pope," it was written by Thomas P. Melady and John F. Kikoski, members of the faculty of Sacred Heart University of Fairfield, Connecticut.[43] The most notable feature of this piece is its complete and uncritical reliance on Claire Sterling, Paul Henze, and Michael Ledeen as authorities on the subject. The article is, in fact, a rehash of the works of these authors. Thirty-three of 78 footnotes are to the works of the Big Three. A further 15 footnotes cite Sterling's version of the Albano Report. The remainder of the citations range from NBC's Marvin Kalb and the *Reader's Digest* to quotations from Henry Kissinger, Richard Pipes, and Zbigniew Brzezinski. Michael Ledeen's *Commentary* article is described as "a thorough treatment of media coverage of this affair and of the reluctance of the 'elite media' to more actively pursue this story. . . . "[44] The au-

41. See Robert A. Brady, *The Spirit and Structure of German Fascism* (New York: Viking, 1937). Chapter 2, "Science, Handmaiden of Inspired Truth," described the accommodation of German scientists to the social philosophy of the Nazi state.

42. *New York Times Book Review*, May 19, 1985.

43. Melady is also President of the University. He has been U.S Ambassador to Burundi and Uganda and a Senior Adviser to the U.S. Delegation at the United Nations.

44. Thomas P. Melady and John F. Kikoski, "The Attempted Assassination of the Pope," *Orbis* (Winter 1985), p. 777, n. 4. The *Commentary* article was incorporated into Ledeen's book *Grave New World*. The contents of that chapter are discussed above in Chapter 6.

thors cite the Albano Report as an authoritative and objective document, and refer to its "exhaustive documentation" of various matters, although they acknowledge never having read the Report. They rely on Sterling's summary and her general inferences based on her own reading of the document.[45] This lures them into citing at length Agca's "remarkable details" on the Walesa plot and Antonov's apartment, oblivious to the fact that the Albano Report acknowledged that on June 28, 1983 Agca admitted that he had either concocted or knew only by hearsay these "remarkable details."

The authors never cite Michael Dobbs's four-part critique of the prosecution's case, nor any other reporter or analyst with a different viewpoint. When ABC-TV in 1983 checked the specifics of the Kalb-NBC claim that the Pope had sent a warning note to Brezhnev, it came up with sharply contradictory facts.[46] Melady and Kikoski give the straight Kalb-NBC version, never hinting that it had been disputed. Agca's claims which Sterling and Henze selectively chose to fit their model are also presented as valid, even where they have been retracted. Henze's version of the alleged Soviet attempt to destabilize Turkey is presented as uncontested truth—alternative facts and an alternative literature are simply ignored. Henze's possible bias is suppressed and the authors adopt Henze's own form of nondisclosure of his background—the former CIA station chief in Turkey is said to have "a strong prior background in Turkish affairs, and presently is a research scholar [sic] with the Rand Corporation."

Melady and Kikoski do not even take into consideration contrary evidence from sources with which they are apparently familiar. For example, they (along with Sterling and Henze) continue to rely on Nicholas Gage's story about the Bulgarian defector Mantarov, long after the *Times*'s foreign editor Craig Whitney had essentially conceded the truth of the Bulgarians' denials and refutations of Mantarov's contentions. The list of problems which the *Orbis* authors sidestepped by ignoring inconvenient evidence is a long one, encompassing all those that would be relevant to a work of serious academic scholarship. In short, Melady and Kikoski provided the academic world with a *Reader's Digest* article salted with a few footnotes.[47]

---

45. "Sterling, who has read the as yet unreleased Albano Report in its entirety, wrote that: 'Judicial belief in Mr. Agca's confession was apparently fortified by a mass of corroborative evidence'." *Ibid.*, p. 799.

46. See the discussion of the ABC program in the preceding section of this chapter.

47. That it was published by *Orbis* is revealing. *Orbis* is published by the Foreign Pol-

The real function of articles like this *Orbis* production is their "echo chamber" service. Relying entirely on Sterling and company, Melady and Kikoski provide a nominally "scholarly article" confirming the Sterling-Henze claims. This is now available for citation as scholarly confirmation of the truth of the Sterling-Henze claims.[48] Thus Henze cites this work in support of his own conclusions in his 1985 update of *The Plot to Kill the Pope*, and it will undoubtedly provide others with a respectable citation for the Sterling-Henze version of the story, despite its wholly derivative and uncritical properties. Readers unfamiliar with the "echo chamber" might conclude that Melady and Kikoski had sifted evidence possibly unavailable to Henze, or that they had examined competing hypotheses and come down on Henze's side. Readers who have not read the *Orbis* article would have no way of knowing that Henze, in citing Melady-Kikoski, is simply citing himself (and Sterling) at second hand. Thus disinformation echoes through the chamber to create the illusion of independent scholarly confirmation.

icy Research Institute, a conservative thinktank affiliated with the International Relations program of the University of Pennsylvania. Its editorial board of 35 academics and thinktank intellectuals includes 24 members currently on the staffs of universities, among them William Van Cleave, Allen Whiting, Robert Scalapino, Paul Seabury, William Griffiths, Richard Pipes. The thinktank members include Colin Gray of the Hudson Institute and Lawrence B. Krause of the Brookings Institution. Presumably this article meets this group's conception of scholarly standards.

48. A fine example of this process was the alleged admission by Khmer Rouge leader, Khieu Samphan, that his government had slaughtered a million people. His statement was reportedly made in an interview with a remote Italian journal, *Famiglia Cristiana*, in 1976. It is extremely doubtful that this interview ever took place, but translations and mistranslations abounded. A mistranslation by John Barron and Anthony Paul of the *Reader's Digest* was cited by Donald Wise in the *Far Eastern Economic Review*, which was then cited by Professor Karl Jackson in *Asian Survey* as authentic evidence. Jackson provided the "scholarly" source to be cited further. For a fuller discussion see Noam Chomsky and Edward S. Herman, *After the Cataclysm: Postwar Indochina and the Reconstruction of Imperial Ideology* (Boston: South End Press, 1979), pp. 172-77.

8. Conclusions

I t is an important truth that "necessity is the mother of invention." This was true of the Bulgarian Connection, which was needed by the New Cold Warriors in the United States, by Craxi, Spadolini, Gelli, Santovito, and the Vatican in Italy, and by others. Thus, as in the case of many inventions, this one had multiple authorship. With the shooting of the Pope on May 13, 1981, a number of different individuals immediately knew in their hearts that the KGB did it—or ought to have done it—and from several independent sources there soon emerged claims that the KGB *did* do it.

The Bulgarian Connection as Western Disinformation

That the idea of the Bulgarian Connection was conceived early and pushed by a number of independent sources, none of whom had any evidence for the Connection, is one of several lines of accumulating evidence pointing more and more conclusively to the Bulgarian Connection as a product of both deliberate disinformation and some form of manipulation and coaching of the imprisoned Agca. It is now known, for example, that the Italian secret service agency SISMI issued a document on May 19, 1981—within a week of the assassination attempt—which claimed that the Plot had been announced by a Soviet official at a gathering of the Warsaw Pact nations in Bucharest, Rumania, and that Agca had been trained in the Soviet Union.[1] This report was pure disinformation, generated from within SISMI or supplied in whole or part from some other intelligence source. It is an important document in two respects: It shows that the idea of pinning the crime on the East came

1. The points summarized here are developed more fully in Chapters 4 and 5.

early to elements of the secret services, and it demonstrates their willingness to forge or pass along false evidence on the Connection itself. This forgery appeared as fact in the first book published on the Plot, by a Vatican priest; and a Vatican official subsequently acknowledged that the hypothesis of KGB-Bulgarian involvement in the shooting had been secretly disseminated by the Vatican very soon after the event. Furthermore, an official Catholic group in West Germany paid substantial sums to a Gray Wolves member and friend of Agca to visit Agca in prison and to persuade him to talk.[2] Testimony during the recent trial in Rome also indicated that the West German police offered money and leniency to Oral Celik (through Yalcin Ozbey, held by the Germans in prison) if he would agree to come to West Germany and help confirm Agca's testimony. In short, the willingness to implicate the Bulgarians and Soviets by disseminating lies and seeking to induce false witness by western intelligence agencies and other political interests was displayed early and often.

We also showed in Chapter 6 that the two primary U.S. sources on the Bulgarian Connection, Claire Sterling and Paul Henze, have demonstrated similar creative propensities in dealing with the subject. Paul Henze is a long-time CIA professional and specialist in propaganda, who has openly admitted impatience with demands for evidence when dealing with hypothetical enemy crimes.[3] Both Henze and Sterling use what has been called the "preferential method of research," which consists of picking out those pieces of fact or claims that are "preferred" for their argument and disregarding all others. Both have a strong penchant for relying on the claims of badly compromised intelligence sources and discredited defectors.[4] Sterling's creativity—and lack of scientific self-discipline—in dealing with the Bulgarian Connection is shown in her response to Orsan Oymen's claim that Agca's lifelong and extensive relations with the Gray Wolves must have had a bearing on his actions. Her answer, that she "could not see how to reconcile that with Agca's summer in Bulgaria," is revealing. His stay in Bulgaria, a thruway for Turkish migrants (and Gray Wolves), proves or suggests nothing. But to one who knows the truth beforehand and employs the preferential method of research, it is a telling point.

Based on Agca's visit to Bulgaria in the summer of 1980, both Ster-

2. This plan was called off after it was found that Agca had already begun to talk. See Chapter 5, n. 3.
3. See Chapter 6, pp. 148-49.
4. See Chapter 6 and Appendix C.

ling and Henze saw an opportunity to create a Soviet Plot scenario.[5] Both were well funded, and they were generously received by the mass media, despite their blemished credentials and demagogic arguments. We believe that the Sterling-Henze model and the western media's eager and uncritical acceptance of the Bulgarian Connection helped shape the case in Rome. Sterling and Henze provided the basic scenario adopted by both Agca and Martella, and the quick upsurge of popular belief and political vested interest in the Plot gave the case an almost unstoppable momentum. Agca's guidance to a proper confession was encouraged and made more effective by the pre-packaged scenarios and the already prepared groundwork of belief.

A second body of evidence suggesting that Agca was manipulated and coached while in prison has been the accumulating data on P-2, SISMI, Pazienza, and the Ledeen Connection. It has long been known in Italy that the extreme Right—the "party of the coup"—has had an important place in the military establishment and secret services. But a spate of new evidence on these topics has surfaced in the past few years, much of it highly relevant to the Bulgarian Connection.[6] This evidence shows clearly the very important role that P-2 had assumed in the military and intelligence services, the frequency with which elements of the secret services have had cooperative relations with terrorists and the Mafia, and their willingness to forge and plant documents to achieve their political ends. There has also been considerable evidence of the involvement of individuals with important links to the Reagan administration, notably Francesco Pazienza and Michael Ledeen, in the dubious practices of the secret services.

A further set of evidence that has strengthened the case for coaching has been the growing number of plausible claims of "smoking guns."[7] A Vatican official has named the prison chaplain Mariano Santini, who was in close and regular contact with Agca, as a Vatican agent attempting to get Agca to confess. (Santini was also close to the Mafia, and was subsequently jailed as a Mafia emissary.) In 1983, Mafia official Giuseppi Cilleri claimed that Francesco Pazienza had been visiting Agca in prison and had given him detailed instructions on proper testimony and identification of the Bulgarians. Agca's cell neighbor, Giovanni Senzani, a Red Brigades terrorist who had rallied to the gov-

5. They may even have believed in the truth of their own creations, although this must remain uncertain. Nobody has yet invented a sincereiometer.

6. See especially Chapter 4 above.

7. See especially Chapter 5 above.

ernment, was in regular contact with Agca. He was familiar with the photo album of Bulgarians from which Agca selected his alleged co-conspirators (it had been used earlier in Senzani's own trial). Giovanni Pandico, a former Mafia official and principal witness in the trial of hundreds of Mafia personnel in Naples, provided details on just how Agca was induced to talk by Mafia chief Cutolo, former SISMI official Musumeci, and various others in the Ascoli Piceno prison. Francesco Pazienza has denied the allegations of his own involvement in persuading Agca to "confess," claiming that he has been made the "fall guy" for the *actual* perpetrators of the induced confession—other members of SISMI whose names and role he spelled out.[8]

These various threads of evidence show that there was an intent to implicate the Bulgarians arising from several different sources, all of whom had access to Agca in prison, and that the interested parties in the Italian secret services and Vatican had no compunction about doctoring evidence. There are also now a number of explicit statements that describe how and by whom Agca was prodded and coached. This aggregate of evidence, when combined with the lack of any support for Agca's frequently revised claims of Bulgarian involvement, leaves little doubt that the Bulgarian Connection was a product of encouragement and coaching.

We believe that the actual plot to kill the Pope—in contrast with the plot to implicate the Bulgarians—arose from indigenous Turkish sources. No other scenario yet advanced has comparable plausibility, let alone such solid empirical support, as one based on Agca's link to the Gray Wolves.[9] The Gray Wolves' hostility to the Pope has demonstrable ideological roots, although the actual shooting was very probably affected by Agca's own psychological peculiarities and "Carlos complex."[10] The Gray Wolves had links to some Bulgarians through the smuggling trade, but they also had links to the CIA and numerous other rightwing groups with whom they had more ideological compatibility. It is our belief that none of these foreign connections had any direct bearing on the assassination attempt.

8. See Diana Johnstone, "Bulgarian Connection: Finger-pointing in the pontiff plot labyrinth," *In These Times*, January 29-February 4, 1986.
9. For details, see Chapter 3 above.
10. See Chapter 3, p. 56.

The Flaws in the Case From Its Inception

We have stressed throughout this book that the Bulgarian Connection was never at any time supported by credible evidence or logic, and survived only by a tacit refusal of the western media to examine closely a convenient political line. Let us recapitulate briefly a few of these fundamental flaws.

• The alleged Soviet "motive"—fear of the Pope's aid to Solidarity—lacked plausibility from the beginning. Rational behavior would have led the Soviet leadership to calculate that the Poles and West would quickly attribute an assassination attempt to them even if it were well covered. There was also every reason to anticipate that the effect of an assassination attempt on the Poles would be adverse to Soviet interests (*i.e.*, it would elicit rage and increased hostility). The purported motive has also never been reconciled with the fact that Agca's threat to murder the Pope in 1979 and the "deal" he allegedly struck with the Bulgarians in Sofia in the summer of 1980 took place before Solidarity even existed.

• A related "paradox" of Soviet involvement has also never been satisfactorily resolved. That is, while the alleged plot was intended to strengthen the Soviet's hand in dealing with Poland, as it worked out in the real world the plot caused the Soviet Union severe propaganda damage (even though the Pope was not killed and evidence of Soviet involvement has not yet been produced). On the other hand, the Reagan administration and western hard-liners have benefitted greatly from the plot. On the Sterling-Henze model, the Soviets must be incredibly stupid. On our model, in which the Bulgarian Connection was manufactured by Sterling-Henze and U.S. and Italian officials, the source of the plot and the resultant flow of benefits are comprehensible.[11]

• According to Sterling, Henze, Marvin Kalb, Albano, and Martella, the Soviet and Bulgarian secret police are highly efficient and try to maintain "plausible deniability." This is incompatible with hiring an unstable rightwing Turk, bringing him to Sofia for an extended stay, and especially with arranging to have him supervised in detail by Bulgarian officials in Rome. Agca did visit Sofia, Bulgaria in 1980. In the

11. In our analysis, the assassination attempt was a fortuitous event from the standpoint of both East and West, but with the imaginative anticommunist Agca in an Italian prison, the West was able to take advantage of this event—through the actions of SISMI and Sterling and company—to construct a "second conspiracy."

Sterling-Henze analyses, this is a key fact showing Bulgarian guilt. But if the KGB is smart and covers its tracks, concern over plausible deniability would have caused them to go to great pains to keep Agca *away* from Bulgaria. Thus, Agca's visit to Bulgaria provides the raw material for creating a Bulgarian Connection only because a propaganda system allows its principals to contradict themselves and one another virtually without challenge. The Keystone Kops arrangements outlined by Agca involving Bulgarian officials *in Rome* would have been laughed off the stage by NBC or the *New York Times*—if this propaganda show had been put on in Moscow.

● As pointed out by Michael Dobbs, "Agca can be shown to have lied literally hundreds of times to judges both in his native Turkey and in Italy."[12] Orsan Oymen estimates some 115 changes in testimony by Agca recorded in the Martella Report. Agca withdrew significant parts of "confessions," which he admitted were based on outside assistance or produced out of thin air. As Agca was for all practical purposes the sole witness in the case, Martella's decision to proceed to a trial in the face of this self-destruction of credibility reflected a broken-down judicial process.

● The Sterling-Henze-Martella school referred frequently to Agca's testimony as having been "independently confirmed." This assumed a properly managed investigation of Agca's claims. But Martella conceded a lack of control over or knowledge of Agca's visitors in prison, and we have seen that Agca's outside contacts were extensive. Furthermore, Martella's *presumption* of the validity of Agca's primary allegations[13] injected an additional element of impropriety into the process of confirming Agca's claims. Given the high probability that Agca was fed information by individuals in SISMI and elsewhere in the Italian prison-intelligence-political-judicial network, "independent confirmation" has to be taken with a grain of salt.

● Not a single witness was produced in more than three years of investigations and trial to support any Agca claim of a contact with Bulgarians, in Rome or anywhere else, although his supposed meetings and travels with them were frequent and in conspicuous places. The car allegedly hired by the Bulgarians in Rome for the assassination attempt has never been traced. The large sum of money supposedly paid by the Bulgarians for the shooting has never been located or traced.

12. "A Communist Plot to Kill the Pope—Or a Liar's Fantasy," *Washington Post*, November 18, 1984.
13. See Chapter 5, pp. 114-17.

• With one exception, every proven transaction by Agca, from his escape from a Turkish prison in 1979 to May 13, 1981, including all transfers of money or a gun, was with a member of the Gray Wolves.[14]

• The photographic evidence of May 13, 1981, one of the bases on which Martella arrested Antonov, collapsed long ago. Martella eventually asserted that the photograph allegedly showing Antonov on the scene was actually that of a tourist, not Antonov, and the matter was dropped. But this tourist has never been located by independent researchers, and the photo of Antonov in St. Peter's Square is a remarkably exact likeness, requiring a phenomenal coincidence. An alternative hypothesis is that the photo of Antonov was faked.[15] In the Lowell Newton photograph, the individual fleeing from the scene, originally identified by Agca as the Bulgarian "Kolev," was later identified as Agca's Gray Wolves friend Oral Celik.[16] It is thus possible that Martella was lured into arresting Antonov by a combination of a fabricated Antonov likeness and one of Agca's lies, which together placed *two* Bulgarians in St. Peter's Square at the time of the shooting. Martella's gullibility quotient on claims of Bulgarian guilt was unflagging up to the submission of his final Report.

• The formal photo identification of Bulgarians by Agca on November 8, 1982, put forward by Martella and the media as compelling evidence of Bulgarian involvement, was rendered meaningless by the statement of Minister of Defense Lagorio on the floor of the Italian Parliament that Agca had already identified the Bulgarian photos two months previously. The dramatic photo show was thus almost surely a staged rerun of a prior briefing and "identification." It should be recalled that Agca took seven months after deciding to "come clean" before naming a single Bulgarian.[17]

14. The exception was that he apparently received a small sum of money from Mersan, who was acting as a courier for Ugurlu. Given Ugurlu's ties with the Gray Wolves, and perhaps even Turkish intelligence, this single exception to the Gray Wolves pattern will hardly bear the weight given it by Sterling-Henze, who claimed that it removes Agca's crime from a Gray Wolves context and points the finger of guilt at the Bulgarian-Turkish Mafia. We argued in Chapter 3 that these links took place within the larger framework of the activities of the Nationalist Action Party and the Gray Wolves.

15. For a discussion of the ease with which Antonov's face could have been inserted into the crowd by a computerized photo-editing machine widely used in the publishing and advertising industries, see Howard Friel, "The Antonov Photo and the Bulgarian Connection," *CovertAction Information Bulletin*, Number 21 (Spring 1984), pp. 20-21.

16. The trial in Rome raised doubts about this second identification, and the true identity of the fleeing individual is uncertain.

17. See Chapter 5, pp. 110-11, for a further discussion of this photo identification.

Conclusion: The Lessons and Future of the Bulgarian Connection

The history of the Bulgarian Connection illustrates well the role of the mass media as a servant of power. The New Cold Warriors were looking hard for a basis on which to assail the Evil Empire in 1981, and the shooting of the Pope and the incarceration of Agca in an Italian prison offered them a marvelous propaganda opportunity. The mass media performance, from the time of Sterling's *Reader's Digest* article in August 1982 up to the time of the trial, allowed that propaganda opportunity to be fully realized.[18] As we have seen, in dealing with the Bulgarian Connection the major U.S. media violated norms of *substantive* objectivity[19] in several ways:

(1) They used as primary sources individuals with badly tarnished credentials, and failed to provide adequate disclosure of their backgrounds and affiliations.

(2) Although the Sterling-Henze analysis and Agca's claims were not supported by independent evidence, were logically faulty, and were ludicrous in their shifting James Bond scenarios and blatant ideological underpinning,[20] they were not subjected to critical scrutiny. Instead they were passed along as "news" even when they were displacing and contradicting earlier versions of the "news."

(3) The media "played dumb" on a variety of important issues, such as Agca's prison conditions, the belatedness of his confession, the possibilities of coaching, and the massive violations of "plausible deniability" in the Plot.

(4) The media also played dumb on the Italian and Cold War context, and suppressed information on a whole string of Italian parliamentary and court reports on the abuses of the intelligence services. Attention to these issues and documents would have raised serious questions about

18. As we point out in Chapter 7, Michael Dobbs of the *Washington Post* and ABC-TV provided partial exceptions to this generalization, but they were relatively insignificant in the total coverage of the case.

19. *Nominal* objectivity may be met by reporting verbatim a statement by Claire Sterling or George Shultz; *substantive* objectivity would require, among other things, an assessment of whether the quoted statement was true or false before it was transmitted as relevant "news." Bias is also displayed in the selection of only those authorities and statements that the journalist-editor-publisher likes to reward with publicity.

20. See Chapter 2, on "The Challenges to the Disinformationists."

the Italian judicial process and the validity of the Sterling-Henze line. In brief, by their gullibility and failure to ask obvious questions the mass media played a central role in allowing a propaganda theme full and uncontested reign. With their cooperation an implausible piece of disinformation was passed off on the public as a truth for more than three years.[21]

With the case for a Bulgarian Connection dismissed by an Italian court following a lengthy trial, can not be said truth and justice have been finally vindicated? The answer is no. We have shown in this book that the Bulgarian Connection is a myth. The court has acquitted for lack of evidence rather than for innocence, making the rectification only partial. The court also has left open an avenue through which the western disinformationists and media can continue to suggest that the Bulgarian Connection was valid but simply could not be proved because of "political constraints" on the pursuit of the case.[22] The western media foisted the myth of the Connection on the public aggressively and uncritically over a three-year period. That myth can only be ousted from the popular mind by a campaign of substantial intensity and duration. But no such campaign will take place. In fact, our forecast is that the loss of the case will be reported briefly and the subject will then be dropped. There will be no extended analyses or retrospectives on how the media sold the public a bill of goods, nor will there be editorials on the corruption involved in uncritical reliance on disinformationists and a coached witness to serve the New Cold War.

21. Herbert Gans contends that "the rules of news judgment call for ignoring story implication," and that journalists follow such rules. The personal values of journalists "are left at home," he tells us, and "the beliefs that actually make it into the news are *professional values* that are intrinsic to national journalism and that journalists learn on the job." "Are Journalists Dangerously Liberal?," *Columbia Journalism Review*, November-December 1985, pp. 32-33. We would submit that Gans's assertions are completely incompatible with the history of news coverage of the Bulgarian Connection.

22. As we noted in the Preface, the disinformationists stress "political" factors anytime they lose. The dominant political forces at work in Italy, however, are strongly pro-western (as described in Chapter 4), and western preconceptions and power played an important part in bringing the Bulgarian Connection into existence in the first place. We believe that the failure of the trial to exonerate fully the Bulgarians reflects similar political bias. In addition to normal western suspicion of the communist powers, we believe that there was an unwillingness to repudiate completely the Italian judges and prosecutors and other western interests with a large stake in the Connection. Dismissal for lack of evidence frees the victims, while affording some measure of solace and protection to the establishment interests that originated and pushed the case.

Instead of Sterling, Henze, and Ledeen being discredited by the trial and dismissal of the case, we believe that they will be given the floor once again to explain it away. With their rationalizations, and with few critical retrospectives, not only will the disinformationists and the mass media come out of this affair smelling like roses, the Bulgarian Connection itself will be salvaged. It will perhaps be quietly placed on the back burner for a while, but the myth has entered popular consciousness by intense and indignant repetition, and it will take on renewed life after memories of the upsetting trial are dimmed.

Looking at the international dimension, the West and the western mass media were guilty of a huge fraud, with Bulgaria and the Soviet Union subjected to an intense and effective multi-year propaganda campaign based on false evidence. With the dismissal of the case, will the West now suffer a severe propaganda blow and will the Soviets and Bulgarians recoup some of their losses? We believe that this will not happen: U.S. and western power and media domination are so great that lies can be institutionalized as myths and *can remain effective even after exposure.*[23] If you are strong enough, just as you are never a "terrorist" but only "retaliate" to the terror of others, so there is no such thing as a losing propaganda campaign. In the words of Alexander Pope: "Destroy his sophistry: in vain—The creature's at his dirty work again."

23. The history of the Soviet shooting down of the Korean airliner 007 in 1983 provided an object lesson and answer. The day after the event, the United States organized a huge propaganda campaign based on the claim that the Soviets had knowingly murdered 259 civilians. Five weeks later, the CIA acknowledged that the Soviets had not realized that the plane was a civilian carrier. ("U.S. Experts Say Soviet Didn't See Jet Was Civilian," *New York Times*, October 7, 1983.) As that information was surely available to U.S. officials within hours of the downing, it is clear that the United States suppressed crucial information to allow it to conduct a propaganda barrage. Following the revelation that the Soviet Union had not recognized that it was shooting down a civilian plane, there were no discernible criticisms of the United States for its propaganda assault based on disinformation, and Soviet villainy in the case has been institutionalized. See Edward S. Herman, "Gatekeeper Versus Propaganda Models: A Case Study," in Peter Golding, Graham Murdock, and Philip Schlesinger, eds., *Communicating Politics: Essays in Memory of Philip Elliott* (Leicester: University of Leicester Press, 1986).

Appendices

A. Did the Western Media Suppress Evidence of a Conspiracy?

Claire Sterling maintains in *The Time of the Assassins* that western governments and the western media quickly backed away from the initial statements of Italian government officials that the assassination attempt on Pope John Paul II was the result of a conspiracy. In the opening lines of her book, Sterling says that "for but a fleeting instant, the truth was close enough to touch . . . , and then it was gone."[1] While space does not allow us to discuss each instance of the misuse of evidence which characterizes Ms. Sterling's book from beginning to end, as the alleged media coverup of a conspiracy is her opening theme, an analysis of that claim provides a valuable case study of the quality of her work.

As we noted in Chapter 2, the conspiracy initially perceived by the western media was a Turkish one. Rather than quickly backing off from any investigation into a Soviet-backed conspiracy, as Sterling maintains, the western media vigorously pursued the abundant evidence that Agca had been aided and sheltered by his colleagues in the Gray Wolves. While the western media can rightly be accused of many things, to say that it did not immediately provide its readers with details about a possible conspiracy in the attempt on the Pope's life is absurd, though tactically of great value to Sterling in her efforts to portray herself as a misunderstood seeker after the real truth, the Bulgarian Connection.

To demonstrate this point, we will summarize the coverage which the unfolding investigation received in the *New York Times* and the *Washington Post* for the period from May 14—the day after the assassination attempt—to May 25. By this latter date Agca had ceased to pro-

1. Claire Sterling, *The Time of the Assassins* (New York: Holt, Rinehart and Winston, 1983), p. 5.

vide his captors with any fresh leads; and on May 25 the *New York Times* provided its readers with a long, summary article which brought the various threads of the investigation together. Our recounting of this coverage by two of the leading U.S. newspapers will serve two purposes. First, it provides us with what might be called a preliminary paradigm, a well-textured first draft of what we call the First Conspiracy. (We elaborate on the background of the First Conspiracy in Chapter 3.) Second, from this summary it will be evident that, contrary to Sterling, the most casual reader of these newspapers in the first weeks after the papal assassination attempt would have been overwhelmed by information about Agca's background in Turkey, and by speculation about the involvement of the Gray Wolves in his attempt on the Pope.

● May 14, 1981: In its initial report on the assassination attempt, the *New York Times* noted Agca's background in Turkey and his earlier threat to kill the Pope. The front-page article connected Agca with the Nationalist Action Party. The *Washington Post*, in a long article by its Turkish correspondent Metin Munir, probed Agca's Turkish background, focusing on his association with the Gray Wolves and his responsibility for the murder of the Turkish newspaper editor Ipekci.[2]

● May 15, 1981: The lead article in the *New York Times*, by R. W. Apple, Jr., was headlined "Police Trace the Path of the Suspect from Turkey to St. Peter's Square." Once again the *Times* noted Agca's connections to the Nationalist Action Party and the failure of the international police to arrest Agca when Turkey had requested it.[3] A second article on the 15th of May, contained the words quoted by Sterling as suggesting that the Italian authorities had abandoned the search for any conspiracy: "Police are convinced, according to government sources, that Mr. Agca acted alone." This article, without a by-line, focused on the Pope's medical condition and was printed on the inside pages. Even

2. The *London Times* focused its article on the Pope's attacker on the Ipekci assassination and his subsequent letter threatening to kill the Pope in 1979. It described Agca as "without doubt the most wanted Turkish terrorist," and quoted Turkish authorities complaining that West European governments had repeatedly ignored the Turkish government's warnings that Agca was in their country and its requests that Agca be arrested.

3. Interestingly, R. W. Apple, Jr. quoted from a letter purportedly found on Agca's person after his arrest—in which he claimed that "I, Agca, have killed the Pope so that the world may know of the thousands of victims of imperialism"—and then went on to describe this as "language that seemed to support his assertion that he was not part of an international plot." The full text of the letter protests against U.S. intervention in El Salvador and Soviet intervention in Afghanistan. These sentiments are perfectly compatible with the ideology of the Gray Wolves, as we discuss in Chapter 3.

this peripheral aside, however, was followed with the observation that
"police do not exclude the possibility that Mr. Agca was backed by an
organization and had the help of friends in some of the countries that he
had visited since escaping from a Turkish prison in November 1979."[4]

The *Washington Post* of May 15 included an article by Metin Munir
headed "Turk Describes Suspected Gunman as 'Determined, Highly
Trained.' " The Turk in question was Hasan Fehmi Gunes, a former
Minister of the Interior in Turkey at the time when Agca was arrested
for killing Ipekci. According to Gunes, "We know he [Agca] was extreme Right because we know that the people who gave him money and
arms and helped him in his crime were extreme rightwing." To this article were appended reports from Turkey and West Germany that elaborated on Turkish efforts to apprehend Agca and the apparent lack of
cooperation they received from West Germany and other countries. The
report quoted a Frankfurt journalist who specialized in the activities of
rightwing Turks in West Germany. He recounted the attempt of a 60-
man squad of Turkish police to track Agca down there, "but it was
given little support by German police and did not find him."

• May 16, 1981: The *Times*'s article noted the conviction of the Italian press—both leftwing and rightwing—that the Pope was the victim of
an international plot. It also quoted the issue of *La Stampa* cited by
Sterling in which magistrate Luciano Infelisi said, "As far as we're concerned, documents prove that Agca did not act alone. He is a killer enlisted by an international group with subversive aims." The *Times*'s article went on to detail the Turkish background of Agca's false passport,
noting that this fact "was just one suggesting links with Turkish political groups." A second front-page article, by the *Times*'s Turkey correspondent Marvine Howe, was headed "Turks in Disagreement on Motive of Alleged Assailant." The debate described in the article pitted
some Turks who claimed that Agca was simply a psychopath and had
acted alone against Gunes and others who pointed to Agca's extensive
ties to the Gray Wolves, and who argued that the assassination attempt
was almost certainly based in such a conspiracy. An article on the inside
pages of the *Times* by John Tagliabue gave many details of apparent
sightings of Agca in West Germany, and of Agca's alleged ties to the
many branches of the Gray Wolves in West Germany.

The *Washington Post* for May 16 headed its main front-page story
"Wider Plot Is Probed in Papal Attack." In it Sari Gilbert reported from

---

4. Given this language, it is entirely possible that the words "acted alone" related simply to the events in St. Peter's Square, and may well be true.

Rome on Infelisi's contention that, because of Agca's well-financed and extensive travels, "we have ruled out the theory that this was a gesture of an isolated madman"; but Infelisi also said "he still was 'not convinced' that there was an international conspiracy." Gilbert noted that Agca claimed he had received his assassination weapon in Bulgaria, but quickly pointed out that Italian police had been able to trace the murder weapon from the Belgian factory where it was made, following its path first to Switzerland and then to Italy. An inside-page article by the *Post*'s Turkey correspondent included an interview with Agca's brother Adnan, who said that his brother "hoped to win world fame and a place at the head of the Moslem world." "If they torture or spiritually oppress my brother," Adnan said, "the whole Islamic world will flock to his side. The crusaders are against the entire Islamic world." The *Post*'s correspondent again noted Turkey's irritation that other countries were so unwilling to cooperate with the martial law government in its attempt to have the many convicted terrorists who had escaped its borders returned to Turkey. The *Post* also noted that several Gray Wolves had been arrested in connection with Agca's passport fraud, a story given a headline and much bigger play in that same day's *London Times*.

● May 17, 1981: On this date, Sunday, the front-page article in the *New York Times* was headlined, "Police Lack Clues to Foreign Links of Suspect in Shooting of the Pope." The burden of the article, however, was the near-universal acceptance of the idea that some kind of conspiracy lay behind Agca's attempt on the Pope, contrasted with the disappointing results of efforts by the police to find clues. "The assertion that Mr. Agca was unquestionably the agent of an international conspiracy," claimed the *Times*, "has spread around the world in the last 48 hours, and official statements of caution seem powerless to counter the impression that terrorists in Europe and the Middle East plotted to assassinate the Pope." The article went on to trace the debate in the Italian press over the nature and extent of the conspiracy, and cited *La Stampa*'s story that Italian investigators believed "Mr. Agca may have been financed and supported by friends belonging to rightwing groups in the large Turkish communities in Western Europe, particularly in West Germany, rather than by a network of international terrorist organizations."

The debate within Italy was clearly not whether Agca was part of a conspiracy, but what kind of conspiracy stood behind the assassination attempt. What some Italian officials seemed to be backing away from was the idea that Agca was linked to a network of international terrorists, à la Carlos the Jackal. The view that Agca's conspiracy was most likely a Turkish one received support from an article by Marvine Howe on an inside page of the *Times* headlined "Turk Is Called a Product of Violence in His Nation." Sari Gilbert, in the *Washington Post*, noted that the police now believed that the man seen running away from the scene of the crime might be Agca's long-time Turkish comrade, Mehmet Sener. (The *London Sunday Times* pursued the same theme in a long article, "The Wolf Who Stalked A Pope," which traced Agca's terrorist record in Turkey.)

● May 18, 1981: On this, the fifth day after the assassination attempt, the *New York Times* had a front-page article by Marvine Howe which was headed, "Turks Say Suspect in Papal Attack is Tied to Rightist Web of Intrigue." This was the longest exposition to date of Agca's ties to Turkey's neofascist Right. Howe drew on the recently released indictment of the Nationalist Action Party, the parent organization of the Gray Wolves, to provide readers with some background analysis. The article focused on the Western European branches of the Gray Wolves, or "Idealists," which led Howe to state that "it is not difficult to imagine how he [Agca] could have traveled widely in Europe and evaded the authorities." She also noted that the martial law prosecutors of the Nationalist Action Party had found links between the party and the West German secret service. The *Washington Post* noted that "Italian magistrates are so convinced that the Turkish terrorist is connected to a rightwing organization that yesterday they assigned five Roman judges who are specialists in Italian right-wing subversive groups to the team carrying out his interrogation."

Also on this day both the *Times* and the *Post* discussed the way that Agca was standing up to interrogation. The *Times*'s article noted Agca's "refusal to answer key questions," while the *Post* said that Italian police were describing Agca as "tough and cool, a professional terrorist who has not yet shown any sign of breaking down under the pressure of interrogation." Both the press and the police were realizing that Agca had provided investigating authorities with an abundance of information about himself, but that only some of it was true and none of it concerned his Gray Wolves associations or any assistance he was given between his escape from a Turkish prison and his assassination attempt. Sari Gilbert of the *Post* noted that "Agca has given the police a six-page deposition in which he is reported to have admitted initial close ties to a rightwing movement in Turkey, but to have added that he subsequently converted to Marxism at a Palestinian base in Syria." This is apparently the same report around which Claire Sterling framed her *Reader's Digest* article some 15 months later; but "Italian investigators," noted Gilbert, "seem to feel there was never any such conversion. 'He is trying to further muddy already murky waters,' one of them was quoted by news agencies as saying here today."

● May 19, 1981: The *Washington Post*'s main headline on the front page announced that the "Italian Police Seek 2nd Suspect." They (apparently erroneously) identified this second suspect as Mehmet Sener, evidently on the basis of the Lowell Newton photograph, which had been provided to the Italian police. The police were also reportedly looking for "Oral Gelik" [*sic*], described as "another Turkish rightwing extremist." The declaration that the Italian police were looking for a second suspect "seemed to lend weight to the growing conviction in some circles that there was a conspiracy against the Pope's life and that a terrorist organization was behind it." But the *Post*'s reporter also noted that the head of DIGOS, the special antiterrorist police, "took a more cautious approach," and that according to this source Agca "may have been a hired killer, or he may not have been. As for an international conspiracy, it's a very remote possibility." In an article on the inside pages—"Probe of Turkish Right Links Pope Suspect"—the *Post* followed the *Times*'s lead of the previous day in using material from the indictment of the NAP to trace Agca's ties to Turkey's neofascist Right. For its part the *Times* reported from Bonn that "Germany Finds No Evidence Accused Turk Lived Here." The *Times*'s reporter, John Tagliabue, also drew on the NAP indictment to ask questions of West German officials about Agca's links to any of the NAP's European branches; but they said there was no evidence that Agca had ever been in West Germany.

● May 20, 1981: The focus of the western media turned to some remarks Agca apparently made during his interrogation on May 18, in which he claimed that he had considered killing other world leaders, including the Queen of England and the Secretary General of the United Nations. "I went to London to kill the King," the police quoted Agca as saying, "but I found he was a woman and decided against it because I am Turkish and a Moslem and I don't kill women." For the same reason, he added, "I did not kill Simone Weil, the President of the European Parliament, after I had been to Brussels to study how the Community works." The *Washington Post* report claimed that Agca's statement "left his interrogators highly skeptical about its veracity"; but R. W. Apple, Jr. of the *New York Times* apparently considered this

statement food for thought, saying that it "lent credence to the thesis that
Mr. Agca's views are essentially anarchistic, growing out of a hatred of
authority, rather than conventionally leftwing or rightwing." The *London Times*, meanwhile, quoted British authorities who denied that Agca
had ever set foot in Britain.

• May 21, 1981: The *Times*'s correspondent John Tagliabue reported
from Bonn on "Militant Views Among Turks Trouble Bonn." The report surveyed the West German government's fears about the large Turkish "guest worker" population, and focused on the activities of rightwing organizations there.

The *Washington Post* story on this day was headed, "Interrogation of
Agca Turns Up Several Baffling Mysteries." This article summarized
what was known and not known about Agca and his travels before
shooting the Pope, and stressed the general bafflement of the police of
several Western European countries in the Agca case. Apparently for
the first time a possible Bulgarian Connection was proposed. The *Post*
quoted a "high-ranking Italian official" who noted that Agca had
passed through Bulgaria after escaping from Turkey. According to this
hypothesis, continued the *Post* story, "the Bulgarians might be upset
enough by the alternative to communism evolving in Poland and the
strong backing of the Catholic Church, as well as of the Polish Pope, to
the Solidarity independent union movement to encourage Agca in his
endeavor. . . . " The *Post* story did not give this hypothesis much credence, however, quickly quoting a "western diplomatic source" who
called this theory "off the wall."

• May 22, 1981: The *Times*'s report for this day was quite short and
was printed on the inside pages. It described Agca's transfer from police
headquarters to Rebibbia prison, just outside of Rome. The story's
headline reflected Agca's shouted remark to reporters that he was
"sorry for the two foreign tourists [who had been wounded] but not for
the Pope." The story also noted that Agca had been interrogated by
police for more than 75 hours over the past 9 days.

A much longer story in the *Washington Post*, datelined Malatya, Turkey, was headed, "Accused Turk Looked for Exit From Poverty." It
traced Agca's life from its beginnings in extreme poverty through his assassination of Abdi Ipekci in 1979. The article noted that Malatya had
been a center of the opium trade, and that the region had suffered se-
verely when the trade was suppressed in the early 1970s. The article
also noted the profound effect on the Malatya region of the formation of
the coalition government in 1976, which was headed by the conserva-

tive Justice Party and included the Nationalist Action Party, and quoted local sources as saying that Agca had been frequently seen in the company of the Gray Wolves. Finally, the article described the wave of rightwing terrorism which resulted in more than 700 shops owned by leftists being burned or looted in 1978, following the murder of the local Justice Party chief. This outbreak resulted in the proclamation of martial law for the Malatya region, the first Turkish province to be put under control of the Army.

• May 23, 1981: The *Times*'s story, by Marvine Howe, followed the lead of the *Post*'s story of the day before "Turk's Hometown Puzzled by His Climb to Notoriety." The article included interviews with Agca's brother and mother (as had the *Post*'s story the previous day); but despite his mother's disclaimer that Agca was "good and honest and brilliant, just an ordinary boy," Howe quoted "political sources that insisted that Mehmet Ali Agca was associated with extreme rightwing organizations known as Idealist Clubs" [the Gray Wolves]. The article also noted that Agca's high school had been taken over in 1975 by the Nationalist Action Party, "naming one of their prominent members as director and filling the staff with militants. Seminars were held on fascism and Nationalist Action Party principles, which were basically anti-foreign, anti-West, and militantly nationalistic."

The *Washington Post* for this day contained only a short report on the Pope's continuing recovery.

• May 24, 1981: Once again, the *Post*'s comments were restricted to a medical note that the Pope was now out of danger. The *Times* focused on Agca's European travels, again highlighting claims by Turkey that European governments had failed to cooperate with their earlier requests for Agca's arrest and extradition. In the "Review of the Week" section, the *Times* noted that "Questions Continue," particularly those connecting Agca to the Nationalist Action Party and the "Idealist Associations" of Western Europe.

• May 25, 1981: By this date the broad outlines of the preliminary paradigm of the case had been established, and both newspapers prepared summary articles. The *Post* headlined their contribution, "Turkey, Searching for Modernity, Offers Fertile Field for Terrorism." It portrayed Agca as a product of the rapid social and economic changes which were drawing Turkey into the modern world economy, while leaving backwaters like Agca's hometown of Malatya to suffer in poverty. For its part, the *Times* wrapped up its coverage of this phase of the case with a very long article by R. W. Apple, Jr., which began on the

front page ("Trail of Mehmet Ali Agca: 6 Years of Neofascist Ties")
and filled up an entire inside page as well. Apple rooted Agca solidly in
Turkey's neofascist Right, and traced his involvement with the Gray
Wolves and rightwing terrorism from his high school days, through his
brief university career, and then on to greater things. Apple found
Agca's motivation puzzling, still stumbling over Agca's claim that he
thought of killing most of the crowned heads of Europe; but he also
quoted Turkish sources who believed that Agca was mentally unbalanced and aspired after greatness or notoriety. Finally, the article gave a
detailed account of Agca's wanderings through Western Europe, sheltered by the Gray Wolves and completely unhampered by the conti-
nent's police forces.

Summary

It should by now be abundantly clear that it is impossible to subscribe to
Claire Sterling's assertion that, for but a fleeting moment, the possibility of a conspiracy was a "truth close enough to touch," and that this
truth was suppressed by western governments and the western media in
the interests of preserving détente. On the contrary, the western media
vigorously pursued the clues that there was a Turkish-based, rightwing
conspiracy which connected Agca through a multitude of threads to the
Nationalist Action Party and the Gray Wolves. The distortion perpe-
trated by Sterling at the opening of her book is characteristic of her handling of all evidence, perhaps because of her confidence that the major
media outlets of the West are content to rely on her testimony, without
even examining the files of their own newspapers.

B. Bulgaria and the Drug Connection

Taking advantage of Bulgaria's sudden prominence in the western media to strike another blow at the Evil Empire, the disinformationists have used the Bulgarian Connection episode to raise sweeping charges that Bulgaria, acting of course as a Soviet instrument, is engaged in a campaign to destabilize the West by flooding it with narcotics. This campaign has been quite successful, resulting in diplomatic setbacks for Bulgaria and adding to the established truth that the Soviet Bloc is behind international terrorism, now expanded to include "narco-terrorism."

In this appendix we address two specific claims advanced by the disinformationists. These are, first, that the Bulgarian state agency KINTEX organizes much of the international narcotics flow; and second, that Bulgaria violates the international conventions establishing the Transport Internationaux Routiers (TIR) truck system, even using a TIR truck to facilitate the escape of Agca's fellow assassin, Oral Celik. To assess these claims we will look at the evidence put forward at two U.S. congressional hearings that were held in the summer of 1984 on the Bulgarian role in arms and narcotics smuggling. Paul Henze participated in both of these hearings, being joined by representatives of the State Department, the Drug Enforcement Administration (DEA), and the Customs Service, and by supposed experts on Bulgarian drug smuggling. These hearings, which allowed only marginally dissenting notes from the main theme of Bulgarian guilt, afforded the proponents of the Bulgarian Connection ample scope to present whatever evidence they had.

225

Background to the Hearings

Charges that Agca was linked to Bulgaria through his participation in Bulgarian-supported drug smuggling had been an integral part of the pre-confession allegations of the Bulgarian Connection. The Ugurlu-Mersan-Agca link had been at the heart of both Claire Sterling's *Reader's Digest* article and the NBC "White Paper" broadcast in September 1982. The link between Agca's attempt on the Pope and Bulgarian support for smuggling was apparently made tighter in early December 1982, when an investigation into arms and drug smuggling in the Italian city of Trent indicted Bekir Celenk, who had already been named by Agca as the person who offered him over one million dollars to kill the Pope. The charge that the Bulgarian state import-export agency KIN-TEX was involved with smuggling was included in Italian Defense Minister Lagorio's speech to the Chamber of Deputies on December 20. And the arrest of Celenk on smuggling charges was featured by both *Time* and *Newsweek* in their January 3, 1983 issues which put the papal assassination attempt on the covers of both magazines.[1] The *Christian Science Monitor* devoted an article to Turkish investigations into Bulgarian smuggling and Bulgarian links to the Turkish "Mafia" on January 20. Four days later *New York Times* correspondent Henry Kamm reported from Sofia on a press conference held there by Bekir Celenk; and on January 28 the *Times* printed another piece by Kamm, "Plot On Pope Aside, Bulgaria's Notoriety Rests On Smuggling."

Probably the most influential of all the media reports on Bulgarian smuggling was "Drugs for Guns: The Bulgarian Connection," by Nathan M. Adams, which appeared in the November 1983 issue of the *Reader's Digest*. Adams, a *Reader's Digest* Senior Editor, claimed that "over 50 percent of the heroin consumed in Europe and much of that in the United States flows across Bulgaria's borders with the full knowledge and direct participation of high-ranking [Bulgarian] government officials." He further claimed that the drugs were "paid for with War-

---

1. In November 1984 the prosecutor in the Trent case issued 37 indictments—of 25 Italians, 9 Turks, 2 Syrians, and an Egyptian—on charges of smuggling drugs and arms, and possibly even an atomic bomb. One of the accused was Bekir Celenk. Another was the Italian film star Rossano Brazzi. See E. J. Dionne, Jr., "Italian Case Uncovers an Alpine Heart of Darkness," *New York Times*, November 24, 1984.

saw-pact weaponry," thus fueling Middle Eastern terrorism. Adams charged that this action by Bulgaria was the product of a 1970 Bulgarian Committee for State Security (KDS, later DS) directive to destabilize the West through the narcotics trade. Adams's article, which he later claimed was based on six months' research in eight nations, became the primary source for the congressional investigation into the Bulgarian role in narcotics trafficking; and although it was deeply flawed, it has gone unchallenged in the West.[2]

Charges that KINTEX was promoting drug dealing were renewed in April 1984, when a Danish television report was picked up by CBS News. In its report for April 26, 1984, CBS quoted from a signed letter from one Peter H. Mulack, a West German national residing in Miami since 1979. Mulack was allegedly involved in trading in embargoed high-technology goods with Eastern Europe, and in shipping East European weapons to African nations, primarily South Africa. According to documents presented by CBS, Mulack told KINTEX that " . . . I can deliver the required electronic material. However, as the material is under embargo, it will take at least three months to deliver. Payment for the consignment may be made in heroin or morphine base. . . . " CBS showed a return letter from KINTEX thanking Mulack for committing himself to "deliver the requested goods and you are willing to accept payment as mentioned."[3] This certainly seemed like hard evidence, and to this day the viewers of the CBS report have not been told a most salient fact: that the documents they were shown were forgeries, as was revealed in the fine print of a U.S. congressional report.[4]

2. Adams was making a career of such allegations. The July 1982 *Reader's Digest* ran a five-page article in which he claimed that vast quantities of drugs were coming to the U.S. from Cuba and Nicaragua. See William Preston, Jr. and Ellen Ray, "Disinformation and Mass Deception: Democracy as a Cover Story," *CovertAction Information Bulletin*, Number 19 (Spring-Summer 1983), pp. 9-11.

3. Cited from *Drugs and Terrorism, 1984*, Hearings before the Subcommittee on Alcoholism and Drug Abuse of the Committee on Labor and Human Resources, Senate, 98th Congress, 2nd Session, August 8, 1984, p. 76.

4. According to the DEA, the correspondence between the Bulgarians and the West German dealer shown on Danish television (and also on CBS-TV) was "probably not genuine," and the DEA "has no corroborating evidence." "Written documentation of illicit activities," cautioned the DEA, "is not typical of the modus operandi of KINTEX" (*Bulgarian-Turkish Narcotics Connection: United States-Bulgarian Relations and International Drug Trafficking*, Hearings and Markup before the Committee on Foreign Affairs, House of Representatives, 98th Congress, 2nd Session, 1984, pp. 113-14). To our knowledge there has been no follow-up on the question of who forged the documents fed to Danish TV, nor an investigation of whether CBS-TV was the victim of a deliberate disinformation ploy.

Accusations that Bulgaria was supporting smuggling, whether for gain or as a means of destabilizing the West, were clearly important in straining Bulgaria's ties with Italy, which withdrew its ambassador from Bulgaria on December 11, 1982; shortly thereafter travel by Bulgarians to Italy was restricted.[5] The United States also acted quickly. In January 1983 the U.S. Embassy in Sofia presented a protest to Bulgaria, citing what they claimed were the activities of known drug and arms smugglers in Bulgaria and demanding that something be done. When Bulgaria's response the following month was judged unsatisfactory, further protests followed. A decade of cooperation between the two countries in countering narcotics smuggling was broken off (see below). Though the State Department successfully lobbied against a bill by Jesse Helms that would have banned U.S. trade with Bulgaria, in July 1984 it banned "nonessential" government travel to Bulgaria.[6]

The Hearings

By the summer of 1984, charges that Bulgaria supported narcotics and arms smuggling had gained a firm foothold in the western media. This provided congressional conservatives with a means of pressuring the State Department on the Bulgarian Connection. A House Foreign Affairs Committee "Task Force on International Narcotics Control" held hearings on the "Bulgarian-Turkish Narcotics Connection: United States-Bulgarian Relations and International Drug Trafficking," in June and July of 1984. One of the goals of the committee members was to urge that the Reagan administration take further diplomatic sanctions against Bulgaria.[7] A second hearing, on "Drugs and Terrorism, 1984," was held by Florida Senator Paula Hawkins in August. The purport of her hearing was to dramatize the global role of Soviet proxies in narcotics smuggling. Both committees heard representatives of the U.S. Drug Enforcement Administration and U.S. Customs Service, as well as Paul Henze and Nathan Adams.

5. Loren Jenkins, "Italy Calls Pope Plot 'Act of War,' " *Washington Post*, December 21, 1982.
6. Clyde Farnsworth, "U.S. Restricts Government Travel to Bulgaria," *New York Times*, July 10, 1984.
7. See Rick Atkinson, "U.S. Links Bulgaria, Drug Traffic," *Washington Post*, July 25, 1984.

At the House Foreign Affairs Committee hearing on the alleged "Bulgarian-Turkish Narcotics Connection" it quickly became apparent that there was little quarrel among the witnesses about the extent of Bulgarian nefariousness. Only Jack Perry, a former U.S. Ambassador to Bulgaria, questioned whether Bulgaria supported narcotics smuggling and illegal arms trafficking as a matter of state policy, noting that he had heard nothing about this before being removed by the Reagan administration in 1981. But the issue of smuggling immediately became entangled with the alleged Bulgarian role in the attempt on the Pope, a charge pressed not only by Henze but by Senator Alfonse D'Amato of New York. This forced the State Department into an awkward position, for the measures which the Foreign Affairs Committee proposed would be tantamount to taking a position on the Bulgarian Connection case in Rome. This was obviously what Henze and D'Amato wanted; but the State Department's appeal to postpone any sanctions pending the outcome of the imminent trial in Italy was finally acceded to by the Committee.[8]

Somewhat lost in this discussion was the weakness of the case for Bulgarian support of smuggling and arms trafficking. For example, the central piece of documentary evidence used by several witnesses to support these charges was Adams's *Reader's Digest* article, "Drugs for Guns: the Bulgarian Connection." As noted above, Adams's most sensational charge was that between 1967 and 1970 plans were formulated by the Soviet Union and Bulgaria to destabilize the West by, among other things, narcotics. The source for this charge was Stefan Sverdlev, a defector from the Bulgarian KDS who fled to Greece in 1971. He claimed that Bulgaria's role in narcotics trafficking was part of a larger Warsaw Pact project initiated in 1967 to destabilize the West. (Sverdlev's dubious evidence is analyzed in Appendix C.) Adams charged that between 1970 and 1980 "billions upon billions of dollars' worth of narcotics and arms were moved or exchanged through Bulgaria by the state trading agency KINTEX, whose clandestine activities were—and are—under the direct control of the First Directorate of the DS. . . ."[9]

8. On September 12, 1984, W. Tapley Bennett, Jr. wrote to the Committee on behalf of the State Department: "Any legislation declaring or implying a U.S. belief in Bulgarian wrongdoing should await the outcome of the Italian judicial proceedings concerning the attempted assassination of the Pope. . . . Senior Italian officials have urged us to maintain this position of strict non-intervention." *Bulgarian-Turkish Narcotics Connection, op. cit.*, n. 4, pp. 90-91.

9. *Ibid.*, p. 74.

It was on the basis of Adams's article that members of the Foreign
Affairs Committee casually bandied about their estimates of the extent
of Bulgarian state smuggling. Adams charged that in the late 1970s
"approximately 25 percent of heroin reaching the United States either
moved through Bulgaria or was in some way abetted by KINTEX."[10]
This preposterous statement was reduced in the Committee's bargaining
with the representative of the DEA to a more modest 10 percent. Yet in
response to written questions at the conclusion of the Committee's hearings, the DEA admitted that they had "no substantive evidence to support these allegations,"[11] and that "there is not enough evidence to indict any Bulgarian official at this time."[12]

The Customs Service's testimony also helped to demystify the TIR
trucking system, whose alleged abuse by the Bulgarians had become
such a central issue in the Bulgarian Connection case. The Customs Service pointed out that (a) the TIR Convention made provision for on-the-
spot inspection where smuggling was suspected, so that the system was
not a *carte blanche* for smuggling; (b) the U.S. shipping industry had a
major stake in the continuation of the TIR system; (c) "recent trend assessments by DEA indicate that overland transportation of drugs has de-
creased considerably over the last decade"; and (d) "U.S. Customs
does not have a documented factual basis to conclude that Bulgaria has
violated the TIR system and we are not aware of any other agency having such information."[13] Thus, whatever allegations were made by the
DEA, the State Department, and by western disinformationists, the
U.S. agency most likely to be aware of Bulgarian violations of the TIR
Convention did not believe there was much substance to them.

Finally, Bulgarian guilt was reinforced for members of the Foreign
Affairs Committee by the frequent reminders coming from both DEA
and the State Department that the U.S. Customs Service had broken off
its earlier relationship with their Bulgarian counterparts—a relationship
which had involved training programs, conferences, and information
exchanges. Once again, however, the fine print at the end of the Committee's report revealed a more complex story. The Customs Service

10. *Ibid.*, p. 75.

11. *Ibid.*, p. 113.

12. *Ibid.*, p. 114. This denial was repeated by the DEA in answer to a similar question
at Senator Hawkins's "Drugs and Terrorism, 1984" hearings later in the summer: "No
direct association between KINTEX and the 'Gray Wolves' has been reported to the
DEA" (*Drugs and Terrorism, 1984, op. cit.*, n. 3, p. 64).

13. *Bulgarian-Turkish Narcotics Connection, op. cit.*, n. 4, pp. 131-35.

acknowledged that the United States and Bulgaria lacked the kind of exchange agreement which Bulgaria had negotiated with several countries, including West Germany and Austria, under which investigations by one country's customs service are carried out at the request of another country's service. Negotiations for such an agreement had been begun by the United States and Bulgaria, but were broken off at the direction of the State Department in early 1983.[14] In answer to written questions the Customs Service stated that it "has no hard evidence that the Government of Bulgaria has conducted illicit narcotics trafficking."[15] Indeed, it apparently maintained this position at an interagency meeting on July 18, between the first and the second session of the Committee's hearings, which was obviously called to iron out the differences in the stories being given the Committee by the two agencies. Noting that the DEA representative at the meeting had admitted that "evidence in DEA's possession would be considered hearsay in an English court of law and that credible evidence would be difficult to obtain,"[16] the Customs Service refused to budge from its position. In fact, in answer to another question, the Customs Service stated that "the cessation of customs contact between U.S. and Bulgarian Customs is a position which is not enthusiastically supported by customs administrations of U.S. allies."[17]

While there are many loose ends in the question of Bulgarian state participation—or even direction—in the smuggling trade that clearly sends vast quantities of drugs and other contraband back and forth between Western Europe and the Middle East, for certain interests in both the United States and Italy these charges constituted a target of opportunity. The availability of uncheckable testimony from defectors, convicted smugglers, and others with real or fabricated "information" to sell provided a ready and endless supply of material to document charges of Bulgarian culpability. Yet without the implication of Bulgaria in the attempt on the Pope it is doubtful that there would have been any market for these charges. A search through the indexes of the *Washington Post* and the *New York Times*, for example, reveals that

14. *Ibid.*, p. 84.
15. *Ibid.*, p. 115.
16. *Ibid.*
17. *Ibid.*, p. 131.

only a few articles published prior to 1982 even allege any Bulgarian participation in narcotics smuggling. Yet following the arrest of Antonov media interest in Bulgarian smuggling blossomed. And even though no new evidence of substance was discovered, publicity about alleged Bulgarian smuggling and charges that Bulgaria was behind the attempt on the Pope were mutually reinforcing, one "confirming" the other.

The Echo Chamber

As with other aspects of the Bulgarian Connection, the drugs-for-guns allegations benefitted from a recycling process that appeared to give the claims independent confirmation. We call this the "echo chamber"; and it has become a hallmark of the work of the disinformationists.

A good example of the echo chamber at work occurred during the congressional hearings on Bulgarian support for narco-terrorism. On June 7, 1984, Paul Henze told the House Committee on Foreign Affairs' "Task Force on International Narcotics Control" that "with Bulgarian help, what came to be called the 'Turkish Mafia' set up elaborate networks, lodged in part among Turkish workers in Europe, for moving opium products westward." On July 17 the *Wall Street Journal* printed a long article by David Ignatius about the ongoing investigation of Agca's links to Turkish drug-smuggling bosses, particularly Abuzer Ugurlu.[18] Ignatius drew on Henze's House testimony and supplemented this with an interview, in which Henze claimed that "it is inconceivable that a widely known criminal operative such as Ugurlu could have lived and worked in Bulgaria without the approval of the Bulgarian intelligence service and the rest of the Bulgarian Communist Party hierarchy." In all other respects as well, Ignatius's article was pure Henze, and was probably inspired by him, as it drew on a Turkish prosecutor's report which had "received little attention outside of Turkey," and was

18. "Turks Closer to Linking Pope's Assailant with Bulgaria." The alleged Agca-Ugurlu link contributed to the reopening of the investigation into the murder of Ipekci in December 1982, just after Agca named Ugurlu. Ugurlu had surrendered himself for arrest in West Germany in March 1981, just before the deadline announced by the new Turkish martial law government for some forty wanted criminals to surrender or lose their Turkish citizenship. West Germany extradicted Ugurlu to Turkey. Characteristically, Henze and Sterling never mention that Ugurlu had surrendered himself voluntarily to the West German police.

translated especially for the *Wall Street Journal.*

Ignatius's long article was then presented to the next meeting of the House investigative committee by Senator Alfonse D'Amato, an adherent of the Bulgarian Connection hypothesis and a collaborator with Claire Sterling since the fall of 1981. D'Amato claimed that the article corroborated the findings of Sterling and Henze. And a little over a week later, testifying before a Senate subcommittee looking into "the link between drugs and terrorism," Henze cited the *Journal* article ("the only U.S. newspaper to report these developments") in support of his Agca-Ugurlu-Bulgaria linkage.[19]

Thus, in the real world of the disinformation process, two congressional committees had heard witnesses testify about the Agca-Ugurlu-Bulgaria link. The testimony had been supported by a *Wall Street Journal* investigatiõn. And the *Journal*, drawing on a previously unknown Turkish prosecutor's report and expert testimony before Congress, had updated its readers on the growing evidence that Bulgarian-backed smuggling formed the root of the Bulgarian Connection. It would be only natural for the creators and consumers of "informed opinion" to believe that a fact of some importance was being confirmed by several sources. It is unlikely that anyone noticed that these apparent confirmations were only the echo chamber at work, reverberating another of Henze's claims to create the appearance of multiple confirmation.

19. *Drugs and Terrorism, 1984, op. cit.*, n. 3, p. 97.

C. The Use and Misuse of Defectors

During the Red Scare of the late 1940s and early 1950s, some ex-communist witnesses briefly made a new career for themselves, testifying and writing about their first-hand experience with the communist menace. Not surprisingly, this new profession fell under the sway of economic laws; and ex-communist witnesses were forced to develop and improve their products once the novelty of their original message wore off. As noted by David Caute, "invention" was "the specialty of renegades, who traded heavily in mounting American popular fears," and Soviet émigrés "were always ready to delight congressional committees with the wildest 'inside stories' of diabolical Kremlin plots."[1] By their assertions and claims of Red evil the ex-communist witnesses helped to legitimate the repression of the Red Scare era; and subsequent exposure of much of their information as completely fictitious had only a marginal impact on the media's receptivity to similar testimony by other witnesses.

What the ex-communist witness was to the era of the Red Scare and McCarthyism, the defector is to the age of "international terrorism" and disinformation.[2] Most of those who leave Soviet Bloc countries or other official enemies of the United States, of course, simply come to the West to start a new life. Some émigrés undoubtedly hope to return, and await the collapse of whatever regime rules his or her homeland. And some take up the cause of counterrevolution, whether it be as *con-*

1. David Caute, *The Great Fear* (New York: Simon and Schuster, 1978), pp. 131-32.
2. To our knowledge there are no studies which scrutinize the sum total of defector evidence analogous to the several useful studies of ex-communist witnesses of the Red Scare era. See, for example, Herbert Packer's *Ex-Communist Witnesses* (Stanford: Stanford University Press, 1962); or Victor Navasky's *Naming Names* (New York: Viking Press, 1980).

tras, as broadcasters for Radio Free Europe, or as analysts for the CIA. The defector may share one or more of these attributes, but to be a defector the émigré must possess certain other characteristics which are of use to the West. The value of defectors is governed by two things: the information that they bring with them, and their willingness to bear witness to the evils of the state they left behind. Some defectors, such as star athletes or dancers, can fulfill this latter category passively, simply by living and performing in the West. But government workers or military officers, having no independent source of fame—and thus salability—in the West, must provide important information and/or be willing to testify publicly about life in the East, and especially about the plans and methods of the Soviet-Bloc rulers.

The testimony of defectors, however, is extremely unreliable and easily subject to manipulation. For one thing, many defectors are bitter and may want to generate hostility against their homeland, which may lead them to inflate or invent negative information. Furthermore, defectors who claim a lot of knowledge about the enemy are more marketable than those admitting that they know very little. Once defectors have been debriefed in the West on their areas of expertise, however, they have nothing else to sell, and must either enter the private economy or "discover" new information to remain employed by the public sector. This provides a market incentive to *create* information.

Sometimes sudden shifts in consumer demand reactivate old defectors. This was the case with the Bulgarian Connection, which breathed new life into the market for Bulgarian defectors. Elements of the security services of the West are often willing to connive with defectors to concoct serviceable points of disinformation, and to use defectors to convey these documents to the mass media. Edward Jay Epstein cites the testimony of former CIA officer Joseph Burkholder Smith, "who disclosed that the CIA had sent a Soviet defector to deliver [*Reader's Digest* editor John] Barron a story it had wholly invented," and which Barron subsequently used in his published writings under *Reader's Digest* auspices.[3]

A timely illustration of the political economy of the defector can be found in the case of former Soviet diplomat Arkady Shevchenko, whose book *Breaking With Moscow* became a best seller in mid-1985. Two fine investigative reports have traced the rehabilitation and marketing of

3. Edward J. Epstein, "The Spy Who Came In To Be Sold," *New Republic*, July 15-22, 1985, p. 41.

Shevchenko. After his defection in 1978, he initially produced material which was then characterized by *Time* magazine as "far less valuable as an intelligence source than had been anticipated." Based on its own intelligence sources, *Time* concluded that Shevchenko "had little knowledge of the inner workings of current Soviet policies or intelligence operations." This estimate was shared by analysts from the Defense Intelligence Agency. Indeed, when the Simon and Schuster publishing house received the completed manuscript of Shevchenko's story in 1979, for which they had advanced $146,000 on their $600,000 contract, they sued for the return of their advance because the book "did not contain sufficient new material about the Soviet Union to merit its publication. There were no revelatory firsthand conversations with Soviet leaders—and no mention of any espionage activities by him."[4]

But in 1984, in a new political climate with a lower threshhold of gullibility, Shevchenko's memoirs returned to the publishers. This time they were repackaged, with entirely new sections on his alleged conversations with Khrushchev, and with the revelation that he had actually been a mole for the CIA all along. Edward Jay Epstein made a point-by-point analysis of the plausibility of several of Shevchenko's claims, characterizing them as "demonstrably fictitious," and calling Shevchenko "the spy who never was." Moreover—and of great relevance to the Bulgarian Connection—Epstein pointed out that Shevchenko's "super mole" activities were first passed on by the CIA to the *Reader's Digest*'s John Barron, and that Barron incorporated them into his 1983 publication, *The KGB Today: The Hidden Hand*. Coverage by CBS's *60 Minutes*, a *Time* cover story, a best seller, a lucrative movie deal, and a position as a regular commentator on Soviet affairs for ABC News soon followed. Shevchenko's marketability has been completely untouched by the exposure of his fabrications.[5] Thus Shevchenko shares with Mehmet Ali Agca this dubious distinction: Two of the most famous disinformation sources of our era have been sold to the U.S. public through a series of fabrications that began with the collaboration of

4. *Ibid.*, pp. 35-36. See also David Remnick, "Shevchenko: The Saga Behind the Best Seller," *Washington Post*, June 15, 1985. The quotations from *Time* are cited in Epstein, *op cit.*, n. 3., p. 35.

5. In November 1985, for example, the *New York Times* published Shevchenko's Op-Ed article on the redefection of Soviet KGB official Vitaly Yurchenko. ("A Lesson of the Yurchenko Affair," November 12, 1985). And ABC called upon Shevchenko to comment on the significance of the Summit. Long after Epstein's exposé, the *New York Times Book Review* gave favorable notice and an unqualified recommendation of Shevchenko's book to its readers. (December 8, 1985; January 26, 1986.)

western intelligence services and the *Reader's Digest*.

Shevchenko's story is illustrative of the role of the defector in fabricating myths about Soviet strategies to defeat the West. Needless to say, writers such as Sterling, Henze, and Ledeen do not pause for even a moment to consider whether defector testimony presents any problems of veracity. A delightful example of this is found in Sterling's *The Terror Network*, where she brings in a Czech defector, Major General Jan Sejna, to support her claim that the Soviets had set up terrorist training camps as far back as 1964. Indeed, Sejna's testimony plays a central role in Sterling's argument about Soviet responsibility for international terrorism. Yet it turns out that Sejna had been debriefed by western intelligence in 1968, and had never mentioned this important information, because (according to Sterling) "nobody ever asked him about such matters." It wasn't until 1980, when Michael Ledeen fortuitously asked Sejna about Soviet plans for international terrorism, that Sejna thought to tell anyone about the terrorist training camps. This convenient recollection coincided with the Haig-Ledeen demand for just this kind of information, essential to make the transition from "human rights" to "international terrorism" as the public relations face of the new administration's foreign policy.

Sejna's testimony, however, does not withstand examination. Leaving aside the absurdity that Sejna would let such an accusation languish in his notes for 12 years before bringing it to public attention, as we noted in Chapter 6, Sejna's claims were so implausible that the CIA concocted a document outlining a supposed Soviet plan for world domination. When it was shown to Sejna, he verified it as authentic.[6] There is evidence that this document, with Sejna as a conduit, served to feed the fires of the anti-Soviet and anti-terrorism crusades of the late 1970s. In 1981 the *New York Times*'s Leslie Gelb was told by intelligence officials, skeptical about information on terrorism coming to them from European intelligence agencies, that "what we are hearing is this 10-year old testimony coming back to us through West European intelligence and some of our own CIA people.'"[7] Alexander Cockburn claims that Arnaud de Borchgrave rushed back from France in 1978 with the exciting new information from French intelligence that the Soviets had a

6. Lars-Erik Nelson, "The deep terror plot: a thickening of silence," *New York Daily News*, June 24, 1984, p. C14; Alexander Cockburn, "Beat the Devil," *The Nation*, August 17-24, 1985, p. 102.

7. Leslie Gelb, "Soviet-Terror Ties Called Outdated," *New York Times*, October 18, 1981.

master plan for world domination, which was the CIA forgery repackaged once again. Alexander Haig had also been delighted with the Sejna-based stories, particularly as cited by Claire Sterling in *The Terror Network*, and was quite annoyed that his own officials kept telling him that "he was basically repeating the stories of the Czech defector."[8]

Between them, Shevchenko and Sejna illustrate several general principles of the political economy of defectors that we noted earlier. They serve a critical role in testifying publicly about the Soviet system. They appear to be the conduits of forged or imaginary documents. And their value is closely tied to market conditions, rising steeply during the Reagan administration. This latter point has been doubly applicable in the case of Bulgarian defectors, whose boats have risen with the tide, but who have been especially lifted by the alleged Bulgarian Connection. In Chapter 7 we briefly noted the useful role played by Iordan Mantarov, the agricultural mechanic who claimed to have been on the staff of the Bulgarian Embassy in France, and to have passed on information on the plot to kill the Pope to French intelligence. Discredited, Mantarov has quietly passed into at least temporary obscurity.

Perhaps the person who has gained the most by the sudden rise in the marketability of Bulgarian defectors is Stefan Sverdlev, a former Bulgarian official who defected to Greece in 1971. Sverdlev was a colonel in the Bulgarian State Security Service, the KDS (now DS). After the arrest of Antonov in November 1982, Sverdlev was the western media's primary source for the claim that, if the Bulgarians were involved, the Soviets must have known about it because the Bulgarian security services are completely dominated by the Soviets.[9] This claim, of course, could only be used so many times before its novelty wore off. And so

8. *Ibid.*,; Cockburn, *op. cit.*, n. 6; and Nelson, *op. cit.*, n. 6.
9. According to Claire Sterling, "lengthy interviews with Col. Sverdlev have appeared in dozens of publications, including the *New York Times*, *Newsweek*, the *Reader's Digest*, the leftwing Paris daily *Liberation*, the conservative *Le Figaro*, and the Italian Socialist Party's *Avanti*." ("An Eastern Defector's Family Is Taken for a Ride Home," *Wall Street Journal*, November 23, 1983.) The burden of Sterling's article, incidentally, was to describe the alleged kidnapping of Sverdlev's wife and 13-year-old son by the Bulgarians on the weekend of November 12-13, 1983. Neither Sterling nor the *Journal* followed up on this sad story. As the *New York Times* reported three weeks later, it quickly became apparent that Sverdlev's wife was unhappy in the West and returned, taking their son with her. "She has done this because she has the nature of an adventurer," said Sverdlev. James Markham, "Bulgarian Exiles Get Reminder from Motherland," *New York Times*, December 12, 1983.

Sverdlev, like the ex-communist witnesses of an earlier era, developed a new product.

Sverdlev's new area of specialization became the alleged Bulgarian role in international narcotics trafficking. He served as the primary source for Nathan Adams's 1983 *Reader's Digest* article, which in turn served as the major documentary "evidence" for the House Foreign Affairs Committee hearing on the "Bulgarian-Turkish Narcotics Connection" in the summer of 1984.[10] Just as Maj. Gen. Sejna suddenly recalled critical evidence on Soviet support for international terrorism when he was interviewed more than a decade after his defection by Michael Ledeen, the most important piece of news that Sverdlev gave Nathan Adams in 1983 was about the existence of a secret 1970 Bulgarian directive to implement a 1967 Warsaw Pact plan to destabilize and corrupt the West through narcotics. Sverdlev had not thought to tell anyone about this directive before his interview with Adams.[11] Needless to say, Sverdlev did not have this directive in his possession; it had been left behind with Greek intelligence, he claimed, when he left Greece for West Germany in 1977. (Conditions in Greece apparently became steadily less comfortable for him after the fall of the Colonels' junta in 1974.) But he did remember the document's date (July 16, 1970) and its number (M-120/00-0500), despite the fact that he had not been called upon to retrieve this information from his memory in over a decade.

Sverdlev's testimony is highly suspect. It seems unbelievable that, given his apparently continuing connection with western intelligence after leaving Greece in 1977, he would fail to mention such a salable commodity. It also seems unlikely that, given the Greek government's connections to the CIA, such a document would have been kept from the Agency prior to 1977. And when former U.S. ambassador to Bul-

10. "Drugs for Guns: The Bulgarian Connection," *Reader's Digest*, November 1983, pp. 84-98. These hearings and their context are examined more generally in Appendix B, above.

11. Paul Henze told the House Foreign Affairs Committee that "Many of Sverdlev's revelations were taken lightly at the time he made them, even by intelligence professionals." (*Bulgarian-Turkish Narcotics Connection: United States-Bulgarian Relations and International Drug Trafficking*, Hearings and Markup before the Committee on Foreign Affairs, House of Representatives, 98th Congress, 2nd Session, 1984, p. 30.) But news of the Warsaw Pact destabilization plan was apparently omitted completely. During Adams's testimony before the same committee, there was some momentary confusion about whether Adams's claim to have been the first to hear Sverdlev's information, as Sverdlev also maintained, was correct. A subsequent insertion into the committee s record agreed with Adams. *Ibid.*, p. 99

aria Jack Perry testified before the House Foreign Affairs Committee's hearings on the "Bulgarian-Turkish Narcotics Connection," he told the Committee that "I read about that [Sverdlev's claims] in the *Reader's Digest*, but I was never aware of it when I was on active duty, and I have never seen that intelligence."[12] Thus it seems most likely that Sverdlev's document never existed, and that Adams and Sverdlev had developed the sort of mutually beneficial relationship which characterizes the contemporary misuse of defectors.

In sum, defectors are now part of the market system, with the demand for particular kinds of evidence eliciting the required supply. This system only works because the mass media refuse to look critically at system-supportive claims. Even devastating exposés of a Sejna or Shevchenko fail to dislodge charlatans or constrain the use of demonstrable fraud. This allows the system of defector mobilization and management to continue unimpaired.

12. *Ibid.*

D. Sterling versus Andronov

The methodology used by Claire Sterling and Paul Henze can be readily employed to prove CIA involvement in the assassination attempt against the Pope. This was done by Soviet journalist Iona Andronov in his monograph *On the Wolf's Track*.[1] Although we do not find it very convincing, Andronov provided a somewhat more compelling case than Sterling and Henze. As he advanced the wrong villain, however, his work has been ignored in the West. A brief comparison of Sterling and Andronov may be instructive in showing the irrelevance of method and the overwhelming importance of proper conclusions in mass media choices of stories to feature.

Red Network Methodology Applied to Bulgarian and CIA Connections.

Red Network methodology starts with the prior knowledge of Red Center guilt. In consequence, it does not require much in the way of supporting evidence. The heart of the method is to find "linkages" and then to search around for someone who will say that the linkages reflect "control" by the Red Center. Thus, after a protracted search described at great length in *The Time of the Assassins*, Sterling found an unnamed Interpol agent who gave "his oath" that the Bulgarian secret services *controlled* the Turkish Mafia.[2] Experts in this area, including the U.S. Drug Enforcement Administration, the U.S. Customs Service, and Turkish journalist Ugur Mumcu, have stated repeatedly that there is no evidence that Bulgaria controls the Turkish Mafia. Sterling *prefers* the claim of the anonymous informant (if he exists) who asserted Bulgarian control,

1. Iona Andronov, *On the Wolf's Track* (Sofia: Sofia Press, 1983).
2. *The Time of the Assassins* (New York: Holt, Rinehart and Winston, 1983), p. 225.

242 THE BULGARIAN CONNECTION

and on this basis Bulgarian control becomes definitive fact for Sterling.[3] The Turkish Mafia works frequently with the Gray Wolves. Based on this association, Sterling says "The Wolves were being run by this huge contraband ring, the Turkish Mafia, unique in the world in that it was really working for a Communist state corporation under the sponsorship of the Communist state of Bulgaria."[4] Thus once again we move from a linkage to control, here without even bothering with the anonymous confirmation. Supplemented by the imputed motive, the Soviet desire to stop the Polish Solidarity movement, the Bulgaria-Turkish Mafia-Gray Wolves-Agca links become a chain of command responsible for the assassination attempt.

Using this same Red Network methodology, it is not at all difficult to put up an imaginative demonstration that the *CIA* was behind the plot to kill the Pope. This is the case that Andronov develops, which is the eastern variant of the Sterling model. Andronov argues, as does Sterling, that the Gray Wolves themselves had no real motive for shooting the Pope; they had to be manipulated by an external power. The purpose of the Plot was to discredit the Soviet Union, in accordance with the new Reagan-Haig anticommunist crusade. It depended for its success on the likelihood that the western press "will jump at the murky fabricated accusations against Moscow and Sofia of complicity in international terrorism."[5] Andronov acknowledges that such an act against the Pope seems incredible even for the CIA, but he notes that the CIA hired Mafia murderers to try to assassinate Cuban President Fidel Castro, and he claims that there is a profascist grouping within the CIA that is capable of anything.[6]

Andronov puts great weight on the linkages built up by the CIA in Turkey with the extreme Right. He points out that former CIA agent Frank Terpil acknowledged supplying arms and training to the Gray Wolves. He quotes Mumcu's statement that Türkes, the head of the Nationalist Action Party, "has always been strongly connected with the CIA."[7] Andronov claims that the Turkish papers were full of reports

---

3. "He [Agca] was picked by a unique criminal band called the Turkish Mafia, which operates out of Sofia, Bulgaria, which, indeed, is under the direct control and supervision of the Bulgarian Secret Service." "Why Is the West Covering Up for Agca: Exclusive Interview with Claire Sterling," *Human Events*, April 21, 1984.

4. *Ibid.*

5. *Op. cit.*, n. 1, p. 46.

6. *Ibid.*, p. 43.

7. *Ibid.*, p. 33.

that the CIA armed the Gray Wolves and that the United States funded Türkes. He agrees with Sterling and Henze that the terror of the late 1970s aimed at destabilization; but, reversing the Sterling-Henze line, he contends that destabilization was rightist in origin and served U.S. and rightwing interests. Andronov claims that the murder of Ipekci on February 1, 1979, was part of this U.S.-inspired destabilization effort. Ipekci was deeply concerned about the destabilization program and had assailed the Gray Wolves as an instrument of murder. Two weeks before his assassination, on January 13, 1979, Ipekci met by appointment Paul Henze, former CIA station chief in Turkey and at the time on the staff of the National Security Council. Andronov proposes that Ipekci was warning Henze and urging him to control his subversive program in Turkey.[8]

For Andronov, a key link in the U.S.-backed destabilization effort was Ruzi Nazar, a former Nazi who worked in the U.S. Embassy in Turkey with Henze and then moved to West Germany. Nazar served in both Turkey and West Germany as the U.S. liaison with the Gray Wolves. Andronov cites several individuals, including Mumcu, who say that Nazar had real influence over the Gray Wolves.[9]

Andronov's scheme of linkages and controls is as follows: Agca's paymaster in Europe was Celebi, a high Gray Wolves official in West Germany. It was Celebi who gave Agca the final go-ahead on the assassination attempt in April 1981. Celebi, however, was a subordinate of both Türkes and Enver Altayli, an associate of Türkes who was in control of all Turkish fascist finances and Gray Wolves propaganda. Andronov quotes from an interview with Orsan Oymen, the Bonn correspondent of *Milliyet*: "According to information I have, Altayli collaborates with the American CIA."[10] The linkages are complete: a CIA-Gray Wolves-Agca connection is confirmed by at least three named sources.

Although we do not believe these arguments to be true, the Andronov case is far stronger than Sterling's. What gives it special strength is the consistency of motive and results. The motive was to incriminate the Soviet Union and discredit it in the eyes of the world, to help Reagan convince the U.S. public to accept a major rearmament and to persuade Europeans of the necessity of Pershing and cruise missiles. What is

8. *Ibid.*, p. 30.
9. Mumcu reproduces a long letter from Gray Wolves leader Enver Altayli to Türkes in which a cooperative relationship with Nazar is made clear. See above, p. 64, n. 49.
10. *Op. cit.*, n. 1, p. 39.

more, the assassination plot worked well to meet these ends. By contrast, Sterling's version requires irrational and exceptionally incompetent Soviet behavior. The Andronov model is consistent with rational CIA behavior and the results of the plot are compatible with Reagan-CIA objectives.

Sterling and Henze, of course, would rule out CIA involvement on the ground that this is not the kind of thing the United States would do. There is some truth in this. Shooting the Pope, even through a hired surrogate, would be an extraordinary act. It is doubtful that the top officials of the CIA would authorize it as a means of helping a propaganda war against the Soviets, even though the CIA has arranged for many attempts to kill foreign leaders.[11] But similar doubts may be raised that the cautious Soviet leadership would be any more likely to engage in such an extraordinary and risky venture than the CIA.[12]

11. See, *Alleged Assassination Plots Involving Foreign Leaders*, Interim Report of the Select Committee to Study Governmental Operations With Respect to Intelligence, U.S. Senate Report No. 94-465, 94th Congress, 1st Session, November 20, 1975.

12. See Chapter 2, pp. 14-15 and n. 13. In a fine illustration of Sterling methodology, in *The Time of the Assassins* she reports a conversation involving Martin Peretz, editor of the *New Republic* and several *New Republic* interns who think the KGB plot far-fetched: "Tell me," pursued Marty. "What do you think of the story that the CIA plotted to kill Fidel Castro?" "Oh, that! Of course!" "Why are you so ready to believe that the CIA would kill Castro, but not that the KGB would kill the Pope?" Marty went on, intrigued." "Because the CIA does things like that."
Sterling fails to note that the CIA's multiple efforts to murder Castro are not "a story" but are on the record, acknowledged by government authorities. By contrast, the evidence for a Soviet connection to the plot to kill the Pope is sorely lacking. Furthermore, the doubting interns may be questioning the logic of the plot, which, as we spelled out earlier, has serious flaws.

E. The Georgetown Disinformation Center

The papal assassination attempt provided a cornucopia of propaganda opportunities for hardliners, both in government and out. A well-publicized report by the Georgetown Center for Strategic and International Studies (CSIS), entitled "The International Implications of the Papal Assassination Attempt: A Case of State-Sponsored Terrorism,"[1] took full advantage of these opportunities to score political points. While the title of the document suggests that readers might expect a serious discussion of the substance of the case, Bulgarian and Soviet guilt were assumed beforehand as a working premise. The big question raised by the report was: What should U.S. responses be *if* the Soviets are shown to be behind the papal shooting? The document thus had the built-in objectivity of a report on an individual entitled: "How should we deal with John Doe if it is established that he beats his wife?"

The Plot was framed in a Sterlingesque setting in which international terror is sponsored by states which aim to "undermine world order." The guilty state is of course the Soviet Union, and the point of the CSIS report was to stress that "the papal case can be used as a symbol" in a propaganda campaign to dramatize the Soviets as the center of terrorism. The authors of the report faced several problems, however. First, there is the issue of whether the United States has clean hands. Are South Africa and Israel terrorist states? Are they U.S. surrogates? Are the *contras* U.S. instruments of terror? Are Chile, El Salvador, and Guatemala engaged in terrorist attacks on their own citizens? Can the Soviets match the CIA's numerous attempts to assassinate Fidel Castro?

1. This is a "Report of the CSIS Steering Committee on Terrorism," Zbigniew Brzezinski and Robert H. Kupperman, Co-chairmen, published in December 1984 by the CSIS in its Significant Issues Series, Vol. VI, No. 20.

This issue is mentioned fleetingly in the report and passed by without serious discussion.

A second problem was that the truth of the Bulgarian Connection had not yet been decided in the Italian courts at the time the report was published. As noted, the conferees assumed Soviet involvement without presenting any supportive evidence. Co-chairman Robert Kupperman smoothly asserted in his Overview that "most thoughtful observers" believe in the Connection. He does not name any such observers nor provide any citations. The issue of Soviet guilt was also dealt with in a manner suggesting the Henze "print": doubts on this point represent a "legalistic and narrow-minded" attitude that "is not politically sound."[2] The report also notes that aggressive U.S. government accusations of Bulgarian and Soviet guilt might be regarded as interfering with Italian judicial processes. This did not prevent the conferees from concluding that there should be an "organized effort on the part of the government to develop as much credibility and access to information about the case as is needed to generate a political attitude."

This perceived need for a more aggressive government propaganda effort was based on an alleged widespread disbelief in the Plot, which was attributed to a "prodigious" Soviet disinformation effort. The conferees agreed that the western media had been penetrated and that Soviet disinformation had "had an effect." The western media lacked awareness "about how disinformation functions." The conferees did not consider U.S. disinformation, which may not exist for them. This stress on Soviet disinformation and western media victimization is a longstanding focus of the Henze-Sterling-de Borchgrave school, which tries to make all dissenting opinion a product of Red influence, not disagreement about the facts. This vision leads naturally to the conclusion that we should bring Big Government into play to deal with this menace: The CSIS report urges the U.S. government to use "informal connections" to "discourage the internal process of imposing more and more skepticism on the Bulgarian (and possibly Soviet) involvement." (Translation: the U.S. government should intervene to discourage dissenting views on the Plot.)

Given the loss of the case in Italy, several questions arise. If, as Kupperman suggested, "most thoughtful observers" thought the Bulgarians and KGB guilty, how did they blunder so egregiously? Could it be that the people the CSIS regard as "thoughtful" are a wee bit biased,

2. See Chapter 6, pp. 148-149.

perhaps even in the disinformation business?[3] Banish the thought! It is obvious that the truth did not prevail in Italy because of the power of KGB disinformation and the West's fear of offending the Soviet Union and disturbing détente.[4] If I win, justice is done; if I lose, the deck is stacked.

The composition of the working group that produced the report enables us to understand its content: Paul Henze, former CIA propaganda officer; Zbigniew Brzezinski, former National Security Adviser to Carter and member of the Committee on the Present Danger (CPD); Max Kampelman, CPD member and Reagan's choice for arms control negotiator; Ray Cline, formerly of the CIA; Robert Kupperman, ''terrorism expert'' of CSIS; Marvin Kalb, author of the extremely biased NBC-TV program on the plot; and Arnaud de Borchgrave, Red Scare novelist and editor of Reverend Moon's *Washington Times*. That de Borchgrave is an Adjunct Fellow of the CSIS tells us a great deal about that organization. So does this report in general.

---

3. Michael Ledeen has been a stalwart of the CSIS, and Kupperman hired as his adviser on Italy Francesco Pazienza, under multiple indictment in Italy for forgery, theft, and collaboration with terrorists. See Chapter 6.

4. This last point is put forward regularly by Sterling. See Preface and Chapter 6.

Index

ABC-TV, 199-200, 204, 213
Adams, Nathan M., 226-27, 228, 230, 239
Adnan (Mehmet Ali Agca's brother), 42, 155, 219
Agca, Mehmet Ali, 1, 10, 16-17, 35, 36, 120, 138, 181, 187-88
    allegations by (later retracted), of plot to kill Lech Walesa, 2, 29, 30-32, 33, 117, 157, 192, 193
    as a longtime rightwing activist in Turkey, 42, 48, 50-56, 65, 137-38, 155, 217, 218, 220, 221, 223, 224; see also Gray Wolves
    as an unlikely recruit for Soviet-bloc secret services, 15-16; see also Agca, as a longtime rightwing activist in Turkey
    as sole witness against the Bulgarians, 2, 157, 190, 211
    claim of, to be Jesus Christ, ix-x, 39, 155, 181, 194, 196
    coaching of, in prison, 3-4, 5, 32, 33, 40-41, 57, 102-12, 119, 121-22, 195, 198, 202
    credibility of, ix-x, 2, 27, 37-38, 59-60, 120-21, 183-84, 189, 191, 197, 200-01, 236-37; see also Agca, retractions by, of previous testimony
    desire of, for public attention, 56-57, 105-6, 108, 196, 200
    escape of, from Turkish prison, 52, 137, 140-41
    identification of Bulgarians by, 2, 21, 22, 23-24, 26-27, 30, 110-11, 116-17
    influence on, of media presentation of Bulgarian Connection, 24, 28, 57, 202, 207

    initial testimony of, 20, 220-22
    long delay of, in naming alleged co-conspirators, 17-18, 23-24, 107
    retractions by, of previous testimony, 17, 31, 32-34, 36, 38, 109-10, 115-17, 138-40, 157, 181, 192, 193, 194, 196-97, 200, 201
    role of, in assassination of progressive newspaper editor Ipekci, 52, 187, 217, 222
    testimony of, in second trial, ix-x, 39, 194-97
    threat by, to kill the Pope in Turkey, 14, 52-53, 156, 186, 187, 196
    trial of, in July 1981, 18-19
    trip to Bulgaria by, 13-14, 16, 20, 53, 184, 187, 207, 210-11
Agca Dossier (Mumcu), 137-38
Agee, Philip, 132
Ahmad, Feroz, 49, 51-52
Aivazov, Todor, 17, 28, 32, 35, 107, 115, 117, 140
Albano, Antonio, 36, 87, 104, 122, 191, 210
Albano Report, 15-16, 36, 109-10, 119, 190-94, 203-4
    coverage of, in western media, 6, 181, 190-94, 200-201
    leaking of, 33, 36, 119, 120, 140
Amnesty International, 151
Andronov, Iona, 64, 133, 141-42, 170, 179, 241-44
Andropov, Yuri, 1-2
Angleton, James, 74, 132
Antonov, Mrs. Rossitsa, 17, 117, 120-21, 140, 176, 193, 200
Antonov, Sergei, 2, 101, 127
    Agca's testimony against, 17, 32-33, 36, 109-10, 111-12, 116-17, 212

248